SHATTERED
BUT NOT
BROKEN

One Woman's Inspiring Story About
Living Beyond Loss and Grief

BETTY MAJOR-ROSE

LifeRich
PUBLISHING

Copyright © 2022 Betty Major-Rose.

All rights reserved. No part of this book may be used or reproduced by any means, graphic, electronic, or mechanical, including photocopying, recording, taping or by any information storage retrieval system without the written permission of the author except in the case of brief quotations embodied in critical articles and reviews.

LifeRich Publishing is a registered trademark of The Reader's Digest Association, Inc.

LifeRich Publishing books may be ordered through booksellers or by contacting:

LifeRich Publishing
1663 Liberty Drive
Bloomington, IN 47403
www.liferichpublishing.com
844-686-9607

Because of the dynamic nature of the Internet, any web addresses or links contained in this book may have changed since publication and may no longer be valid. The views expressed in this work are solely those of the author and do not necessarily reflect the views of the publisher, and the publisher hereby disclaims any responsibility for them.

Any people depicted in stock imagery provided by Getty Images are models, and such images are being used for illustrative purposes only. Certain stock imagery © Getty Images.

Scripture quotations marked KJV are from the Holy Bible, King James Version (Authorized Version). First published in 1611. Quoted from the KJV Classic Reference Bible, Copyright © 1983 by The Zondervan Corporation.

Scripture taken from the New King James Version®. Copyright © 1982 by Thomas Nelson. Used by permission. All rights reserved.

Scripture taken from the Holy Bible, NEW INTERNATIONAL VERSION®, NIV® Copyright © 1973, 1978, 1984, 2011 by Biblica, Inc.® Used by permission. All rights reserved worldwide.

Scripture taken from the Holy Bible, New Living Translation, copyright © 1996, 2004, 2015 by Tyndale House Foundation. Used by permission of Tyndale House Publishers Inc., Carol Stream, Illinois 60188. All rights reserved.

ISBN: 978-1-4897-4073-1 (sc)
ISBN: 978-1-4897-4072-4 (hc)
ISBN: 978-1-4897-4071-7 (e)

Library of Congress Control Number: 2022904148

Print information available on the last page.

LifeRich Publishing rev. date: 06/01/2022

Navigating through the road of grief is never easy, and there are no quick fixes. This road, for some, can be a long and lonely journey. There are no words that can alleviate the pain you may experience after the death of a loved one. And yet, it is one of the greatest sorrows that can occur in one's life. Betty Major-Rose shares her experiences with death and her journey through grief. As you read through the pages of this book, I pray it will help you through your grief journey.

DEDICATION

This book is dedicated to the members of my family who have gone on to be with the Lord.

My beautiful and amazing daughter, Ginneria, who in the midst of her short life was the epitome of grace, strength, courage, and compassion.

To my beloved first husband, Lionel, who gave me five beautiful children to carry on his legacy. I thank him for being such a dedicated husband and an amazing, loving father. He took fatherhood very seriously; there was nothing he wouldn't do for his children. He made clear that he would assume the responsibility of leadership in our marriage, and that those responsibilities fell squarely on his shoulders. He led our family in truth. He walked in integrity. He had a positive attitude and lived with purpose. He was a strong and God-fearing man. Yet, he was the most gentle, kind, and caring person I have ever met. If it had not been for Lionel, this book would not have been written. Lionel's death was life-changing. I had to rebuild my life and myself, and because of him, it made me more resilient and stronger than I ever thought I could be. His death taught me in the most profound way the importance of the love of family.

To my much-loved siblings; Roland, Eloise, Edna, and Janet; for their unconditional love and support. My devoted mother, Bertha, and loving grandmother, Edna, who taught me how to love, how to give without expecting anything in return, how to love my family unconditionally, how to serve others, and always look for the good in them. My aunt, Velma, whom I lived with during my teen years, she loved me as her own. She taught me life lessons that I will hold with me forever. My great-grandson, Cyler, who I was blessed with the opportunity to love on him in his short life. Also, to my many family members; my stepfather, aunts, uncles, nephews, nieces, and cousins; your hearts have touched mine, and you lived to be missed.

ACKNOWLEDGMENTS

While this book is about my personal, spiritual, and emotional healing journey through the many traumatic losses I have experienced in my life, I thank God for walking with me as I struggled through these seasons of grief and pain and getting me through the darkest and most painful hours of my life. He also gave me the strength to go through this grief journey and brought me to a place of inner peace and healing. I also thank Him for giving me the fortitude to write this book. Without Him, it would not have been possible.

Every accomplishment in life is a result of the contributions and influences of others. During the process of writing this book, I am indebted to my loving and dedicated husband of fifty years, James, and my wonderful and awesome children; Deshone, Michelle, Lionel, and Kim; who are the joy of my heart and love of my life. They believed in me, encouraged me, supported me, and inspired me to push forward to fulfill the vision that God gave me over thirty years ago. I want to add that Kim was instrumental in the practical manifestation of this book, working by my side to help me see my dream come to fruition.

To my beautiful, loving grandchildren and great-grandchildren; Ayana, Tony, Gabrielle, Bennie Jr. Clive, Chardonnay, Christina, Blair, Olivia, Alyssa, Adonijah, Lauryn, Anahkah, Lionel, Blake, Kadrian, Victoria, Rebecca, and Layla; who I love dearly. To my surviving siblings, Doris, Joanette, John, and Dwanda. To my sons-in-laws, Anthony, Bennie, and Patrick, and my daughter-in-law, Liliana. To all the families I have had the pleasure and honor of supporting throughout the years who lost family members to murder and other tragic deaths through the Cook County State's Attorney Office, the Family Trauma Advocacy Counseling Center, and other agencies and organizations.

SPECIAL THANKS

To Amber Travis, thank you for your support and encouragement.

To Kimberly Applewhite, thank you for the wonderful design of the book cover.

To Marc Anthony, thank you for the wonderful photograph.

INTRODUCTION

One thing that is certain in this life is death. The Bible underscores this in Ecclesiastes 3:2, NIV highlighting that everything has its time "A time to be born and a time to die." Essentially, we are born, and we die. Death is inevitable, and people cannot prepare themselves for it or avoid it. Death is one of the hardest, if not the hardest, thing we live through in this life, and a sudden tragic death comes with even more unique challenges. When someone we love dies, the pain of loss can be immense.

Death and grief are not strangers to me. Over the years, I have experienced several losses and have grieved in many different ways. Each grief experience was not the same due to the nature of my relationship with each family member or friend, with some losses requiring a different adjustment, while other losses left me feeling like my whole world was shattered. I experienced a combination of emotions I had never experienced before and some with an intensity that even scared me. At times, my psychological, mental, emotional, and physical pain was so deep I felt like lying down and never getting up. At times, I felt I couldn't endure the excruciating agony anymore or go on with my life feeling depressed, hopeless, and empty. Nothing could take away the pain. As much as people tried, no one could come up with any words to make me feel better or make the hurt go away. I didn't know what to do or how to act in front of my family, my children, and friends. I was so afraid of making others feel uncomfortable that I didn't let anyone know how I felt. I didn't know how to talk about how I was feeling or what I was experiencing, and all of this became overwhelming for me.

I had to learn how to release my pain and embrace my grief. The only way I could do that was to sit humbly before God and be open and honest about my pain, sadness, anger, and fears. As soon as I acknowledged those feelings and released them to God, I felt a burden lift off me, and I received inner peace and healing. The word of God says in Psalm 34:15-18 (NIV), "The eyes of the LORD are on the righteous, and his ears are open to their cry. The righteous cry out, and the LORD hears and delivers them from all their troubles. The LORD is near to the brokenhearted; He saves those crushed in spirit." This comforted me because God saw me and heard me when I cried out for help, even when no one else did. He knew my heartache, and He saw my pain. My heart was broken, and I felt crushed from all sides. God's word promised me that He was going to be close to me, and He was. I'm so grateful that the devil couldn't take my mind.

Even though I have grieved deeply, God's generous grace and my willingness to allow Him to heal my heart, a heart that was severely torn open again and again, He continued to give me the peace I needed. Some of the losses I experienced included my brother who drowned at age twelve; my first husband who was killed in an automobile accident; my grandmother, who was diagnosed with cancer, had a stroke and died less than an hour later; Three of my sisters, the eldest died from cirrhosis of the liver and a collapsed lung; another sister (I was her caregiver) died from Huntington's disease, and the third sister had a brain aneurysm and later died from an accidental overdose from prescription medication. I have also experienced the deaths of eight close aunts, six uncles, three nephews, two nieces, three sisters-in-law, six cousins (two were murdered, and they were brothers); one niece (her husband and son both were murdered prior to her death) two mothers-in-law, two brothers-in-law, (one killed by a drunk driver), my biological father, and my stepfather, who died while cleaning the church for Sunday's service. The pastor found him sitting in the pew. I also lost my best friend of thirty-six years. She died from cancer, and her son was murdered six years earlier. Moreover, within one year, my sister, nephew, and mother all died suddenly and unexpectedly.

The most devastating loss of all was the murder of my daughter. Nothing has affected me more than hearing the words "Your daughter is dead." Losing my child was the most painful and profound loss of all. Grieving her death has been a lifelong journey. Her legacy and future died along with her. I know without a doubt that if it had not been for the grace of God, I would not have been able to get through her death and still be in my right mind. Yet, through God's love and grace, He kept me from being consumed by her murder. My heart still aches for my baby, and it's been over thirty years since her death. My grief journey has been a long winding road. There was a time when I could not imagine my world without her, but the key to my healing was acknowledging my pain and giving myself permission to grieve. This was not an easy process. However, despite everything I've been through, I eventually made it through healthy and strong with a sense of hope.

If you are struggling with the emotional, mental, and even physical pain of grief, I hope you take comfort in the fact that God has your pain in the palm of His hands. He will not let you go, and He will not let you down. A word of hope is found in I Peter 5:10 (NIV) "And the God of all grace, who called you after you have suffered a little while, will himself restore you and make you strong, firm, and steadfast." As difficult as it was for me to experience the many losses in my life, I am here today to tell you that I survived and eventually thrived. Take heart. I thank God for walking alongside me through my journey through grief, and my greatest desire is that you allow Him to join you in your journey. My prayer is that the pain you experience today will be your ministry tomorrow. The God of love will carry anyone through loss, and I can say He never left my side, and He will never leave yours.

My purpose in writing this book was to share my grief journey and open up a dialogue to have conversations about death and grief. A section in this book will assist you in understanding what to expect and normalize what you may be experiencing during your grief journey.

Grief isn't something you get over. It's something you have to go through and learn to *live* with.

My Journey Through Grief
**Surely, he hath borne our grief. And carried
our sorrows-Isaiah 53:4 (NIV)**

CONTENTS

Chapter 1   Death Uninvited 1
   Reflecting/Remembering 1
   New Orleans—The Lived Experience 3
   Childhood Experiences 4
   Transitioning 5
   Appreciated Our Differences 6
   The Advantages and Disadvantages of a Large Family ... 7
   Feelings of Inadequacy 8
   Blended Family 8
   Growing Up in the South 9
   My First Experience with Death 10
   She Was My True Friend 11
   The Call 12
   This Can't Be True 13
   On My Way Home 13
   Search and Rescue 14
   Clowning Around 14
   The Waiting Period 15
   Not Good News 16
   Unimaginable Pain 16
   Feelings of Loneliness 17
   The Funeral 17
   Having to Accept Reality 18
      Reflection Impact of Losing a Sibling 20

Chapter 2   California Dreaming 23
- A Life-Altering Offer 23
- Saying Goodbye 24
- A Turning Point in My Life 25
- On One of My Visit's Home 26
- Love at First Sight 27
- Developing a Friendship and Relationship 27
- My Summer Winding Down 28
- Developed a Friendship and Relationship 28
- Proposal 29
- My Wedding Day 29
- Reminiscing 30
- Our First Home 31
- Planning Our Family 31
  - Reflection Building A Strong Marriage 32

Chapter 3   Stormy Clouds Ahead 35
- We're Having a Baby 36
- Approaching Due Date 36
- Baby on the Way 37
- That Special Moment 38
- Our First Night Home 38
- Working out Kinks 39
- Hurricane Betsy—Stormy Night Ahead 39
- Hurricane Arrival 40
- Settling Down for The Night 41
- Woke Up Immersed in Water 41
- Preparing to Make Our Escape 41
- Begin Making Our Way to Safety 42
- Forceful Winds and Heavy Rain 42
- Rescuing My Sister and Others 43
- Making Our Way to Safety 43
- A Mother's Determination 44
- Crying Out for Help 45
- Mama Rescued from Drowning 45
  - Reflection The Devastation of Hurricane Betsy 46

Chapter 4   Tears In a Bottle 47
   Hoping We Could Salvage Some Things 47
   Starting Over and Surprise Baby Number Two 48
   Preparing for The Arrival of Our Second Child 48
   Pregnant with a Toddler 48
   Approaching the End of My Pregnancy 49
   Progressing in Labor 50
   Almost There 50
   The Birth of my Second Child 50
   Bringing Ginneria Home 51
   Growing Family 51
   Baby Number Three—Including My Girls with the New Baby 52
   Excited for Another New Life 52
   Start of Labor 53
   The Birth of My Third Child 53
   Bringing Michelle Home 54
   Family Adjusting to Third Child 54
   Family Continues to Grow—Baby Number Four 54
   Adjusting and Making Adjustments 55
   Burst of Energy 56
   Settling Down for the Night 56
   Baby Number Four on The Way 57
   Bringing Lionel Home 57
   Raising Four Children 57
   Our Dream Home 58
   My Life Was Forever Changed 58
   Wasn't His Norm 59
   Saying Our Final Goodbye Without Knowing It 59
   The Dream 60
   My Nightmare Came True 60
   Embracing My Children 61
   Telling My Children Their Dad Was Dead 62
   Wrapping My Heading Around: The Days Following 62
   Hearing the Details 64
   Preparing to Say Our Final Goodbye 64
   Seeing Him for the Last Time 65

Remarks from Family and Friends 66
Making Adjustments 67
Grandmother's Love 67
One Life Taken—Blessed with a New life—Baby Number Five ... 68
Going It Alone 69
Holidays Approaching 69
Returning Home 70
Getting the Kids Ready to Return Home 72
First Day Home 72
Preparing Dinner 74
Having Family Dinner for the First Time Alone 74
Learning How to Cope with My Pain and Emotions 76
Beginning to Feel Abandoned 78
I Realized That I Was Not Alone—It Was Hard on My
Children Too 79
Bittersweet Moments 79
Moving Forward to Make Sure I Had a Healthy Pregnancy 80
Beginning of Labor 81
Arrival at the Hospital 82
Final Gift of Love 83
My Fifth Baby—Bringing Kim Home 83
Adapting to Being Widowed and a Solo Parent 85
    Reflection Being Widowed 86

CHAPTER 5   NAVIGATING THROUGH THE FIRST YEAR 89
Making My Way Through 89
Adjusting and Readjusting 90
Grieving in Different Ways 90
Sharing Their Memories 91
Overtaken at Times 92
Unbearable Loneliness 93
I'm Stronger Than I Thought 93
Approaching the Second Year 94
Transitioning from a Stay-at-Home Mom 94
Stepping Out into the Workforce 95
It Was Harder Than I Expected 95
    Reflection Supporting Children After a Parent Dies 96

CHAPTER 6   ONE MORE CHANCE AT LOVE 99
   An Admirer 99
   Seeking Guidance 100
   A Lot to Think About 100
   Embracing the Change 100
   It All Started 101
   Invited to Lunch 102
   Dating Challenges 102
   Getting Acquainted 103
   Guilt, Shame, and Betrayal 104
   Feeling Guilty 104
   Progressing in Our Relationship 105
   Revealing My Relationship 105
   Returned to Chicago 106
   Chicago Here I Come 106
   Taking Everything into Consideration 107
   Headed Back to Chicago 108
   Took the Chance at Love and Marriage Again 108
   Choices and Decisions We Make 109
   Stay or Run? 109
   Periods of Abstinence 110
   Co-dependency 111
   Grieving Once More 111
   Concealing the Truth 112
   For Worse for Sure 112
   Experienced Family Life Differently 114
   Turbulent Ride 115
   The Question Is Why 115

CHAPTER 7   THE STRENGTH OF A WOMAN 117

CHAPTER 8   HER NAME WAS GINNERIA 123
   The Unimaginable 124
   Who was Ginneria? 125
   We Called Her Toby 126
   She was a Go-Getter 128

The Call that Changed Our Lives Forever..................................128
The Call..130
The Ride to the Hospital...132
Unsupportive and Un-Empathetic 133
Why the Deception? 134
Having to Tell the Shocking News...138
Lingering Regrets..140
Dreading What's Ahead..141
Not Looking Forward to the Days Ahead 142
Something I Was Not Looking Forward To… 142
Murderer in Custody 148
Walking Around in a Fog 148
Support is on the Way...150
An Uncomfortable Moment...151
The Visitation/Funeral 153
I Wasn't Ready..153
Finalizing Arrangements for Burial.......................................157
Our Final Goodbye 159
The Burial...162
Not Looking Forward to Returning or Looking Forward to
Christmas..163
Navigating Through the First Several Months After
Ginneria's Death...167
Processing the Unimaginable 168
Saying Goodbye to My Sister...169
Unsure of My Emotional State..170
Encouraged to Move On...172
Felt Abandoned...173
The Rollercoaster Ride Continues 174
A Spur-of-the-Moment Decision 175
Approaching the First Year..175
Second Year 178
The Third, Fourth, and Years Beyond 181
    Reflection The Death of a Child............................184
    Reflection Coping with the Murder of a Loved....................186

Chapter 9   Remembering My Sisters 189
    Eloise 189
    Edna 193
    Janet 195
        Reflection Coping with the Death of a Sibling 200

Chapter 10   I'm Ready to Go 203
    Reflecting on the Impact of This Incredible Woman 205
    Beginning of 207
    Persuading Her to Leave 208
    Events Leading Up to Her Death 209
    Never Got a Chance to Talk with Her 210
        Reflection Coping with the Death of a Parent 212

Chapter 11   His Name Was Cyler 215

Chapter 12   The Birth of a Ministry 219
    The Death of a Stranger 219
    Encouraging Scripture Verses While Coping with Grief 224

CHAPTER 1
Death Uninvited

"Even though I walk through the darkest valley, I will fear no evil, for you are with me; your rod and your staff, they comfort me."
Psalm 23:4 (NIV)

What sound is that I hear? It's a scream that is horrifying and scaring me. I've never heard it before. Wait, it's coming from inside of me. Oh, I can't catch my breath, and I can't go any further. My heart is racing and pounding. My chest is burning. My heart is going to pop out of my chest or stop all together. My legs keep moving, and I can't stop running.

As I touched my chest, I collapsed to the ground, and tears exploded from my eyes like water running from a faucet. I couldn't imagine what I had just heard. Was it true? My ears must be failing me. I could not have heard that correctly. This must be a dream? Wake me up, somebody, PLEASE! In this moment, my life forever changed. I never imagined that when I woke up seven hours earlier, I would hear that my only brother was dead.

Reflecting/Remembering

Looking back over my life, I have many fond and pleasant memories of my childhood growing up in the 1950s and 60s in New Orleans, Louisiana, even with everything that took place. My family and I grew up with a sense of community where neighbors looked out for one another, families respected each other, and people spoke as you walked by. During that time, people sat on their front porch and watched all the children in the neighborhood. Simply—people cared. If one family was experiencing hardship, other families in the community would raise money by participating in "fish fry's" (preparing dinners to sell) and would give the money to the family that was in need so they could purchase groceries, pay their rent, or meet whatever needs they had. Neighborhood grocery stores would even allow you to run a tab with their store. They called it "on the books," where families could shop for groceries and pay their bill at the end of the week when they got paid. In this way, no one went hungry.

I also remember the "watermelon man" who came to our neighborhood selling fresh fruits and vegetables. He would drive down the street in his truck with his head leaning out of the window, singing about all the food he had available. He would sing, "Watermelon man, watermelon man, I got the watermelon red to the rind, try 'em fo you buy 'em. I got the greens, the cabbage, the tomatoes, and the potatoes." The watermelon man also sold the weekly newspaper and Jet magazines. He would sing, "Weekly and the Jet, buy 'em in a set, fifty-five cent, I'mma say it again, weekly and the Jet, buy 'em in a set, fifty-five cent." During the summer, your teeth would be stained from eating snowballs and Hucka-Bucks (a frozen favored ice cup) all day long to stay cool because of the heat and humidity. I also remember our curfew was when the sun went down. When the streetlights came on, you had to be inside without an excuse.

Mardi Gras "Carnival" season was our favorite holiday. It was a time to let loose, enjoy yourself, listen to great music, eat a lot of food, and spend time with family and friends. Families would gather to celebrate this festive time. Most families always tried to set up in the same spot each year under the Claiborne Bridge. They would bring folding chairs, tables, blankets, ice chests, tents, and grills. The most exciting part for me was seeing and hearing all the high school marching bands "battling it out" as they marched along the parade route. There were also flag girls, the dance team, the majorettes, and the color guard. They were awesome. I remember my sister, Janet, was a majorette when she attended Booker T. Washington High School. I had an opportunity to see her marching with her high school band as the lead majorette. She was stepping high as the band played, and the Mardi Gras floats moved slowly down the street behind them. At times, during the route, floats stopped to throw Mardi

Gras paraphernalia such as beads, candy, cups, toys, and doubloons to the crowd as the bands continued playing their selections. The crowd was full of excitement, dancing along to the music as the majorettes were stepping to the beat of the music. At that point, my sister, Janet, broke out and threw her baton high in the air and immediately did a cartwheel followed by a whirl-turn and a split. She then caught her baton as it spun down, and the crowd went wild. Just as the floats started moving again, Janet was back in stride and never missed a beat.

Two of my most favorite events during Mardi Gras were the Zulu parades. Zulu is New Orleans' largest predominantly African American carnival organization known for its blackface krewe members. Krewe members wore grass skirts and threw out unique hand-painted coconuts. Everyone wanted to walk away with one of them. The Indians were among the most colorful. No one in the city wore more elaborate costumes or took it more seriously than Mardi Gras Indians. Their costumes were unforgettable with amazing hand-sewn creations of intricate beadwork and dramatic images. Their costumes take an entire year to create, with hundreds of thousands of beads, brightly dyed ostrich plumes, sequins, velvet, and rhinestones sewn on by hand—some weighing as much as one hundred fifty pounds! And they wore their costumes only once. There are more than fifty Indian tribes in the city, and each march to the beat of their own drummer, literally. With a formal hierarchy of chiefs, spy boys, flag boys, big chiefs, wild men, and other unique monikers, the Indians grace the streets of New Orleans' neighborhoods in a friendly competition over which chief is the "prettiest." With boastful singing and threatening dances and gestures, on Mardi Gras Day, the tribes go out seeking other tribes to do "battle" with. My sister Doris' husband was a member of one of the tribes.

New Orleans—The Lived Experience

I believe New Orleans is called "The Big Easy" because people who live there are viewed as laid back. They are also seen as knowing how to live in the moment, relax, and just take life in stride. There are actually several stories about how New Orleans became known as "The Big Easy," all of which probably have some truth to them. In the early 20th century,

New Orleans was known as a haven for struggling musicians playing jazz or blues. It was an "easy" place to find work and earn a living performing music. The other story is that New Orleans had extremely lax or nonexistent enforcement of drinking laws during Prohibition, and so it became known as a place where it was "easy" to get a drink, party, and have a good time. This continues today. New Orleans is one of the few cities in America where one can wander down the street in the French Quarter with an open container or cup of alcohol and not be breaking the law. However, this is not the everyday lived experience for those living there. For "Orleanians," it is quite different than the fantasy world held by tourists.

Childhood Experiences

My childhood experiences in the 1950s and 60s were marked by the Jim Crow era. Jim Crow was a system designed to keep black people separated from whites in public facilities, housing, transportation, you name it! Essentially, its discriminatory practices were to exclude and restrict black people's rights and civil liberties across the United States, and we certainly lived through these experiences in the South. New Orleans may have seemed to be an integrated city, but an NAACP official's description of segregation published in an article in the Louisiana Weekly summed it up best. He stated that segregation was, "A modernized, streamlined slavery that replaces ankle irons with 'For White Only' signs; that replaces slave quarters with the slum ghetto; that replaces three meals a day with the starvation wage of maids and porters; that replaces the master's bullwhip with the torch of the mob and the policeman's club." I also remember during this time that black folks had to address white people as "sir" or "ma'am," a courtesy never reciprocated, and we had to eat in different restaurants, lunch counters, and drink from different water fountains. We had different restrooms, and the buses and streetcars were also segregated in New Orleans. I remember there were removable wooden signs that divided whites and colored people. The signs stated, "Colored Area," which was attached to the back of the seat, separating the black and white seating areas. This was done to ensure that white and black passengers would be kept separate. When the bus was crowded, any white passenger could move the sign back, giving themselves more seating space and forcing black passengers further behind, thus limiting their seating. When this happened, blacks had to give up their seats and stand. I vividly remember the days when riding the bus. We had to get on the bus in the front to pay our fare and then get off and go to the back door of the bus to get on and find a seat. However, the day came when I was twelve years old, in 1958, and the "whites only, and colored only" signs on buses and streetcars were officially removed. But even after the desegregation of buses and streetcars, I still felt uncomfortable. I remember seeing blacks on the bus seated, and the seat next to them was empty. A white person would rather stand than sit next to a black person.

Segregation also spilled over into religion. The Catholic Churches were also segregated, and blacks were expected to sit in the rear pews. Most hospitals were also for whites only. There were only two hospitals I remember where blacks were able to receive medical attention: Charity Hospital or Flint-Goodridge Hospital. Public housing developments were no different. The public housing projects reserved for whites were the Florida, Fisher, St. Thomas, and Iberville developments, and the Magnolia, Lafitte, St. Bernard, and Calliope were for blacks. My eldest sister, Eloise, moved into Calliope housing development after Hurricane Betsy.

The beaches were the same. Pontchartrain Beach was for white families, and Lincoln Beach was open to both blacks and whites, but whites never came over to Lincoln Beach. However, Audubon Zoo was open to both races, and every so often, my mom and stepdad would take us to Audubon Park Zoo. I remember whenever we went to visit the animals, we'd visit the reptile house, but Mom would never go in because she was afraid of snakes. My mom would always say that she was afraid of four kinds of snakes, the large ones, the small ones, the living ones, and the dead ones. There was also City Park, which I later learned was one of America's largest urban parks, which banned black people. Thinking back, it's amazing that at the time, I did not know this park existed.

Transitioning

My grandmother, Edna, moved to New Orleans when my mom was in her late teens from Laurel, Mississippi because my grandfather was emotionally and physically abusive. He was an excessive drinker and often became violent. With sadness and hurt in her eyes, my mom would often talk about witnessing her mother being physically attacked several times a week. My grandmother didn't have an easy life. In reality, she was a very broken woman inside, but you would never know it by looking at her.

My mother shared with me that her mom and dad began arguing one night after dinner, and the argument escalated. She witnessed my grandmother being thrown against the wall repeatedly, punched on the arms and chest, and then slammed to the floor, causing her glasses to fall off her face and shatter. The arguing continued for a while until he went to bed. My mother shared this was the night my grandmother made the decision to leave. My grandmother struggled to hold onto her marriage, but when the problems and pressure became overwhelming, she understood how little control she had, and things would not change. Therefore, she decided to leave Mississippi and initially left my mother and her sister and brother behind with her aunt. My grandmother later explained that she was going to New Orleans and would come back to get them after she was settled. My mom understood it took a lot of courage for my grandmother to leave and start a new life for her and her children. She believed her mom just wanted to try to put the past behind her and start over. In 1940, my mother and her brother followed, but her sister stayed behind with my grandmother's aunt.

Appreciated Our Differences

I am the third of nine children—yes, nine. Several years after Mom moved to New Orleans, she had my sister, Eloise, the nurturer, then came Roland, but we all called him "Sonnyboy." There really is no way to truly describe Sonnyboy except to call him the jokester of the family. In fact, it's hard to remember a time when Sonnyboy was ever serious. Sonnyboy was always considered average in height and small in stature for his age. He had big, dark-brown eyes, smooth dark skin, and a humorously boisterous personality that made him stand out. Everyone loved him. I came two years after Sonnyboy, which explained our close relationship. As much as I would have enjoyed life as the youngest in the family, six more came after me. There was Doris, the socialite; Edna, the carefree one; Joanette, the curious one; Janet, the athlete; John, who we called "Champ," the spoiled brat; and Dwanda, the unpredictable one. We all had very different emotional temperaments and needs. The experience of having to navigate through these variations enabled me to respect the different psychological differences of my siblings. Although, having siblings with so many different personalities, I came to deeply appreciate each of them and their uniqueness. As I grew up, I gravitated toward individuals most similar to me.

The Advantages and Disadvantages of a Large Family

Growing up in a large family has its advantages and, yes, difficulties, as well as rich experiences that come with it. We were taught how to compromise, the ability to share with one another, and to be self-reliant. It was we, not me. Everything belonged to everybody else. We looked out for each other, and we were never bored with all the craziness going on all the time. I cannot remember spending any substantial amount of time home alone. I was so accustomed to being around my siblings, except when I went to my godmother's house on the weekend and weeks at a time during the summer. We would all go to church on Sunday and midweek service. I don't ever recall going out with the entire family to dinner because Mama couldn't afford it. However, we always ate dinner together at home. Sunday was always special. My siblings and I did a lot of things together that didn't cost much. We would go with our friends crabbing and crawfishing, and later we would have a crab and crawfish boil in the backyard with our friends. We would dance and just have a good time. Although there were a lot of things we didn't have, there were more things we did have. The most important thing was we had each other.

The only downside of being part of a big family is sharing a bedroom, a bathroom, and sometimes clothes. Honestly, despite the many ups and downs, there is not a single thing I would change about the size of my family or how we grew up in it. It's been said that the sibling relationship is the longest and one of the most influential relationships that most people will have in their lives, and I truly love the tight family bond I share with my siblings.

Feelings of Inadequacy

With this many siblings and all of their personalities, I'm sure you're wondering where I fit into the equation. Who was Betty as a little girl? Well, unlike some of my siblings, I was somewhat of an average kind of kid. I was never what you would consider "popular." I was extremely shy, quiet, and introverted. I did not have many friends growing up since I was very selective of whom I hung out with. In fact, the other kids often made fun of me because I was extremely tall and skinny with big eyes.

Being introverted with an awkward appearance wasn't the best combination, so I was often made to feel inadequate. I felt my peers thought I wasn't smart enough or pretty enough. The constant scrutiny was excruciating, but my relationship with my siblings, mother, and grandmother helped soften the blow a bit, but most importantly, they made me feel special. As long as I can remember, I have had a strong sense of who God is. I always knew He was my source, and I never questioned that despite everything I've gone through in my life. My strong faith can be attributed to the fact that we, my siblings and I, were brought up in the church. It is fair to say we were in church two to three times a week unless there was a church revival. In that case, we were there every single night. But unlike a lot of adolescents who spend a substantial amount of time at church, I didn't run from the church as I grew old enough to make my own spiritual choice. For me, it was the total opposite. Once we moved to another area of the city, our regular church was quite a distance away. On some Sundays, there were times when my mom was working, and my siblings wouldn't attend church service. However, there was a Catholic church within walking distance from where we lived, and I would go there on my own Sunday mornings.

Blended Family

My mom was a very strong woman. Her strength came from being tested by life's unpredictabilities. Having to raise nine kids, she did an incredible job financially, emotionally, physically, and spiritually. There is no doubt that being a single parent is one of the toughest jobs to have. I didn't grow up in a two-parent household in the early years of my life, and I didn't know my father at all. Mama never talked about him. All I knew was my father wasn't around, and that was that. Mama used to say, "I'm your mother and your father." It wasn't until my mom married my stepfather, John, and they had my other siblings, that I finally get to experience living in a two-parent household. My mom and stepfather had grueling work schedules, especially Mama. Come to think of it, I don't ever recall a time when my mom didn't work. In the 1940s, it was extremely common for black women to work as housekeepers, and that's what my mom did. My mom took on various jobs to make ends meet, and later she received training and began working at Charity Hospital as a nursing assistant in the pediatric department. Years later, she became a surgical technician at Touro Infirmary Hospital and retired from West Jefferson Medical Center. Mama invested all she had in us down to her last penny. There were many times when she had extra money to give to us, but when she didn't, we understood. Yes, Mama insisted on instilling her hard work ethic into her children extremely early.

I remember having chores as young as seven years old, washing dishes and sweeping the floor with a broom almost twice my size. And the work didn't stop there. Mama added to my domestic skills a few years later when she taught me how to cook. As you can imagine, I was less than amused with the extra work, but I realized later in life, Mama was trying to teach me critical skills I would need to know later in life. With these simple chores came life lessons of self-discipline, cleanliness, responsibilities, and the value of family. Yeah, Mama had a heart of gold, but she wasn't the best at expressing her love in a physical way to us. Even though my mom hardly said it, we knew she loved us. In fact, it wasn't until she got older that she really started saying, "I love you, and truly I do."

Growing Up in the South

A lot of my memories of living in the South have faded over the years, but a lot haven't. I remember living in several neighborhoods, including the Desire Housing Projects. Our days of living in the Desire Projects are nothing like how it is documented on television today as a crime-ridden community. My family moved into the projects after my brother, Sonny Boy's, tragic death. The Desire Projects was a newly developed government-housing complex in the Upper Ninth Ward of New Orleans. They were actually nice, nothing like what you would typically call "the projects." Some of the buildings were two stories with a courtyard in the center. The area where we lived had an elementary school directly across the street. In my mind, we were a typical middle-class family. As far as I was concerned, we lived in a nice, two-story apartment complex. In retrospect, I guess it really wasn't what I thought it was. In fact, the Desire Projects was the poorest housing development in New Orleans. It's funny because I always knew we lived in the projects, but none of us ever thought we were poor—perhaps Mama did, but we didn't feel like it. Like many parents, especially Negro parents of the South, Mama did a really good job of disguising our reality, including issues that were affecting thousands of African American children in the '40s, '50s, and '60s. I have such wonderful memories of my siblings and me in our living room playing our favorite seventy-eight records and gathering around the radio to listen to the Lone Ranger, Roy Rogers, the Cisco Kid, and Amos "n" Andy on the radio. At that time, we didn't have a television, but eventually, we did and were able to have access and see what was going on in the world around us, especially current events. Even today, the history books only tell a portion of what was really going on in the South prior to the Civil Rights movement. It seems like an eternity ago to the average person, but many people, especially children, don't realize just how recent the days of so-called "separate but equal" policies were. Of course, we'd hear all about the lynching and beatings that killed thousands of people in the South, but for some reason, I don't recall any of that going on in New Orleans. See, there it is again. Mama was really good at doing that. There really weren't any worries in my world, but all of that would change soon enough.

My First Experience with Death

I was nine years old in the summer of 1954, and like many summers in New Orleans, it was extremely hot. While most of the children in the neighborhood spent the better half of their day inside, later during the day, they would come out, and some would play jump rope, hopscotch, or spin the bottle and tag while others would go swimming in the Industrial Canal located about a mile or so from our neighborhood. For me, I spent most of my time with my godmother. I already mentioned that I was somewhat of a loner, so opting to spend time with my godmother was a lot more appealing to me than hanging out at the canal swimming or staying inside. Actually, I couldn't swim anyway. In fact, this had become routine for me until everything changed that August.

On this particular day, I was hanging out at my godmother's house when she got a call from her daughter, Virginia, who they called Virgie, that her neighbor of four years, Ms. Grace, who lived in the same building complex next door from her, had died. Ms. Grace had family, but my godmother's daughter always checked in on her. She did her grocery shopping and sometimes even cooked. She made sure Ms. Grace was taken care of. As I stated earlier, neighbors took care of each other. They were like family, so you can imagine how upset we were by the news of her death. My godmother's daughter had a key to Ms. Grace's apartment, and when she went to check on her later during the day, she found her dead. Ms. Grace was my first childhood death experience. Upon hearing of her death, I was in shock and tried not to believe it. I had just seen her two days prior. I cried at the thought she was gone; however, I was so thankful that I had an opportunity to see her before she died. Somehow, I still felt as though a dark cloud covered over me. I kept wondering how someone who looked so strong and healthy could be dead. She wasn't sick, and I couldn't understand why she died. I remember feeling numb and sad all at the same time. I was also afraid and anxious, and I didn't know why. After hearing the news, my godmother and I walked down to her daughter's house, which was a block and a half away, to be with her. Once we got there, it was hard for me to stay, knowing Ms. Grace was across the hall dead. I knew I had to leave my god-sister's house because I overheard the family talking about someone coming from the coroner's office to remove her body. After hearing that, I knew I could not stay any longer. I had to do something to get my mind off what I was feeling because it was so overwhelming for me.

She Was My True Friend

Before the coroner's office arrived to remove Ms. Grace's body, I left because I didn't want to see her being taken out of the house. I told my godmother I wanted to go back to the house, and I would come back after Ms. Grace's body was removed. As I started walking back to my godmother's house, I began remembering Ms. Grace and all the conversations we had. I thought about all the things she told me and the secrets we shared. I was so lucky to have had her in my life. She was one of many strong women who helped shape my life. She was a kind and compassionate person. I felt honored to have known her. I loved Ms. Grace. She was my best friend even though she was a senior citizen. It's funny because you think you would not have anything in common with someone eighty years old, but age didn't matter. It was not something that held me back from connecting with her. Ms. Grace really enjoyed my company, and I enjoyed being around her. She was truly there for me. She took the time to listen to me and made me feel really good.

What I loved most was she would tell me the truth whether I liked it or not. She'd comment on my clothes if she liked what I was wearing or on the way my hair was combed. We would sit on the front porch talking for hours while drinking lemonade, eating snowballs, or enjoying a slice of watermelon. After she finished her watermelon, she would take the rind and wipe her face with it. When I first saw her do this, I asked her why she was wiping her face with a watermelon rind, and she would say it made her skin smooth. She talked about her late husband and how she missed him. She would also tell me how her children didn't like that she lived alone, and they wanted her to move in with one of them. She talked about when she was younger and how she liked fashion and mostly food because she liked to cook. She also would tell me how she thought I was talented and special and that my future held great things.

The Call

Upon arriving back at my godmother's house, I told her son what was happening and that I was going back to my god-sister's house once Ms. Grace's body was removed. To pass the time, I began watching television because I didn't know what else to do. After about a half-hour or so, I decided to go back to my god-sister's house. As I was halfway down the street, I remembered I had left my keys. I immediately turned around to go back to the house to get them. Upon entering the house, I got my keys and walked back out the door. While walking down the steps, I heard the phone ring. As soon as I began walking down the street, I heard my godmother's son yelling for me to come back to the house because I had a phone call. I returned to the house, picked up the phone, and said, "Hello." The person on the other end of the line was the voice of an unfamiliar female.

This Can't Be True

As she began talking to me, she said Sonnyboy had gone swimming in the Industrial Canal with a group of his friends earlier during the day, and he had drowned. She also told me the rescue team was unable to locate his body. The only thing I remember was dropping the phone and running out the door screaming. I had no idea where I was going, but I had to run. So, I did. I think I only ran about a block, but those few minutes were the most painful moments of my life. My godmother's son was running after me while calling out my name and telling me to stop running. I finally stopped running, and he tried to calm me down. He then walked me back to the house. Once we got back, the only words to describe my emotions were shock, anger, and guilt. I felt guilty for not being there to save my brother. This experience created an internal chaos I had never felt before. After all, the worst possible thing just happened. I had just lost my only brother and my best friend on the same day. Part of me died that day too.

On My Way Home

Once my godmother was told my brother had drowned, she took me home so I could be with my family. Upon arriving home, everybody in the neighborhood had already heard what happened to my brother. As my godmother drove up to the house and parked the car, my friends came over to tell me how sorry they were. As I entered the house, I heard my sisters crying, and I saw my mom sitting in the living room in her favorite chair. I immediately ran over to where she was sitting, fell to my knees, placed my head on her lap, and began sobbing. I could hear her saying, "It's going to be okay, Jiddy. (That's what my mom called me.) It's going to be okay." When I finally raised my head from her lap, I saw the house was full of people. Neighbors were everywhere trying to figure out what they could do to help. People were coming in with food and bringing it into the kitchen. People were also telling my sisters and me to let my mom get some rest. I then noticed my godmother and two ladies walking over to my mom and leaning over her. They began rubbing her back, and I could see the tears streaming down her face. One of the ladies got a towel and wet it. She started wrapping my mom's face with it and asking her if she was in any pain or needed to go to the hospital. I assumed they were asking her this because my mom was pregnant. My stepdad tried to get Mom to lie down and rest, but she said she wanted to wait to hear if they found my brother, and she needed to pray, hoping he may still be alive.

Search and Rescue

Later that evening, police officers came to the house and told my mom and stepdad that the rescue team was unable to locate my brother's body. They also stated they had to stop the search because it became too dark for them to see, and they would continue the search the next morning. At that time, my mom fell to her knees and started screaming, "No, he's not dead, No, he's not dead." My stepdad leaned down, picked Mom up off the floor, and laid her on the couch. Once the officers left, my stepdad tried to get Mom to lie down. After everyone else left, we stayed up for a while, hoping to hear a different kind of news, but we didn't. Finally, we all got ready for bed. My sister, Doris, and I got in bed together and just laid there praying that Sonnyboy swam to safety and was waiting for someone to find him. It was hard for us to fall asleep. Eventually, Doris fell asleep, but I just laid there staring at the ceiling. My sister, Eloise, assumed we were asleep. As I looked over at her in the bed across from us, I noticed her taking her pillow and pressing her face into it. I could hear her screaming, "Not Sonnyboy, not Sonnyboy, please Lord, let it not be him. Let him be alive."

Clowning Around

As mentioned earlier, during the summer, most of the neighborhood kids would get together and go to the Industrial Canal to swim, and whenever my brother was with them, he would go into the water, and he would clown around. He would go under the water, stay underneath for a few seconds, and then come up to the surface laughing. The kids would always say that he was a show-off because he was an excellent swimmer. Later, I learned that on this particular day, he did his usual clowning around and joking while he was swimming, but this time it was different. He went under and never came back up. The group of kids with him said he dove into the water, came up, and went under again, "pretending to be drowning," waving and flinging his arms. He did this several times. The last time he went under the water, he did not come back up. They also said they didn't immediately think anything was wrong when he didn't resurface because they thought he was still kidding around. After waiting for a few more seconds, they realized something was wrong. Some of the boys dove into the water, hoping he was somewhere in the area, maybe tangled in some weeds, but they couldn't find him. Some of the girls ran back to the neighborhood and told what happened. The police were called, and they arrived with a rescue team. The rescue divers tried for several hours until it was dark, but they were unable to locate my brother's body.

The Waiting Period

My brother was an excellent swimmer, and I just could not understand why this happened. After searching for days, my brother's body had not yet been recovered, and I refused to believe he was gone. I remember we prayed for him to still be alive, but our prayers went unanswered. For days, we waited and kept our faith, but our faith began to fade away as the days passed. About five days later, on June 24, a man was fishing and spotted a body floating in the water about a mile or so from where Sonnyboy went under the water. On that day, the man who found the body floating in the water told my family he initially wasn't sure if it was a body or not in the water. However, as he got closer, it became clear that it was a body with crabs surrounding and covering it. He said that he then notified the police, and once the rescue team arrived, they confirmed and recovered the body. He added that the police notified the coroner's office, and they transported the body to the morgue. He then gave his condolences to our family and said he hoped it wasn't our family member. My stepdad thanked him for reporting it, and if it wasn't Sonnyboy, it was someone's family member.

Later that day, the police officers came to the house and notified us that a young black male had been recovered from the Industrial Canal and that the body was taken to the morgue. We were also told it would take about a week or so for the body to be identified because his body was so badly decomposed from being in the water for so long. They further stated that the body would have to be identified through dental records.

Not Good News

The hardest part for my family was waiting and not knowing if it was my brother's body they found floating in the water. Once the body was identified, an officer came to the house and informed my family they had made an identification of the body that was found in the canal, and it was indeed my brother. Upon hearing this, my mom fainted. For me, I could not comprehend in my mind that my brother was dead and that he was never coming back. It was especially hard for me to accept this, given I did not see his body. I was tormented by the thought of never having a chance to say goodbye.

Hearing he was dead made the loss a bit more real because, before this, my family and I lived with hope and then later, hoping against hope. Learning this caused us to feel his absence, and there was a new heaviness all around the house. The laughter was gone, the music was gone, and there was no clowning around. He was the jokester of the family and clowned around a lot. I would sit and just wait for him to come out from one of the rooms or come from behind the door, put his hands over my face, and say, "I got you," and then explode in laugher. I could see those big brown eyes and that contagious smile.

Unimaginable Pain

I can still remember watching my mother's face when she was told the news of my brother's death. I recall all of the strange events that happened after Sonnyboy's death. My mother never seemed the same. You could see the pain in her eyes and even in her body. It was as if a piece of her heart had been cut out on that tragic day. I felt like my family had been ripped apart, especially my siblings. There were four of us, my eldest sister

Eloise, Sonnyboy, Doris, and of course me, but now a part of us was gone. Each morning waking up to the horrible fact that he was dead was unimaginable. However, I was blessed to have my sisters, Eloise and Doris, walk alongside me. We loved each other unconditionally, and we had an unspoken bond that no one could match. My brother was two years older than me and was always there for me. He stood up for me countless times when kids made fun of me for being so tall and skinny with big eyes. He would also encourage me and tell me my eyes were big and pretty like his. When he got in trouble, I was there for him. Sonnyboy and I hung out a lot. We went fishing, crawfishing, climbed trees, and picked mulberries and blackberries together. When we brought them home, Mom would make a blueberry pie. The family would get together in the backyard, make a fire, and boil the crawfish and crabs along with potatoes. Those were fun days, and I could not bring them back.

Feelings of Loneliness

Weeks following my brother's death, I would see him in the places we went together. Although we supported each other, I felt he mostly supported me. I felt completely alone, and even though I had my sisters, I still wished my brother and best friend was there. It was unbearable to think he would never be at my side again. My eldest sister was my lifeline. When I was quiet, she would do something she knew I enjoyed to pull me out of myself. She and I would go walking and just talk about Sonnyboy. She even tried clowning around with me to make me laugh, and even though I laughed, it wasn't the same. I laughed at her trying to act like him, and I really appreciated what she was trying to do.

The Funeral

The day of the funeral was the toughest. It was the time of letting go of his physical body and accepting the idea we would not be seeing him again—seeing those big brown eyes looking at me and smiling. This was the saddest day of my young life. I remember my mom walking behind my brother's casket crying as they carried it up a steep flight of stairs to the chapel.

Once we were inside the chapel and seated, I recall a lot of crying. As I looked at my mom, she was rocking back and forward, and all of a sudden, she stood up, walked over to my brother's casket, and laid her body over it. She started calling his name, "Sonnyboy, Oh my baby." I just sat there crying and looking at her and her body lying over my brother's deep brown casket. My stepdad got up, walked up to the casket, and wrapped his arms around my mom, and just held her for a few minutes. He then led her back to her seat. Sitting there watching my mom, I just felt so overwhelmed with sadness and loss, and I worried about her. I was also angry that I wouldn't be able to see him again and desperately wanted to understand why him, why my brother had to die.

Sitting there, I was having a hard time trying to understand my only brother was inside that box. I kept thinking to myself, my brother is not dead; he's not in that casket. After all, how can one box contain such a larger-than-life person? It just didn't make any sense to me. How could he be dead? This question continued to play in my mind. I never got to see his body because it was a closed casket. How was I to accept the fact that he was really dead without proof? During the service, I kept telling myself over and over, "I know he's gone; my brother is dead." I struggled in a state of disbelief.

Having to Accept Reality

I think that sense of disbelief and shock is what allowed me to function, to survive. It was as though my brain was telling me that Sonnyboy was just gone away for a little while, but not forever. Realization finally set in, and I eventually accepted he was gone forever, and I had to learn how to live with it.

For the next few months after Sonnyboy's death, I didn't know how I would be able to get through this and move forward. He was my best friend and one of the greatest heroes in my life. My world as I knew it seemed to stop. I wanted to be alone in my pain and try to stay connected to my brother in any and all ways I possibly could. A part of me was lost. At night I would cry until I finally fell asleep, hoping that when I woke up, his death would have been a dream. I often wondered, "What was he thinking when he went under the water?" Was he frightened, or did anything pull him under? How long was it before he actually died?

There was a huge void when my family lost Sonnyboy. At first, Mom would take out Sonnyboy's picture and just sit and hold it close to her chest. She would cry for long periods. In fact, that contributed to my siblings and me not talking about him as much because we didn't want her to be sad and see her cry. Of course, we talked about him among ourselves during the first several months, but then we just stopped. It wasn't until I was an adult that I remember us finally talking about him comfortably again with our mom. That's the thing about grieving. Once someone's gone, people think it's best not to talk about the person who has died because of the pain it brings. That's what we were taught to do. We were told through actions, not words, that you just have to get on with your life and not let it get you down. The hardest part was not being able to talk to my mom about him. There was so much pain in her eyes. So, I had to keep everything inside, and it hurt so much trying to pretend I was okay when I wasn't.

Reflection
Impact of Losing a Sibling

When my brother died, my whole world changed. I had no idea what grief was and certainly didn't know how to deal with it. I was angry that he had left me, and this led to guilt. What my brother and I had was a special bond and an awesome relationship. His death affected me in so many ways, and it left a gaping hole in my heart. Talking or even thinking about him was painful. There were times when I thought I was moving on and the pain and sadness were getting better, but then at times, something or someone would remind me of him, and I would fall back into those feelings of sadness, loneliness, and guilt. I realized I had to be open and honest about where I was emotionally rather than trying to hide how I was feeling. I also had to allow myself to receive the love and support I was given. When I was ready, I had to give myself permission, time, and space to feel and heal. I chose to focus on the love my brother and I shared and for having him being a part of my life for as long as I did. Moreover, I had to focus on the endless memories he gave me, which was healing in itself for me.

At a young age, I had to remember not only did my siblings and I were grieving the death of our only brother, but my mother was grieving the death of her only son. Therefore, it was hard for her to provide adequate emotional support to my sisters and me.

Whether the death you are experiencing was sudden or expected, the shock, disbelief, and pain can be overwhelming. Know that everyone copes differently, and each person will have their own way of working through their pain. There is no right or wrong way to grieve, and there is no specific amount of time it takes to get through the grieving process. To the readers who have young children, I want to share with you that children grieve too, but sometimes can grieve in silence for many reasons including, but not limited to, not wanting to upset other family members, not being invited to be open to sharing their thoughts and feelings, or being unsure how to grieve.

- ❖ You have the right to feel what you feel.
- ❖ Regardless of what type of relationship you had with your sibling, you have a right to grieve.
- ❖ Your grieving experience is only one of its kind and it's unique and personal.
- ❖ Communicate how you are feeling with other family members.
- ❖ There are no "right" and "wrong" way to grieve.

CHAPTER 2
California Dreaming

"To everything, there is a season and a time to every purpose under the heaven."
Ecclesiastes 3:1(NKJ)

Each and every person who enters our lives serves a purpose. Sometimes, we may not understand that purpose right away, or we may not even understand why they are a part of our lives in that particular season. But it is important for us to keep in mind that every person who will ever come into our life is a part of God's divine plan.

A Life-Altering Offer

After Sonnyboy's death, I tried to go back to being my "normal" self until the summer of 1959, when I moved to Oakland, California, with my aunt, Velma, and my uncle, Quinton. My aunt was my mother's older and only sister. Aunt Velma was one of three strong women who had influenced my life in significant ways. When she was around, she would encourage me to stand up for myself and never give up on my dreams. Aunt Velma would also give me guidance on things I was concerned about. When I was young, she used to read to me for hours and made me read as well. She would also quiz me on my weekly spelling and history tests. Now that I look back, I realize she instilled in me the importance of reading. My aunt and I always had a special relationship, and I'm forever grateful for her and my uncle for making a difference in my life.

My mom informed me my aunt and uncle were coming to New Orleans for a visit. My aunt usually came around every two years or so, but she was always alone. However, this time she came with her husband. After they arrived, my mom shared with me, she and my aunt had been having conversations for some time about me moving to California to live with my aunt and uncle. My aunt and uncle didn't have any children at that time. Mom asked me how I felt about moving to California and expressed she felt there would be more opportunities available to me. Mom told me to think about it and to let her know if I wanted to go. She also told me if I decided I didn't want to, it was okay, and they would understand. Although I was excited, I didn't understand why my aunt and uncle chose me and not one of my others siblings. Although my aunt and I had an amazing relationship, it was a surprise she didn't ask one of my younger sisters.

After thinking about the offer for a few days, I decided I wanted to go with my aunt and uncle to California because it sounded like a great opportunity for me, not to mention, I loved both of them, and we really got along well. I knew this would be a turning point in my life, moving so far away, especially to another state, and leaving my family behind. Nevertheless, I was willing to take that chance and opportunity and experience something different. The hardest part for me was leaving my family, especially my siblings.

Saying Goodbye

When the day finally arrived for us to leave, I was both excited and frightened at the same time. I struggled with saying goodbye because "goodbye" felt like forever. The thought of being so far away from home and from my family and friends was scary. The trip to California took about four days driving. My aunt and uncle had a blue and white 1957 Chevy Impala. During the drive to California, we stopped in several places. I remember stopping in Austin, Texas, Albuquerque, and Arizona. Somewhere along the way, I remember coming across a sign, and my aunt, Velma, looked over at me and asked if I could read the sign, which was written in Spanish. She said, "Do you know how to speak Spanish?" and surprisingly enough, I read the sign that said, "Si Hablo Española."

Immediately after reading the sign, I realized where we were. Who would've thought I would have the chance to visit Juarez, Mexico, during that time?

My aunt and uncle decided to use our brief stops as an opportunity to do some siteseeing. I even remember trying on a sombrero, a wide-brimmed hat made of straw, and taking a lot of pictures. I was definitely out of my element, but the experience was like nothing I had ever seen, and the memories have stayed with me after all these years. It was like my own youthful awakening. All I had ever known was New Orleans, so our brief visit to Mexico was a life-changing adventure for me. To see other things, other cultures, and people of different nationalities had a major impact on my life. As much as I would have enjoyed staying in Mexico a little longer, we still had quite a way to go before arriving in the Bay Area of California.

A Turning Point in My Life

After hours upon days of driving, we finally arrived in Oakland, California. It was absolutely beautiful! Before then, I had never been outside of New Orleans, and to go from being one of several children at home to being the only one in sight was truly a chilling experience. Once we arrived, the neighborhood looked impressive. The house looked quite nice as we pulled into the driveway. I got out of the car, walked to the front door, and waited on my aunt to open the door. Upon entering the house, I walked around and loved it. It felt so peaceful. My aunt and uncle made me feel so incredibly comfortable and welcomed. Living with them was awesome, and Aunt Velma made me feel like this was my home. Although I heard all about the glitz and glamour of my aunt and uncle living in the Golden State, in reality, and to my surprise, they had a normal simple lifestyle. Aunt Velma worked at the naval base in Alameda, and my uncle worked for the Kaiser Corporation in Oakland. After settling in, it felt strange having my own room, bathroom, and television. Back home, I barely had a closet for myself. I had to move all the way to California to finally get space of my own. The quiet and solitude kind of drove me nuts for a while, and even though I loved living with them, I wished one of my siblings was there with me. Eventfully, I became accustomed to the environment.

California was certainly a different place. I was introduced to a new lifestyle and culture. I realized just how unique the experience of living there would be for me. This was the first time I had seen black and white people walking down the street together, holding hands and dining together in restaurants while laughing and talking. Of course, there was the huge culture shock of seeing so many biracial kids who didn't just identify with their black heritage but their white lineage as well. The list just goes on and on. For the first time in my young life, I was able to go anywhere my heart desired without feeling like I was unwelcomed. The schools were also integrated, which was a far cry from the current policies of the Jim Crow South. I no longer found myself in an establishment where whites sat on one side and blacks on the other.

On weekends, I recall going to the local roller derby skating rink to hang out. Who would've thought there was actually a sport where a group of people skated around in a circle and intentionally knocked each other over the railing? It may not seem like much, but just being there provided a sense of liberation for me. I was like a kid in the candy store. To be able to participate in all of these activities with different people and cultures and not have anyone look down on me felt amazing. During this time, I realized I didn't have to accept things people just threw my way. Throughout the time I lived in California, it showed me a different way of life. I made a conscious decision to never look down on another person because I knew the feeling all too well. To this day, I still choose to treat people with respect.

On One of My Visit's Home

During one of my summer visits back to New Orleans, I met a boy named Lionel through my best friend Georgia's boyfriend. Georgia and I were best friends, and I met her when I came home for summer vacation. She lived across the street from my family, and we kept in touch with each other over the years. We also made a point to get together whenever I came home. One evening, Georgia came over to my house to see if I'd go with her so I could meet her new boyfriend. My initial thought was to make up an excuse to get out of going, but I did want to meet this new guy of hers. Georgia had to meet up with him at the local sweet shop, which was within walking distance from our house. Once we got there, we encountered a group of boys across the street from the sweet shop, and my anxiety level immediately went up. As I glanced at the group of guys standing across the street, I saw "him," and it was definitely something different about him.

Love at First Sight

My eyes glanced at him, and I quickly grabbed Georgia by the arm to ask about this stranger who immediately caught my attention, "Girl, who is that?" She said, "That's Lionel." In a matter of minutes, I quickly learned that Lionel was actually Georgia's boyfriend's best friend. He was eighteen years old and had just graduated from high school. We then walked across the street, and she introduced me to him. I soon learned I knew his brother, Brimp. Brimp lived directly across the street from my mother's house and next door to Georgia's house, but I don't ever recall seeing Lionel visit his brother when I was home on visits. I knew if I had, I would have definitely remembered—trust me. It wasn't every day I'd encounter someone like him. We both connected instantly, and I really liked him. Although it was my first time ever talking to Lionel, there was something unique about him. I wouldn't necessarily call Lionel a quiet person, but he was certainly a more laid-back type of guy. I think that's why we got along so well. Unlike those moments you read about in your favorite romance novels, that initial conversation wasn't filled with any magical moments, but everything with us just came naturally. To be honest, I couldn't recall one thing we talked about during our first conversation, nor did it matter. All that mattered was that I met this guy, and he made me feel safe and secure. That guy would eventually help lay the foundation for the rest of my life.

Developing a Friendship and Relationship

After that day, Lionel and I hung out the entire summer just getting to know one another. We would hang out with our friends at the local Sweet Shoppe, which had all the trimmings, including snacks, burgers and fries, milkshakes, a jukebox, laughter, and a lot of fun. Oh boy, there was nothing like choosing a song on the jukebox and dancing to the songs of music greats such as Barbara George, James Brown, Aretha Franklin, Mary

Wells, Sam Cooke, Jackie Wilson, and Frankie Lymon. We also went to the movies and Lincoln Beach. Lincoln Beach was a spot similar to Great America but had an area across the street from the rides for dancing. It was moments like those that I hoped would never end, but it didn't change the fact that I still had a life outside of our relationship and would need to return to California after summer vacation.

My Summer Winding Down

Before returning to California, Lionel invited me to meet his family. This was the first indication our relationship was really getting serious. At first, I was a little nervous about meeting his family, but once I met them, they were really nice. I could tell he had a very loving and close family, and they were very welcoming. Lionel was the youngest of three brothers and two sisters. His grandmother stayed with them as well. A week later, I took him home to meet my family, and as I stated earlier, Lionel's brother lived across the street from my family, and they knew his brother and his wife. Afterward, we decided we would continue our relationship and build on it even though we were going to be more than 2,000 miles apart. We also agreed we wanted to give our relationship a chance because we loved each other.

Developed a Friendship and Relationship

After returning to California, Lionel and I spoke almost every day on the phone for hours, and this was where our courtship really took place. He was a great guy. He was caring, he was compassionate, and he was concerned about every aspect of my life. We truly enjoyed talking and getting to know one another. He became my best friend, and our feelings for each other grew stronger and stronger each day. I firmly believe you can make anything work if you want to, and we wanted our newfound relationship to work. There is an old saying, "Absence makes the heart grow fonder." I can honestly say this statement was true for us. We got to know each other more intimately during our phone conversations and a lot quicker than we otherwise would have. In the months that followed, I felt like I had known Lionel for years. Lionel was gentle, soft-spoken, an excellent listener, and had great morals. Most of all, he was a Christian. He was not perfect, but he was good-hearted and a charismatic man who had a strong inner-core underneath his exterior, and I believe this is why I loved him, faults and strengths alike. Yes, his jokes were certainly one of his flaws. Lionel had the corniest jokes that sometimes didn't make any sense, but I loved them anyway. I used to wonder what marriage would be like with him. As many young girls do, I used to imagine what my wedding day would be like, who I would marry and how great it would be. I looked forward to my wedding day as being this dreamy, spectacular experience with romance, a stunning wedding cake, and dazzling lights and candles flickering into the night as I danced with my prince charming. You can tell I read a lot of modern romance books. For most of my adolescent life, I was obsessed with the idea of love and being in love. I couldn't wait until the holidays to return home so Lionel and I could be together again. During our many conversations, we often talked about the possibility of getting married once I returned to New Orleans.

Proposal

Upon returning to New Orleans, it was as if Lionel and I had never been apart. We were inseparable. On one particular day, Lionel told me he would take me to a movie and dinner. I had no idea he was considering proposing when he did because we went out quite often. After dinner, we went to the movies, and on our way home, he then pulled the car over and parked. At that time, he said he wanted to talk to me about something. I asked if anything was wrong. At that moment, he said, "Would you marry me?" He told me he knew from the first time he saw me he wanted to marry me and spend the rest of his life with me. I leaned over, kissed him, and said, "Yes, I'll marry you." I was so excited because the first time I saw him, I felt the same way.

My Wedding Day

One year later, we were married. Lionel and I had been planning and eagerly waiting for over a year for this day to come. Finally, I was marrying the love of my life, my soul mate, my best friend, and the man

I wanted to spend the rest of my life with. It was the happiest day of my life. Our wedding day arrived! We were married at St. David Church, and our wedding day was more wonderful and lovelier than I ever could have imagined. Lionel and I stood before our family and closest friends and exchanged the most heartfelt wedding vows. The part of the wedding I was most nervous about was the ceremony, and it ended up being my absolute favorite part of my wedding day. Rather than being nervous or emotional, I had a wave of euphoria, and I was so excited to walk down the aisle and say my vows. The room was lit up with beautiful candlelight and the smiling faces of our loved ones and friends. As we walked down the aisle, I couldn't stop smiling. I felt so relaxed and happy. I could smell the sweet scent of roses that filled the room and saw the flashing lights of the cameras. As we exchanged our vows, we stood under an arch adorned with lace, chiffon, and flowers. It was like we were nestled in our own little world made just for us. While the priest blessed us, all I could hear was the beat of my heart. It was no longer pounding with anxiety. I was happy, and I was in love. There was nothing else in the world that mattered.

Reminiscing

As I pondered my relationship with Lionel and all of the moments that led us to this day, I'm amazed at how fast time had gone by. I thought about all of the beautiful moments we shared and that I was going to be his wife. I thought, "This is so surreal, and it was really happening." Even though I was not anxious, my palms were sweating, my mouth was dry, and my heart was pounding so hard I could not hear myself think. Once I said my vows, I began to feel a sense of calmness come over me. It was as if I was on a cloud. The only face I saw was my husband. When we exchanged our vows, I knew everything was perfect.

After our vows were said, our candles were lit, and our rings were exchanged, we stared in one another's eyes as we promised our lives to each other through sickness and in health, till death do us part. Our love was about commitment, loyalty, long-suffering, and hard work. When the priest pronounced us husband and wife, I thought, "I would forever be Betty Ann Major!" Once the ceremony concluded, we turned to face our family and friends and walked down the aisle as husband and wife. Our first dance was the way I dreamed it would be. We danced to Etta James' *At Last* and talked about our love and our commitment to one another. The tenderness between us as we gazed into each other's eyes was mesmerizing. I was so excited. Just listening to him, I knew I found "The one." What more could I ask for in a partner?

Our First Home

After getting married, we settled into our new married life together and moved into our first home, a one-bedroom apartment. The first time we walked into our apartment, all I saw were wonderful things that I loved, from the big open living room to the oversized closets. When you first entered on the right, there was an eat-in kitchen with a white stove and a simple one-door white refrigerator. We loved it because this was going to be where our first memories would take place. We stayed in that apartment until I became pregnant with our first child, six months after getting married. Once this happened, we knew we had to get a larger place, but it was hard leaving because we had so many memories there, and we made this place our home for sixteen months. I was so grateful for every one of those special memories, and I carried them to every place we live.

Planning Our Family

Before getting married, Lionel and I talked about having children, and we both were open to having a large family. Lionel and I both came from large families and wanted to begin having children early on in our marriage, with them also being close in age. After getting married, I was without question ready to start a family sooner rather than later. We agreed to try for a baby right away. When we became pregnant, members of the family were concerned it was too soon. They thought we needed time to get used to married life together first, but I always wanted to be a young mother. I wanted to be able to enjoy my kids and be young enough to do things with my grandchildren and great-grandchildren.

Reflection
Building A Strong Marriage

During the first year of our marriage, I learned that being married, you become a unit, part of a team. I came to realize there are going to be differences of opinion and maybe even some challenging times. However, we learned to work through them together. I also realized that when we had disagreements, my husband never allowed me to shut down even when I wanted to. Marriage is a commitment and a bond with major work, but amazing rewards also come with it. Lionel and I agreed we wanted to really build a strong and committed marriage. The key was we did almost everything together. We also found hobbies we both enjoyed and spending time together helped us grow stronger and build a strong relationship as a married couple. Together, we learned the true meaning of marriage and what it's all about. Lionel also showed me that love transcends all physical boundaries, and that was felt and enjoyed between two people. We had a really great love for each other. It was deep, long-lasting, and super strong. We believed it would last for years to come. It was important for us to make our marriage a top priority and live every moment to the fullest. Here are some suggestions that Lionel and I did to strengthen the foundation of our marriage:

- ❖ We always said I love you
- ❖ We encouraged each other
- ❖ We kept commitments
- ❖ We never went to bed angry
- ❖ We kept the communication lines open at all times
- ❖ We responded with love and respect even when we disagreed with one another
- ❖ We didn't let resentment build
- ❖ We had patience with each other
- ❖ We respected each other
- ❖ We accepted each other's differences
- ❖ We complimented each other

- ❖ We acknowledged little things that was done
- ❖ We laughed together
- ❖ We cried together
- ❖ We prayed together

CHAPTER 3
Stormy Clouds Ahead

"Then he got up and rebuked the wind and waves, and suddenly there was a great calm." Matthew 8:26 (NTL)

Six months after Lionel and I were married, I became pregnant. I had always wanted to be a mom, and the day I found out was one of the happiest moments for me. I took a home pregnancy test—as a matter of fact, I took four just to be sure. I was ecstatic about my first pregnancy from the moment I saw those two lines and the excitement about seeing this little person my husband and I had created. Upon finding out I was pregnant, I ran into our bedroom and pounced on the bed with joy and happiness, telling Lionel, "We are going to have a baby." We were so happy. I was so excited to enter this new chapter in our life. Before we started trying to get pregnant, we talked about the baby we would have. I told Lionel I just knew we would have a girl, and he said he didn't care if our baby was a boy or a girl; he just wanted to be a father. However, there was something inside of me that said it was going to be a girl, so much so that I had a little girl's name all picked out before I even became pregnant. I remember telling Lionel about a lady and her son I had met on the train going back to California to see my aunt, Velma. Her son's name was Deshone, and I thought it was such a beautiful (and different) name. I asked Lionel if we ever had a girl whether it would be all right if we named her that. (I spelled it differently than the mother spelled her son's name.) He said, sure, if that's what I wanted.

We're Having a Baby

I always knew I wanted to be a mother. Even as a young girl, I was a mommy to my dolls. I know now that motherhood is more than having children, and in reality, it's not about me. I was just a vessel and a steppingstone. God created the family. His design was for a man and a woman to marry for life and raise their children and to know and honor Him. My mom inspired that in me. My mom not only had that responsibility but an assignment from God to impart His values and truth into our lives. She had an opportunity to direct our path toward God, shepherding our hearts as we grew into adulthood. She accomplished that. The Bible also tells us that children are a gift from the Lord (Psalm 127:3 NLT). God entrusts to us these precious gems for a short time. As a parent, I too, wanted the same thing for my children. As parents, we too had our part in helping our children, just as our parents helped us discover our God-given purpose. As parents, we are the most influential people in our children's lives. We knew we could either help or hinder their ability to live out God's purpose for their lives. We make the decision to teach and instill in them the love of God into their lives and never let a day go by without showing them the love we have for them. I knew my life would be much richer and more significant because I would cherish every moment of every day being the best Mom I could be and love them like no other.

During the course of my pregnancy, I felt my absolute greatest. I had very little morning sickness, and I felt emotionally calm throughout my pregnancy. In my early stages, I was so excited about seeing the first ultrasound. Seeing my baby on the screen for the first time made it so real for me. At that moment, it hit me like, "Wow. This is really happening." I had a tiny little human growing inside of me. It was awe-inspiring, totally unlike anything I had ever experienced. I was enthusiastic about being a mom and having our first baby. My baby's first kick was the most remarkable and indescribable feeling.

Approaching Due Date

As my due date was approaching, Lionel set up the baby's crib and a bassinet in our room for the first few months so we could keep an eye on the baby. It was also convenient when I had to breastfeed. While Lionel was getting the crib and bassinet together, I started putting all the baby's clothes in the dresser drawer and washed and folded all the diapers (back then, we had cloth diapers) because I wanted them to smell fresh. I just went overboard preparing for our baby. I packed the baby's diaper bag and my hospital bag too.

I will never forget the moment my labor began. This moment marked the step in my journey into motherhood. I can remember feeling completely normal when I woke up that morning, but later during the day, I started feeling a little crampy. I didn't have the slightest idea my baby was ready to come. It just felt like I was having menstrual cramps. Later in the evening, after dinner, I felt a wetness in my underpants, and I thought I was peeing on myself. When I checked to see, I noticed I had a slightly bloody discharge. I realized at that moment I might be in labor. I then woke Lionel up and called my mom. This was the most exciting day of my life, the day I had been waiting on for the past nine months. I was finally going to become a mother.

Baby on the Way

We had been waiting for this day for months, and now finally, it had come. We would be meeting our baby soon, and I couldn't wait. The day I went into labor, I remember waking up around six o'clock in the morning because I had a restless night and I hardly slept. I went to bed that night feeling a little crampy, and I tossed and turned because I was uncomfortable with sporadic contractions. I timed them, and they varied from fifteen minutes apart to an hour apart. I could tell things were happening when the contractions continued. I realized that they were real contractions. Later that evening, Lionel drove me to the hospital. I was nervous for the simple fact that my life was about to change and would never be the same. Soon, no longer would I be known as just Betty. I would take on a new title, a title that I had been waiting for a long time. I would be known as Mommy.

Upon arriving at the hospital, I was checked in and was taken to labor and delivery. Shortly thereafter, I was given a hospital gown and placed on a monitor. I was then told I was in active labor, about four centimeters dilated, and the baby was fine. After four hours or so, my contractions were coming closer and more intense. At that time, I was told I would be given an epidural to help me relax and lessen the pain. Finally, my water broke, and they began prepping me for delivery. I was excited and nervous all at the same time. At that moment, I felt the urge to push almost instantly, but I had no idea what I was doing. I just remembered hearing a nurse say I should be able to meet my baby really soon.

That Special Moment

Once she was born, and as they laid her on my chest, I thought I was going to actually burst with love and excitement. She was the most beautiful baby I'd ever, ever seen. The first few minutes, I just kept thinking how wonderful it was to have her here. She was so tiny with such big and bright eyes. Her birth was a moment like no other; it was amazing to think I brought a new life into this world. When Lionel saw Deshone, I'll never forget the expression of joy on his face and the way he could not stop smiling and looking at her. He picked her up, cuddled her in his arms and gave her a kiss on the forehead, and said, "I can't believe I'm a father. It feels so good." I asked him what it felt like to hold his baby girl. He said, "Incredible." I was so excited. I couldn't believe I had my handsome, charming husband and a brand-new beautiful baby girl. Everything was great. What more could I have asked for? Even though I was exhausted, ecstatic, and overwhelmed all at the same time, I couldn't wait for them to clean her up and actually hold her in my arms. When they did, I'll never forget the warm, tingling sensation that engulfed my entire body. The emotions I felt are beyond words.

Our First Night Home

Upon being discharged from the hospital while driving home, I couldn't help but think how anxious I was bringing Deshone home. It was an emotional and life-changing time for me because I wanted to do everything right. There were just too many things I didn't know, and I felt overwhelmed. When we arrived home, Lionel carried Deshone into the house, and when I walked in, I was surprised to see several family members there to welcome our bundle of joy. The family had prepared food to last a least a week. It was so much food I didn't know where I was going to put it all. After everyone left and we settled in, I put Deshone in her bassinet and sat on the bed and just stared at her. At that moment, she opened her big brown eyes and began moving her head and making squawking sounds. I guess she was letting me know that she was ready to eat. I picked her up, held her close to my heart, and I felt so much love. I sat on the bed with my new baby girl and began breastfeeding her. This was a special moment, and breastfeeding was like establishing closeness with my baby, and I so enjoyed it.

Working out Kinks

No matter how much you prepare, there's no way you can fully be ready for everything that comes with caring for a newborn for the first time. Since I had never raised a baby before, I was scared and terrified I might do something wrong. I didn't know what I was doing or should've been doing. Though the first two weeks of motherhood were nothing short of amazing, all I did day and night mostly consisted of breastfeeding every two hours and changing diapers. Deshone slept most of the time. I couldn't believe I had fallen in love with being a mom so quickly and taken to it with relative ease. Eventually, all my fears and anxiety dissipated. However, the weeks that followed were no small undertaking. Lionel and I struggle with being deprived of sleep, but it was only for a short period.

During the first six weeks, Lionel would help during the night with diaper changes, and after, he would give her to me to breastfeed. I never had any doubts he would pick up this whole fatherhood thing really quickly because he looked forward to being a dad. I also had to take a back seat at times while he figured out his new role as a daddy. I was completely mesmerized by his ability to manage both roles as a husband and a father. I think he grasped at the beginning that the best thing he could do for our daughter was to make sure her mom was taken care of, and he made that his priority. He made sure we had everything we needed before leaving for work. After six months, I found out that being a wife and mother was a roller coaster ride, and I was learning as I went, but it began to get easier once I establish a routine.

Hurricane Betsy—Stormy Night Ahead

Shortly after Deshone was born, we moved into a much larger house located in the upper Ninth Ward on France Street. The complex had four units that sat on a flat, level foundation. I liked this because I didn't have to walk up any stairs to enter the apartment. My eldest sister, Eloise, and her two girls, Pamela and Ginnel, also lived in the same complex. We were there just two months before Hurricane Betsy hit New Orleans.

On September 9, 1965, Hurricane Betsy hit New Orleans. It was a category four storm producing the city's worst flooding in decades and the deadliest and costliest to hit New Orleans. There had been breaches on both sides of the Industrial Canal, causing dramatic flooding in the Ninth Ward, St Bernard Parish, the Seventh Ward, Gentilly, and parts of New Orleans East. It was very similar to what occurred during Hurricane Katrina in 2005.

Hurricane Arrival

The day Hurricane Betsy hit New Orleans will forever be etched in my memory. I had never been through a storm like this before. The winds were blowing so hard it shook the foundation of our building complex as if it was an earthquake. I can still recall the days after, seeing the flooding and destruction all around us.

On the morning of Hurricane Betsy, there was nothing unusual that stood out from any other day. I remember Lionel went to work and worked a half-day due to the weather forecast, and my sister and I began preparing to go to the store to get things for the house. After Lionel arrived home, he and I, along with my sister, went shopping. We purchased ready-to-eat food items, canned goods, several big bags of ice, an ice cooler, drinking water, candles, and kerosene for our kerosene lamps in case the electricity went out. We were preparing just in case we would be shut in for a few days. Our families had been through several hurricanes before, so we decided not to leave our home. We had always felt safe and saw no reason to leave this time. Therefore, we decided we were going to ride this hurricane out just like before. Since our best friends lived in a two-story apartment building directly across the street from us, Lionel and Clarence (a friend) had already discussed a plan should we need to evacuate. I shared the plan with my sister, and Clarence informed other neighbors in the complex.

Settling Down for The Night

After dinner, we checked on my sister and her two girls. We watched television to get updated information about when the hurricane would make landfall. Before settling in for the evening, I filled the bathtub with water just in case we had problems with the plumbing so we could have water to bathe and flush the toilet. Lionel and I went to bed around 10:30 p.m. after the news. Although it was raining, everything was calm.

Woke Up Immersed in Water

It was nothing but God who woke me up around 4:00 a.m. to use the bathroom. As I got out of bed and my feet touched the floor, I immediately felt water around my ankles. I then walked over to turn on the light in the bathroom, and the power was out. At that time, I woke Lionel up and told him there was water in the house. Lionel jumped out of bed and picked up the flashlight that was on the nightstand. We then checked on Deshone. We both walked into the kitchen area and looked out the window to see what was happening outside. To our surprise, the water was at the ledge of our window ceil. We were like, "What in the world is this?" It looked like we were in the middle of a river. We were surrounded by water. We looked down and could see the water bubbling up through the floor, probably because our apartment laid on a flat foundation. At that point, we immediately scrambled to get dressed as the water was continually rising inside the apartment.

Preparing to Make Our Escape

I instantly picked up Deshone's infant bathtub, placed it on the counter in the kitchen, and placed her inside it. Within minutes, the water was up to my knees. Lionel then told me to get some things together, as we were going to try to make it to our neighbors' house, Clarence and Rosetta, as we had planned. We knew if we stayed much longer, it would be tragic for our family. My mind was racing. At that moment, I knew I had to get in touch with my sister. The building was structured in a way where her apartment was on the opposite side of the building, and my kitchen was on the side of her bedroom. We would often knock on the wall to communicate with each other. I now thank God for that source of contact. I started knocking on the wall and calling out her name. Eventually, I was able to make contact with her, and I asked if she and the girls were okay. She said the water was rising in her apartment, but they were all right. I then told her to get whatever she could for her and the girls and that Lionel was going to come and get them as soon as he got Deshone and me to safety. As the water was continually rising, I gathered some of Deshone's things and put them in the infant bathtub. As we prepared to leave, I got a blanket to place over Deshone's face to shield her from the wind and rain. The water continued rising, and by this time, it had risen to my waist. I looked around the apartment and saw the bed floating, the chest of drawers slumped forward, and a few of the drawers had fallen out of the chest. I also saw our garbage can from the kitchen floating past me into the living room area. All I could think of was, "Are we going to make it over to our friend's apartment building?" I was also wondering if my sister and nieces were still okay.

Begin Making Our Way to Safety

Once I finished getting some things for Deshone, Lionel said he would climb out of the window, and he wanted me to hand him the bathtub with Deshone in it. He also instructed me to climb out once he and Deshone were out. Lionel knew I couldn't swim, and I was afraid of water. At that time, he began to encourage me, saying that I could do it. He assured me everything was going to be okay. Once Lionel climbed out of the window, I handed him Deshone. He then instructed me to turn around so I could climb out the window backward. As I was climbing out, I thought my feet were never going to touch the ground. As soon as my feet touched something solid, I grabbed hold of his arm. Despite me being terrified, I quickly joined my family in the water. Lionel then told me to wrap my arms around his neck so I could be on his back.

Forceful Winds and Heavy Rain

As we started making our way through chest-high waters, there was a sense of calm as the rain lightly came down. By the time we made it into the middle of the street, the water was about to my shoulders. Suddenly, there was a downpour of torrential rain, and then the winds began to pick up and became so forceful it snatched Deshone's bathtub out of Lionel's hands. He couldn't hold his grip any longer because of the forcefulness of the wind. All I could do at that moment was scream as I watched my baby girl float away in the water. Lionel told me to just stand still where I was, and he immediately started swimming to catch hold of the bathtub. After what felt like an eternity, he eventually was able to grab hold of the bathtub and secure it in his arms. He then came back to where I was and told me to hold onto him as we continued to make our way through the water. By the time we made it to the building, the water was up to my neck. I had to hold my head up high enough to keep the water from entering my mouth. As soon as we made it to the building and inside, the rain and the forceful wind subsided and were not as forceful. After Lionel made sure Deshone and I were okay, he and Clarence went back to the apartment complex to get my sister, Eloise, and my two nieces.

Rescuing My Sister and Others

As Lionel and Clarence went back to get my sister and my nieces, I prayed they were still alive and that they make it back safely. I was told that Lionel instructed my sister to have my nieces climb out the window backward. Once they were out, Lionel had one, and Clarence had the other. He then told my sister he was going to come back and get her. Once he got the girls to safety, he went back to get my sister. After Eloise and my nieces made it to the building, Lionel and Clarence went back to rescue other neighbors. Altogether, there were four families in Clarence and Rosetta's apartment. The four men later went back to each apartment to gather canned goods and other items that were not badly damaged by the water. Lionel was also able to get Pampers and some more clothing for Deshone. Thankfully, the items were not damaged because they were in the closet on the upper shelf. We stayed with our neighbor's for four days.

Making Our Way to Safety

When the water finally began to recede, along with my sister and nieces, Lionel and I were able to make our way through the water to my grandmother's house. My grandmother lived in the uptown area. We learned via the portable radio that the city's uptown area was not seriously affected by the hurricane and was unaffected by the floodwaters. We kept Deshone in her bathtub so she would be safe as we began making our way through the water. The water was nasty and full of snakes swimming and hanging from the trees. We had to be extremely cautious not only for ourselves but also for my nieces. There were also power lines popping in the streets. As we got closer to Claiborne Street, we saw boats that were rescuing people. By the time we made it to St. Claude Street, there was little to no water. As soon as we arrived at my grandmother's house, which was about twenty miles from where we were, we were exhausted but so happy to be alive and to know that the rest of my family was safe. I later learned my mom was not able to make it home before the hurricane hit. Mom worked at Charity Hospital. At that time everyone was asked to stay because of the weather conditions. However, she told the staff she had to leave because she was unable to get in touch with her family to see if they were all right due to the power outage. Mom said she told her supervisor she had to get to her children if that meant dying while trying. She then left work after the hurricane made landfall and she believed it was clear for her to go.

A Mother's Determination

Once the hurricane had passed, Mom told us she had to walk because there was no bus service. Initially, this was okay because there was no flooding when she first started her journey home, but as she traveled closer to the upper Ninth Ward, she began to see the floodwaters. As she made her way through the rising water, she saw a man with a boat. He offered to take her as far as Pity Street and Florida Avenue because he couldn't go beyond that point. Given this would bring Mom five blocks from the house, she agreed to be taken that far. When they made it to Pity Street and Florida Avenue, she climbed out of the boat into waist-deep water. As Mom was making her way toward the house, she spotted a long, broken pole in the water and grabbed it to keep her balance. As she came closer to the house, the water became deeper and deeper, and by then, it was to her chest. At that time, she was about ten feet or so away from the house, which was on the opposite side of the street.

Crying Out for Help

My sister, Joanette, shared she was awake at the time because she was afraid the world was coming to an end. As she was sitting in her room, Joanette heard a lady screaming for help (not knowing it was Mom). She ran into Mom's bedroom and told my stepdad a lady was outside screaming for help. He told Joanette to be quiet so he could hear because he thought he heard someone screaming too. As Mom began making her way toward the house, the pole she had in her hand hit the end of the curb, and she lost her balance. She fell and went underwater. Mom was able to keep hold of the pole to pull herself up, and because she could not swim, she began screaming once again for help. Joanette then ran back to her room, looked out the window, and saw the lady holding onto a pole trying to balance herself. Joanette then realized she was witnessing Mom going under the water.

Mama Rescued from Drowning

At that moment, Joanette screamed, "Daddy, that's Mama. That's Mama." As Joanette continued screaming, she saw Mama going underwater for a second time. She thought Mom was going to die. By this time, all of my siblings were aware of what was happening and watched as my stepdad dove out the window to rescue Mom. As Mom went under the third time, he grabbed her arm. Mama began to fight him as he was trying to pull her up. He told Mom to try to stay calm. He then wrapped his arm around the upper part of Mom's body and swam back to the house. Given the house was actually built on pillars, it stood about three feet off the ground. My stepdad was able to pull Mom up onto the porch to safety. When he got her inside the house, he laid her down on the bed to make sure she was all right. After Mom calmed down, my stepdad helped her out of her wet clothes and gave her a hot cup of tea to warm up. We could have died that dreadful night if it was not for my husband and my stepdad. They were our heroes. Lionel not only saved our daughter and me but my sister and nieces, as well as our neighbors. Likewise, my stepdad saved our mom. I also realized God protected my family and me as He has done so many other times.

Reflection
The Devastation of Hurricane Betsy

On September 9, 1965, Hurricane Betsy hit New Orleans. Betsy was a category four storm when it made landfall with winds exceeding one hundred ten mph. This was the worst hurricane to hit New Orleans and the surrounding areas I had ever experienced. It has been said the city's back levees broke open, and some say they were breached on both sides of the Industrial Canal, flooding the Ninth Ward, St. Bernard, New Orleans East, and the area between Franklin Avenue and the Industrial Canal. Because the hurricane made landfall during the night, families woke up to find their homes already flooded. Water reached the attics of houses and over one-story roofs in the lower Ninth Ward. With their homes flooded, some fled to their attics, and unfortunately, some people died due to the rising water. It was reported that 164,000 homes were flooded in New Orleans.

I still remember the roar of the winds and the forcefulness of the water that almost carried my baby away. I also remember the floodwater stood for more than two weeks before people could return to their homes. It took even longer to restore flooded houses to a habitable condition before moving back in. Those who didn't have families or friends who had homes that were not damaged by the floodwaters had to stay in shelters while waiting for the federal government to provide emergency relief. Seventy-six deaths were a direct result of Hurricane Betsy.

CHAPTER 4

Tears In a Bottle

> "You keep track of all my sorrows. You have collected all my tears in your bottle. You have recorded each one in your book."
> Psalm 56:8 (NTL)

After Hurricane Betsy, along with my sister and her children, Lionel and I stayed with my grandmother for two months. The Red Cross gave families vouchers that allowed for replacing furniture and appliances. In addition, the federal government provided Small Business Administration loans without collateral, and many took advantage of these accessible loans, which were later forgiven.

Hoping We Could Salvage Some Things

Once the floodwaters receded, we went back to our home to see if anything was salvageable. When we arrived home, we were unable to get in because the door was stuck. Lionel had to kick the door several times to open it. As we entered the house, it was a total mess. Mud was everywhere. We walked through and noticed the sofa had floated across the living room and was turned upside down. One of the kitchen chairs was in Deshone's crib. Other chairs were scattered around the house, and the television was lying on the floor. There was nothing we could salvage. We lost everything—our car, furniture, appliances, and our clothing. However, most of Deshone's clothes that I had stored away in the closet on the top shelf were not damaged.

Starting Over and Surprise Baby Number Two

Eventually, we moved from my grandmother's house into a three-bedroom house with an extra-large yard for Deshone to play. Two months later, I was surprised to find out I was pregnant with our second child. I had missed my period, but I thought it was due to the stress of the hurricane and being displaced. However, we could not be happier. I later found out that three of my sisters-in-law were also pregnant; we called our babies "Hurricane Betsy babies."

Preparing for The Arrival of Our Second Child

During my second pregnancy, I felt like my first pregnancy allowed me to understand better what to expect the second time around. The happiness and love our first child brought into our lives were beyond what we anticipated, and now we were expecting and preparing for our second child, and it was as rewarding as our first. We knew there were going to be some changes in the family. I knew having a second child and taking care of two children might be a little challenging. On the positive side, having my second child gave me confidence in my ability to handle things that were a little difficult for me with our first. We also needed to prepare and help Deshone understand she would be having a sister or brother. I really didn't talk to her about that until she was about thirteen months old, which was the time my baby bump appeared bigger, and she took notice. I would tell her that her baby brother or sister was inside. At that time, she started patting my belly, and other times, she would put her head against it. I would tell her to say "Hi" to her baby sister because I again felt I was having a girl. Whenever the baby started kicking, I would put Deshone's hand on my stomach so she could feel her sister kicking, and whenever she laid her head on my stomach, I told her to sing or kiss her baby sister. This was giving her an opportunity to start bonding with the baby, which I wanted her to continue once the baby arrived.

Pregnant with a Toddler

Being pregnant for the second time was harder during my first trimester. Even though my morning sickness was about the same, it was a different experience. Between the exhaustion and the morning sickness, it was a bit challenging for me to manage. I had morning sickness that began around the eighth week. It's not like I actually felt sicker the second time around. I just couldn't manage my uncomfortableness with a toddler bouncing around all the time. Also, with my second pregnancy, I gained more weight even though I was way busier. Furthermore, caring for a toddler while pregnant is no easy task. Deshone was barely seven months, and I was still getting used to being a new mommy. At no time did I ever consider how challenging it was caring for a toddler while carrying another baby.

Even though I was fortunate to be able to take a nap whenever Deshone took her nap, I sometimes took advantage of that quiet time to read or watch a movie. With limited time for myself during the day, once Lionel came home from work, and after dinner, he took care of Deshone so I could have time for myself and relax. He even got her ready for bed.

Approaching the End of My Pregnancy

As I was approaching the end of my pregnancy, I had the urge to clean and organize and reorganize everything in the house. I started getting everything ready for our new bundle of joy. I began rewashing all the clothes we had stored away that were Deshone's and washed the additional baby clothes we purchased. We added a new crib, a dresser, and a highchair. I was excited about adding a new addition to our family. I would sit and wonder whether I would have a boy or girl even though I told Deshone she was going to have a baby sister. You see, back then, we weren't told beforehand about our baby's gender. I feel that's a good thing because in this way you can be surprised. I also wondered who the baby would look like. My mind was all over the place. I couldn't wait to have my new baby home. Lionel and I decided if we had a girl, we would name her Ginneria. Of course, if we had a boy, his name would be Lionel. The last few weeks were really tough but also exciting and special. I had no idea how hard the last few weeks could be with a toddler. After cleaning and chasing her around the house, I would run out of breath, and I could not hold Deshone while standing for long periods.

Progressing in Labor

When I was pregnant with my first child, childbirth was completely mysterious. Everyone said it would be really painful, and yes, I came to agree, especially when real labor began. As I neared the end of my second pregnancy a year and a half later, I figured I had a little experience. The truth is, I still had no idea what I was in for. This time around, my mucus plug came out a day before I went into labor. After putting Deshone down for a nap, I decided to sit on the front porch and have a glass of iced tea. Suddenly, I started to feel a little uncomfortable in a crampy way, and later I felt like I needed to use the bathroom. I noticed that when I stood up to go to the bathroom, my mucus plug came out, but there was no sign of any blood. When Lionel arrived home from work, I told him what happened earlier. During dinner, I shared with Lionel I was still feeling a little crimpy, and he shared that I may be in labor or we were approaching labor. After taking a shower and getting ready for bed, the cramps did not subside. I continued to have what felt like menstrual cramps, but the pain grew intense and unbearable. I could barely walk, and I could not sleep. I finally could not take it anymore and decided to wake up Lionel. I told him we were about to have the baby and needed to get to the hospital. He just about jumped out of bed and said, "Let's go." I called my sister, and she came to stay with Deshone.

Almost There

When we arrived at the hospital, I was checked in and taken to labor and delivery. After being examined, I was told I was indeed in labor and had dilated four to five centimeters. Shortly thereafter, the doctor came in and broke my water bag. The contractions came faster and stronger and stayed longer. I was given medication to ease the pain.

The Birth of my Second Child

It's a girl. At that time, the doctor spanked her bottom, and I heard her cry. It was like a sweet melody to my ears. As they placed her in my arms, all of the pain I felt was instantly gone. Lionel and I decided to name her Ginneria. The emotional bond I felt for my daughter had me speechless.

She was gorgeous. Her beauty just took my breath away. Ginneria had a head full of hair. It was a dark brownish-black, which laid strength down her neck, and she weighed six pounds, eight ounces.

Bringing Ginneria Home

Once I settled in, I realized that taking care of a newborn and a toddler wasn't as hard as I thought it would be, especially since Lionel took a two-week vacation. This made things much easier—for a little while. After Lionel returned to work, it was a bit uncomfortable because my body was still sore, but once I found a routine that worked for me, I started feeling more relaxed with my two little girls. Deshone welcomed her baby sister with a lot of hugs and kisses. Seeing the love she had for her sister was so precious to watch. She was obsessed with Ginneria.

Ginneria slept most of the time, and when she was awake, Deshone was constantly running and grabbing diapers and bringing me the baby's wipes and her pacifier. After several weeks, Ginneria started to show her personality. She was calm, not really fussy, and she didn't cry very much. When Ginneria was awake, she would lay in her crib and just look around. She had the most beautiful eyes. On the other hand, Deshone was a different story. Deshone wanted to play, and she wanted to play with Ginneria. One positive change that my second child brought was an increase in my confidence in being a mom.

Growing Family

A year and a half later, I had a feeling I might be pregnant again. I started feeling a little nauseous, my breast was tender, and I was feeling somewhat fatigued. At one point, I told my husband I felt like something was really wrong with me, and I was going to make a doctor's appointment to see what was going on. To which he joked, "Maybe I knocked you up again." I laughed and said, "Yeah, right." Sure enough, two weeks later, I went to the doctor and found out I was pregnant. We couldn't be more excited to be having another member of our growing family. We were overjoyed and extremely blessed. With our first baby, we were learning so much, and everything was really new. Having our second baby was a little tough because we were dealing with an infant and a toddler for the first time, along with all the dynamics that went along with it. Now that our third child was on the way, we thought we finally had it all together. I'd learned so many things going through my last two pregnancies. I felt so much more prepared the third time. The third pregnancy was completely different in so many ways. It actually was a really laid-back pregnancy. I was far less anxious than my previous pregnancies, and I had fewer issues. It was a really good feeling to not be the worried first-time Mom anymore.

Baby Number Three—Including My Girls with the New Baby

After finding out I was pregnant, I began to prepare Deshone and Ginneria for the arrival of their new brother or sister. I wanted to get them ready for the changes and include them in the process. Therefore, I decided to include my girls in the preparations and get them excited about their new sibling. I would take them to my doctor's appointments so they could hear their new brother or sister's heartbeat. They would sit next to me, rub my stomach, and say, "Hi, baby." It was important to me to have my girls share in this special and exciting moment with me. They began to understand (as only a child can) they would have a new little brother or sister and that the baby would be coming soon. I told them they would be able to help me with their sister or brother when he or she came home and all the ways they could help. I even talked to them about feeding the baby, and they began practicing with their dolls. As I watched my girls play in their room, my heart was filled with joy and excitement.

Excited for Another New Life

Even though we would have three kids under five, I was up for the challenge. One thing I can say, pregnancy and delivering my babies were absolutely miraculous to me. I'd experienced pregnancy twice before, but then again, listening to my third baby's heartbeat and feeling him or her move around still took me aback. I felt so blessed to have this experience again for the third time. Even with all the discomfort and every crazy craving, it was all worth it. I felt I was well prepared to take care of my two girls and our new arrival.

Start of Labor

Two days before I went into labor, I prepared a bag for Deshone and Ginneria to take with them to my sister's house. I also rechecked the bag I was taking to the hospital and the baby's bag. The morning leading up to going into labor, I made breakfast for the girls and me. After breakfast, I felt a little crampy, so I laid on the couch and let them watch Sesame Street. After lying there for a while, the cramps seemed to go away. I later got up and started making the beds, cleaning, preparing for lunch, and prepping dinner. After lunch, I put my girls down for a nap, and I took a nap myself. Once Lionel made it home from work, and we had dinner, I started feeling the crampiness again. The cramping started getting worst, along with some spotting. After a while, I started having light contractions, but nothing I thought was a big deal. I knew then I was in the early stage of labor. Later that evening, an all too familiar gush came through as my water broke, but still, I thought I had more time. In the meantime, Lionel called my sister to come over to the house to be with the girls so he could take me to the hospital. Once my sister arrived, we left for the hospital, and my contractions became stronger and stronger.

The Birth of My Third Child

Once we arrived, Lionel parked in the emergency room entrance, ran in, and a nurse came out to help me out of the car and into a wheelchair. After this, everything happened at lightning speed. The nurse rushed me to the delivery area, where a team of nurses assisted me onto the bed. They began taking off my clothes and putting me in a hospital gown. At this time, my contractions were coming every two to three minutes. The doctor came in and began examining me. The only thing I remember was the pain and him instructing me to push while saying, "The baby is coming" At that moment, I screamed and pushed and pushed, and the next thing I heard was "It's a girl." My baby was born. The nurse then placed her on my chest, and I kissed her on her forehead. She was beautiful, and I fell in love all over again for the third time. We decided to name her Michelle.

Bringing Michelle Home

When we brought Michelle home from the hospital, the girls were so excited to meet their baby sister. At first sight, Deshone asked, "Is that the baby who was in your tummy?" The both of them then climbed on the couch and just stared at her. Ginneria grabbed her hand, held it for a minute, and then placed Michelle's hand on her face, moved it toward her lips, and kissed her hand. Deshone was eager to hold her sister. She was sitting next to Ginneria with her arms extended out, waiting for me to place Michelle in her arms. As I placed Michelle on her lap, she then leaned over and gave her a kiss on the forehead and said, "My sissy." After becoming a mother of three, my world totally changed again. It became a little more hectic, and most days it was pretty awesome. I wouldn't trade it for anything in the world.

Family Adjusting to Third Child

I had concerns about my first child, Deshone, after Ginneria was born, like whether she felt she was getting enough attention. Once I came home from the hospital, I decided to have her help me with Ginneria and would read books to both of them in hopes she would not feel neglected. So, once our third child was born, I did the same thing with them. They helped me with Michelle, and I read to the three of them. However, because they had each other to play with, they had a built-in playmate. The balance worked well, and I was pleasantly surprised with how well our family adjusted to having a third child.

Family Continues to Grow—Baby Number Four

Several months after Michelle was born, I discovered I was expecting our fourth baby. Yes, you heard me correctly, a fourth baby. It was all so surreal. When Lionel and I found out I was pregnant with our fourth child, he said, "It's a boy. I know it's a boy." After having three girls, I just had a feeling this baby was going to be a boy. For a while, thoughts were whirling around my head, wondering if I was going to have twins because Lionel was a twin (his baby sister died at birth), and I was gaining weight so fast.

Throughout the next few months, I found myself feeling extremely tired. I presume that's what happens when you're pregnant with three small children, all under five. With two toddlers and an infant who constantly needed all my time and attention, I was often left worn out. At times, I had no idea what was going on inside this belly of mine. Sometimes, it felt like somersaults were taking place, and other times I was so active I didn't notice any activity. Even though my children were on a routine schedule that I followed very early on since they were born, I was still tired. The nice part of following a strict schedule was they all took a nap at the same time, which allowed me to be able to take naps during the day as well. I also enjoyed having quiet time because it was during those moments of quiet time that I tried to soak up every moment of my pregnancy. The girls also went to bed around the same time and mostly slept throughout the night. Having a predictable daily and evening routine helped with children so close together. In fact, it even made it pleasurable. Of course, various things sometimes made it difficult, like colic, colds, teething, or other illnesses.

Adjusting and Making Adjustments

It was not difficult for me to adjust to the additions to our growing family. Since becoming a mother, I had become more organized, more disciplined, and intentional with my time. But I have to admit there were times I doubted whether I could step up again to the new demands. Motherhood taught me more about my strength, discipline, and becoming more organized than I ever could have imagined.

I would be remiss if I did not acknowledge it takes both parents. Lionel was a hands-on dad, and I was really blessed. He was an amazing father. He was present in every aspect of our children's lives. This was important to him, and having a large family was something he wanted too. I loved watching the way he responded calmly to our children when they had disagreements. With his help, the adjustments went smoothly.

With each new addition to our family, we had to make adjustments in our home. We had a three-bedroom house. We had our two older girls, Deshone and Ginneria, share the larger bedroom, and Michelle was in the smaller bedroom, which was set up as a nursery now that we were having our fourth baby. There was very little prep we needed to do. The only thing we did was put another crib in the room where Michelle was.

Being pregnant for the fourth time brought so much joy, unlike the first two times when joy and happiness were mixed with nervousness. My two older ones were more independent and wanted to do everything for themselves, to a certain extent. Yet, with each pregnancy, I could not wait to be full-term and hold my baby in my arms.

Burst of Energy

Leading up to me going into labor, I got a burst of energy. I began cleaning the kitchen, refrigerator, cabinets, and the stove. I then went into the living room, tidied up the bedrooms, and folded the laundry. I felt like Super Woman. I couldn't believe the energy I had. That night was a blessing because I was able to sleep without any discomfort. The next morning, I prepared breakfast for Lionel. Mornings were always our time together before he left for work. After Lionel left, I had quiet time before the children woke up. Once the kids were up, I prepared their breakfast, dressed them, and cleaned the kitchen. After making the beds and getting myself dressed, we left so I could run a few errands. After returning home, I made the girls their lunch and later put them down for their nap. I took a nap for a little while as well. While the children were still napping, I decided to get up and begin preparing dinner. As I was preparing dinner, I began to feel mild cramps, and although they were not consistent, I thought it was best to call my sister to give her notice. She decided to come over until Lionel came home from work, in case I had to go to the hospital.

Settling Down for the Night

After dinner, I got the girls ready for bed, and Lionel and I watched television. After the news, we went to bed. Just before midnight, I started having contractions, and as I turned over in bed to change positions, I felt a small gush of liquid, and I instantly knew—its time. Every time before giving birth, it started the same way—a gush. Like the other times, I tapped Lionel on the shoulder and whispered, "We're having our baby," and as before, he got out of bed and started getting ready. By this time, my trusty sister knew the drill too. She came over to be with the girls while Lionel and I headed to the hospital.

Baby Number Four on The Way

On the way to the hospital, my contractions began to get stronger, and at this point, I was hoping for a speedy delivery. Once we arrived at the hospital, I was taken to labor and delivery. After quickly examining me, I was told the baby was coming. The doctor told me to relax and take deep breathes. Lionel leaned over and said, "I can see our baby's head," and after three quick pushes, our baby boy came out and was placed on my chest. After seeing my son, I thought I was actually going to explode with joy. All Lionel could do was stand in awe. All he could say was, "I have a son, "I have a son. My son has arrived." He was so proud. After baby Lionel was cleaned up, Lionel just held him and could not stop kissing him, as he kept repeating, "I have a son. This is my boy." Finally, a boy after three girls. God blessed us with a son, and he was absolutely beautiful.

Bringing Lionel Home

Upon being discharged from the hospital, I was so excited about bringing baby Lionel home to meet his big sisters. Lionel had baby Lionel in his carrier. I sat down on the couch, and Lionel placed baby Lionel in my arms. I then opened the blanket covering his face and lowered him down for the girls to see him. I told them to say hi to their baby brother. They all began kissing him, and Michelle told him to wake up. At that time, all three girls climbed onto the couch, and while leaning over my shoulders, they just stared at Lionel, while Michelle continued telling him to wake up.

Raising Four Children

Our family grew—and it grew quickly! In a five-year period, I gave birth to Deshone, Ginneria, Michelle, and Lionel. Having four little ones was a lot, but with Lionel helping with the kids, it really wasn't so difficult. He was always there for his children, and he spent a lot of quality time with them. He was not afraid to jump in and change diapers or wake up with them in the middle of the night, even if he had to wake up earlier to get ready for work.

Lionel wanted nothing more than for me to be happy and for our children to be happy too. We both wanted to raise loving kids who felt the love of both parents. Therefore, for us, that meant having dinner together and Saturday and Sunday morning breakfast. Having family time and teaming up for bedtime routines was always exciting. Now here we were, happily raising four children. Some days were pretty awesome, and other days not so good, but I wouldn't trade it for anything. Since becoming a mother, my world has changed. Children have a way of shifting our lives in many different directions, and it can become more hectic and unpredictable. I was constantly trying to figure out what I was doing with my children, who I cherish. In the process, I was learning more than I ever thought I would. I was so grateful to be afforded the opportunity to be a stay-at-home Mom during my children's formative years.

Our Dream Home

After Lionel was born, we noticed a house that was being built in the same neighborhood where we lived before. As soon as we saw this house, we knew this was the home where we wanted to raise our family. The house was a one-story single home with a huge front porch that extended across the front of the house. Lionel said the porch was for those lazy, laid-back evenings after the kids were in bed. We both looked forward to waking up there and having the milkman deliver our milk and cream cheese, and of course, we had to get chocolate milk for the kids. The backyard provided plenty of space for the children to play and to have a swing set. What more did we need? Lionel and I decided right then and there that this would be the house, and we jumped at the opportunity and purchased our dream home.

My Life Was Forever Changed

On Saturday mornings and afternoons, Lionel always made it a priority to do things together as a family. After breakfast, we all would go grocery shopping, and afterward, he would help around the house. Once we finished, we did actives with the children. After dinner and putting the children to bed, he would go out for a couple of hours and be home no later than 10:00 p.m. just in time to catch our favorite weekly television show, "Creature Feature." We always ate pecan shortbread cookies with vanilla ice cream while we watched the show. On Sundays, we all went to church, followed by dinner with my grandmother. Life was about as perfect as it could be.

Wasn't His Norm

Friday, October 20, 1969, my life forever changed. I experienced the kind of pain that I would never wish on another human being, ever. On that particular night, Lionel said he was going to hang out with his cousin. This being a Friday, it was unusually strange that he wanted to go out since he typically went out on Saturdays. Therefore, we decided that the kids and I would go over to my mom's house, and he would pick us up later that evening. During the ride over to my mom's, I didn't have a good feeling about him going out that evening. This is why we had a few words, and I became very angry. When we arrived at the house, my mom had not made it home yet. Only my younger siblings were. So, Lionel asked me if I wanted to stay or if I wanted him to take us back home. At that point, I told him the kids and I would go to my grandmother's house instead. He then asked if I wanted him to drop us off at her house, and I said, "No, I want to take the bus." Besides, I thought the kids might enjoy a bus ride.

Saying Our Final Goodbye Without Knowing It

Upon arriving at my grandmother's house, and as the kids and I walked in, I heard the telephone ringing. My grandmother answered the phone and told me it was Lionel. I took the phone, and immediately he apologized for the disagreement we had earlier. I apologized as well. Looking back, I thank God we were able to talk with each other that night. He told me again he was going to his cousin's house who lived in Plaquemines Parish, which was about forty-five minutes from my mother's house. I then told him to enjoy himself and that the kids and I would just stay at my mom's house, and he could pick us in the morning. We ended our conversation feeling much better and laughing. The last thing he said to me before we ended our conservation was, "I love you. Kiss the kids for me, and tell Deshone she needs to listen to her mother." Of course, I didn't think anything of what he said because he would always say, "I love you," but it was strange for him to tell me to tell Deshone she should listen to her mother. So, I assured him that I would kiss the kids, let them know he loved them, and tell Deshone what he said. We then said goodbye for the last time, and I hung the phone up. The kids and I stayed with my grandmother for about an hour and then headed back to my mom's house.

The Dream

After we arrived at my mom's house, I was tired, it was late, and it was time for me to put the kids to bed. I gave them a bath and took one myself, and we all laid down on the sofa bed in the living room. Sure, the sofa bed might sound a bit uncomfortable, but it was just enough room for my babies and me. What was supposed to be a restful and peaceful night quickly turned into a nightmare. It started with the strangest dream I had. I remember waking up in a state of panic. Like most of my dreams, I was only able to recall certain details, but the details I was able to recall most was the one that caused a sense of unrest in my spirit. In my dream, Lionel had died. The only other detail I was able to remember was my four children dressed in black and white at the funeral. Seeing this, I abruptly awakened. The dream seemed so real at the time. I had no idea what the details of this dream meant, but the idea of something like that happening was almost too much for me to comprehend.

My Nightmare Came True

As I sat up on the sofa bed, still slightly shaken by my dream and struggling to gain my composure, the phone rang. As soon as my mother answered the phone, I knew it was my brother-in-law, Brimp, on the other end of the line. After taking a quick glance at my mother, I could immediately tell there was something wrong. My mother hung up the phone, and I heard her say, "Lionel is dead. He was killed in a car accident." Those words pierced my heart. This wasn't happening! It felt as though someone had plunged a knife into the pit of my stomach. I didn't want to hear that, and I definitely didn't want to believe my husband, the love of my life and the father of my children, was dead. My thoughts immediately turned to my children. How would I tell them their dad was dead when they were expecting him to pick us up in the morning? My nightmare had come true. He was dead. I couldn't believe what I just heard. I didn't want to believe it. All I could do was run. I found myself yet running again. The last time I ran was because of my brother's death, and here I find myself this time running because of my husband. I ran through the house yelling and screaming out, "I just saw this! I just saw this!" The pain was more than I could handle. After I stopped running through the house and finally sat down, I felt emotionally drained. My heart was thumping. I could hear blood rushing through my ears like a thump, and I could see my chest moving up and down under my clothes. My heart was pounding fast and hard, and I noticed my hands were trembling. As I tried to stand up again, my arms and legs began shaking, leaving me unsteady on my feet. I tried taking deep breaths to calm myself down, but my breaths were sharp. My mom came over to where I was standing and helped me back onto the sofa bed while one of my sisters gave me a glass of water. Mom also gave me a Valium to calm me down. I felt as though I had been hit by a ton of bricks. My poor babies, my poor babies. Looking at my children after hearing the news of Lionel's death was very hard and very emotional for me because all I could see was their daddy in each of their faces. They were all so little and wouldn't understand what this would mean. They had no idea what was going on.

Life as my children and I knew it ended on that fateful early morning hour when Lionel was killed, and having to explain the death of their dad was difficult and heartbreaking. I knew I had to look at each one of them in their bright eyes and tell them, but I didn't know how. What do you say to a four-year-old, three-year-old, eighteen-month-old, and a nine-month-old, knowing that they cannot understand what death meant?

Embracing My Children

I remember sitting on the sofa bed rocking back and forth, crying uncontrollably while holding and comforting my babies (well, they were actually comforting me), and Deshone and Ginneria asking me, "What's wrong, Mommy? Why are you crying?" As I held my baby boy, I looked at him, our only son, and I thought about how proud his daddy was to have had a son. Lionel was ecstatic when Lionel Jr. was born. He just held him and could not stop kissing him on the forehead, saying, "I have a son. This is my boy." He did everything for him. He fed him, changed his diapers, and gave him his evening bath. He would talk about taking him to get his first haircut and playing ball with him. The thought of him never getting to do those things or see Lionel take his first step or hear him say his first words broke my heart. All I could do was cry. Those tears weren't just for me. They were for my babies. I had to tell them that their dad was not coming to take us home. Deshone and Ginneria were the only ones who may have had lasting memories of their dad, and they had the strongest reaction to his death. Unlike them, Michelle and Lionel would never have the opportunity to really know and truly experience the love their dad had for them.

Telling My Children Their Dad Was Dead

After I got control of my emotions and stopped crying while still holding them close to me, I told them that I had some very sad news about their dad. Deshone and Ginneria just stared at me. I then explained that their dad had been in an accident and died, and he would not be coming to pick us up to take us home. Although I realized they didn't fully understand what was happening or what I was saying, Deshone's response took me off guard. As she continued staring at me, she said, "We can wait. He will be here later to pick us up." I was lost for words, so I didn't say anything. The only thing I could do was cry while I continued holding them close to me. The feeling of knowing that my children would grow up without a father was devastating. I only found solace in the fact that we had that final conversation. I was thankful and grateful that the Lord allowed us that precious moment, but it still didn't help the pain. It didn't stop me from asking myself the same question over and over again "Why him?" I was reminded of our wedding day and remembered the vow we made, "Till death do us part," but do we really take those words seriously?

Wrapping My Heading Around: The Days Following

The rest of the day, I was in a heavy fog. I can't describe the pain, except it was an enormous, heart-rending pain, and a tidal wave of emotions. I would cry until it was hard to imagine that there was any water left in my body or any hurt left in my soul. But there was. One minute, I felt I couldn't breathe, and the next minute, I plummeted into a panic attack. My heart would race, and I would shake all over. Then all at once, I was filled with sadness and an insurmountable feeling of loss like nothing I ever felt before. I couldn't eat, sleep, or even think clearly. I couldn't imagine Lionel was no longer here with us. My brain couldn't take that in. I felt completely unable to imagine a future without him. I was angry with myself and so angry with him for going out that night. I felt guilt, this horrific, suffocating guilt. Why didn't I insist that he not go out that night? Even though I was a Christian, I was angry with God. To be honest, I was angry with Him for a while. This was something I wrestled with. With such a tragic loss, I had to ask God, "Why?" Not so much "Why?" but "Why me, God?" "Why my family, Lord?" and "Why Lionel?" I felt abandoned and could not overcome the thought that he was supposed to be there with me to help me take care of our children. Although I was angry at God, I knew He was still the source of my strength, and I knew I had to surrender my pain, my angry, guilt. I had to surrender everything because if I didn't, I would not be able to make it.

The days following Lionel's death felt as if I was having an out-of-body experience. I kept thinking that if I would just go to sleep when I wake up, all of this would be just a horrible dream. I was often unaware of what was going on around me and was in a daze as I walked through the things that needed to be done (i.e., plan Lionel's funeral, choose a casket, go to the cemetery, and pick out his clothes). All I wanted to do was sit and cry. My life felt empty much of the time. I was broken, alone, and afraid. Lionel was our rock and a crucial part of our life. With him gone, I was instantly and solely responsible for our home, finances, and our children. I wasn't ready. My kids went from having two parents to one parent in the blink of an eye, and I became a widow and a single mom. I wasn't sure how I'd survive or if I even wanted to, but when I looked at my children, even though I felt completely lost, I knew I had to survive for them. My children were my life, and I was solely responsible for them now.

Hearing the Details

Eventually, more details began to surface in the coming days after the accident, and even in my emotional state, I was still unable to put the pieces together as to what happened to my husband that night. I was told during Lionel's trips from Plaquemines Parish he took the shortcut. I knew that to be true because he always took the shortcut whenever he would go to visit his father's side of the family. I never liked going with him because the road wasn't well lit and often dark when we drove back in the evening. Not to mention, it was very little traffic and a bit scary to the average person who was unfamiliar with driving down that road, but not for Lionel. He loved shortcuts. He had taken that route hundreds of times before, so this particular drive was nothing out of the ordinary.

I was also told that while driving, Lionel suddenly hit a huge bump with a force strong enough to throw him through the windshield of the car. However, it wasn't being thrown from the car that actually killed him. It was the moment the car flipped over and landed on top of him in the ditch. Lionel's cousin was traveling with him, and he was also thrown from the car, but he didn't land in the ditch and survived. All I could think about was what was going through his mind in those final moments? What was he thinking after he was thrown out through the windshield and into that ditch? Would the outcome have been different if the car hadn't landed on top of him? These thoughts were continually going through my mind.

Preparing to Say Our Final Goodbye

The morning of the funeral, I just sat on the edge of the bed and cried. I cried for myself, I cried for my kids and cried for the dreams Lionel and I had. I knew that this day was going to be the hardest day of my life. I just couldn't imagine a life without him; we did everything together as a family. He was my best friend, and although I was surrounded with love and support from my family, I just felt so alone. I just wanted my husband back. Knowing that I would not ever see him again was unbearable. The thought of having to dress my children to go to their dad's funeral was the worst feeling. As soon as I got myself together and dressed, then I began dressing my girls. Even though my family wanted to help me dress them,

I wanted to dress them myself. However, my sister insisted she would dress Lionel.

After dressing Deshone, Ginneria, and Michelle, I explained to them that we would be going to see their daddy and say goodbye to him for the last time. I also explained to them that their daddy was going to be in a beautiful colored casket, something like a box. I tried not to think about Lionel being crushed underneath that car, and I prayed his face would not be disfigured for the sake of the children. If it were, it would have forever been ingrained in my memory.

Seeing Him for the Last Time

When we arrived at the funeral home, my sister, Eloise, took me by the arm and helped me out of the car while my cousin, Alice, helped Deshone, Ginneria, and Michelle. My grandmother had Lionel. As my sister and I walked, she led me through the front door and to the chapel. As I slowly walked down the aisle toward the casket, and as I moved closer and closer, I begin to see him lying there, and my legs literally gave out beneath me. My sister grabbed me around my waist to keep me from falling. As I finally made my way to the casket, I stood there looking at his lifeless body. I couldn't believe he was gone, and I would never see his caring face or hear the sweet sound of his voice again. All of a sudden, fear overtook me, and I felt so scared. All I could do in that moment was lean over his body and weep. As I lifted up my body and looked at his face, he was as handsome as I remembered. The fear that I had about his face being disfigured was gone. At that moment, I leaned over him again and kissed him gently on the lips while telling him that I loved him. As I was kissing him, I noticed blood oozing from the side of his mouth. It startled me, and I began to feel uneasy. The sight of blood oozing out of his mouth was traumatizing. I began to think he wasn't dead and that maybe he was in a coma because he was still bleeding. My sister had someone get the funeral director. Once he got there, I told him that Lionel was bleeding, and he explained to me that because Lionel's body was badly crushed, they had to put extra embalming fluid, which was why a blood-like substance was oozing out of the side of his mouth. At that moment, I remember my uncle Herman coming up to the casket, taking me by the arm, and leading me to my seat alongside my children. I then noticed the chapel was filled with so many people, some I knew and some I didn't know. As I sat down with the girls on each side of me, and Lionel was on my lap, I couldn't stop staring at the casket.

Remarks from Family and Friends

During the funeral service, I felt like I was a bystander looking in because it seemed so unreal. As I listened to all of the wonderful tributes paid to Lionel, I could feel the tears streaming down my face as they acknowledged his kindness, his giving nature, and the love he had for his wife, children, and family. Some of his co-workers and employers also commented on his work ethic. They remembered him always having a smile on his face and how much he loved life. So many people got up to say such wonderful things about him, and it made my heart smile even through the pain. One of his co-workers said that after Lionel Jr. was born, he came in handing out cigars, saying, "I finally have my son." I was so grateful to hear the amazing remarks. This made me so proud to have been his wife.

Once the service was over, I took Deshone, Ginneria, and Michelle up to the casket for them to say goodbye to their dad. It was very emotional seeing our kids stand at their daddy's casket, looking at his lifeless body. While standing there, Deshone placed her hand inside the casket and began shaking her dad's arm, telling him to wake up. This was really hard for me to watch as she tried to wake him up. The images of those final moments with my children standing at their dad's casket will forever be etched in my memory. It was the most heart-wrenching part of this whole experience. It was impossible to hold back my tears as I told the girls that their dad wasn't asleep but that he was dead and had gone to heaven. Yet, I knew they were too young to understand. Though I said goodbye to my husband, I did not say goodbye to our love for each other. Everyone then started coming up to me, giving their condolences and saying how sorry they were. Many said they knew how I felt, and although they meant well, they had no idea how I was feeling.

Making Adjustments

The hardest journey of my life began the day after Lionel was placed into the ground. As the casket was lowered, the girls and I threw the rose we had onto his casket. As we walked back to the car, it was at that moment the realization struck me that I was a solo parent, and although I was experiencing a wide range of emotions, I knew the Lord was going to get me through this. I sensed He was walking with me every step of the way, as His Word says in Psalm 23:4 (NIV), "Even though I walk through the darkest valley, I will fear no evil, for you are with me; your rod and your staff, they comfort me." In the quiet moments, I felt comforted.

Following the funeral, Lionel's family really didn't know how to approach me, nor did they know what to say to me. I told myself it must be because they were grieving for him as well. At first, I didn't know how to handle it. A few of them called to check in on us, while others did not call to say a word. I realized that Lionel's family was hurting too, and my loss wasn't greater than theirs. I lost a husband, my children lost their father, but they had lost a brother and a son. However, my mother-in-law called me on the phone, and we talked about how hard it was for her to have to deal with the loss of another son through such a tragic loss (Lionel's brother, Eugene, was killed by a hit-and-run driver in 1968 a year before Lionel's death). Lionel's mother wanted me to understand that there are times when she, as his mother, was in horrendous pain as well, and as much as I wanted her to be there for me, she just needed time. I told her I understood that she needed time to grieve. I sympathized with her because I knew how it was for my mom when my brother died. The greatest pain for a mother is the loss of their child.

Grandmother's Love

The kids and I later moved in with my grandma because she wanted to make sure the children and I were being looked after, and she didn't want us to be alone. I know that what she really wanted was to have baby Lionel and the girls around so she could spoil them. I didn't mind; I loved being around my grandma. As we settled in, I thought I would be able to get some sleep, but I couldn't, no matter how hard I tried. I was consumed by

Lionel's death. I continued to replay everything over and over in my head. I thought about the night I had my last conversation with him right here in my grandmother's house and how he died. Not only that, I wondered how I was going to manage all of this. I ached for my husband every day, and when I tried to sleep, I would reach over for him, as I used to do, and he wasn't there. I just wanted him back! He was gone forever. How do I move past this? How do I move on? Also, I had feelings of being inadequate to face the challenges of raising my children alone. I knew that I had to pull myself together for the sake of them. Even though I was hurting, I just couldn't put my children on hold while I drowned in my pain and sorrow. My children needed stability, and I had to realize that they were dealing with the loss of their dad as well. Unfortunately, I just had to face the reality that he was gone. I could not afford to wallow in my grief if for no other reason than that my children needed me to be emotionally intact. As I continued to have difficulty sleeping, my grandma would give me a glass of warm milk, and surprisingly, I would feel relaxed and eventually fall asleep.

One Life Taken—Blessed with a New life—Baby Number Five

A month after Lionel's death, I often found myself feeling sick. Of course, I just thought it was part of me grieving. I wasn't eating or sleeping, so I went to the doctor to get a checkup, and to my disbelief, I was pregnant again. It was a huge surprise. I never would have seen this one coming, not even in a million years. I was extremely excited and full of joy because this was another legacy of Lionel; yet, I was sad because he would not be here to share in the joy of our new life. He died not knowing he was going to be a father for the fifth time. I was sad not because of the pregnancy but going through it without him being at my side. How was I going to find the physical and emotional strength to take care of five children alone? I knew it would be a tremendous job, but I also knew God would give me the strength to do whatever I needed to do. I loved being pregnant, but it did bring a somber mood during my prenatal visits. It saddened me that he was not going to be there to hear our baby's first heartbeat. I remember with every pregnancy, he had always been there when I had an ultrasound, and I missed being able to kick around names with him.

Going It Alone

During my pregnancy, it was extremely hard and upsetting for me knowing that Lionel wasn't aware that I was pregnant, that he was not going to be there to accompany me to the hospital during the birth of our fifth baby (as he had always done), and he would never know whether we had a boy or a girl. The more I thought about this, the more I felt really alone. Despite the intense grief, sadness, and anxiety that overcame me, I knew this would be a joyous period in my life. I was determined to remember the happiness I felt previously being pregnant and knew that maintaining my health and sanity were the most important things for our baby and me. While there with my grandmother, she made sure I had balanced meals and got plenty of rest for the time we were with her.

Holidays Approaching

At the beginning of November, I started to feel somewhat anxious because the holidays were quickly approaching, and these holidays were going to be our "first." Lionel had only been dead for several weeks, and Thanksgiving was around the corner. As I reflected on Thanksgiving, it has always been a festive occasion for our family. Before his death, we looked forward to the upcoming holidays and spending time with the family. We always had dinner at my mom's house, and she always prepared a feast. So, keeping with the tradition, the kids and I went to my mom's house on Thanksgiving Day, and it was more difficult than I could have imagined. Everyone tried to put on happy faces and act as if everything was normal, but it wasn't the joy and laughter we experienced each year—it just wasn't there.

The next holiday was about a month away, and I was really stressing out. Christmas for the children without their dad and with him dying only two months earlier was going to be extremely hard not only for me but also for the children. Christmas was our favorite time of the year. I didn't know if I was up to putting up a tree and decorating it, but my grandmother told me that even though Lionel was not there, the children and I were, and if he was alive, he would want us to have a merry Christmas. She added, "And we are going to have a wonderful Christmas." My grandma suggested that the children could celebrate their dad by making him a memory ornament, which I thought was a great idea. I then told her she was right. The children needed to have something to look forward to. They always enjoyed Christmas and so looked forward to opening their gifts. My grandma said she was determined to create a magical Christmas for them. I then told her I would do the same because they deserved it. I'm not even sure how I made it through wrapping their gifts without them seeing me. My grandmother had the house smelling so good with all the baking she had done. They were so excited when they woke up on Christmas morning and saw all their gifts under the tree. I thank God for using my grandmother and giving me peace while taking away all of my anxiety to enjoy that awesome day alongside my children and grandmother.

I made it through Thanksgiving, Christmas, and with the New Year approaching, I started feeling anxious all over again. We celebrated New Year's Eve every year by allowing the children to stay up even though they were young so that we could all bring in the New Year together. I felt awful turning the page in my life and bringing in a new year without my husband. I suddenly realized that within seconds I would be living and breathing in a year that Lionel would never experience. It was devastating, but here again, my grandmother was there as we welcomed and celebrated the New Year. She baked cookies and made homemade eggnog. I thanked God again for my grandmother and allowing all of us to see another year. I just loved Grandma; she was with me through it all.

Returning Home

The children and I stayed with my grandmother for five months, and I was so grateful that she took care of the children and me during the early stages of my pregnancy. I knew that I could not have handled it alone. After five months, I told my grandma that I felt I was strong enough to go back home and take care of my children and me. She told me if I needed anything, she was only a phone call away, and if I wanted to get out, she would take care of the children.

After deciding to return home, I called my sister, Eloise, and asked if she would help me freshen up the house before bringing the children home. I also told her that I needed to go grocery shopping because I wanted to get everything my children enjoyed eating. I picked her up, and we went grocery shopping. After we finished shopping, we headed to the house to start cleaning. As I got out of the car and approached the door, I froze. I had not been home since Lionel died, and it was hard for me to put the key in and turn it in the lock. Once I got the courage to unlock the door, I walked in, and it felt lonely, empty, and cold. It seemed as though all the love had been sucked out. As I started walking through my house, it was really hard because everything we cherished and the times we shared as a family were in this house. Now it didn't feel like home anymore. There was an emptiness that hit me in the pit of my stomach. It felt like Lionel had just died, and I was grieving his death all over again

Every room I entered was a reminder that Lionel's physical presence was no longer a part of what I called "our home," and I couldn't access any of those old home feelings. Losing those feelings of my home was another part of my grieving that I didn't expect and was not prepared for. I stood there devastated. In that moment, it was apparent and without question that everything that was a part of our lives, the memories we had shared, could never be replaced. Our home, our physical space, all changed in the blink of an eye, and the life we had ended because there was a missing link. The challenge was saying goodbye to what was and beginning a new journey to rebuild our lives. I had to make our house a home again for my children and me and to make more memories.

After my sister helped me bring in the groceries, we began cleaning the house. I began cleaning frantically so that my children could return to a clean and fresh house. My sister cleaned and mopped the kitchen, cleaned the cabinets and refrigerator, and the strove. I started in the bedrooms, changed the bed linen, and polished the furniture. As I went through each room, I could see Lionel all over the place. As I started cleaning the dining room and polishing the dining room table, I reflected on my daughters, Deshone and Ginneria, sitting beside their dad at our dining room table, putting together puzzles with him, and us having dinner. Tears filled my eyes, and my heart ached because they would not have those moments with him ever again. Those memories could not be reconstructed. Once we finished cleaning, my sister asked if I wanted her to spend the night. I told her "No," and that I needed to do this alone. I was so thankful my sister was there with me and for having her support throughout the most difficult time in my life.

Getting the Kids Ready to Return Home

After returning to my grandmother's house, I gathered the children and our things so we could return home. I really didn't want to leave my grandma. For one, I felt safe, and two, I was afraid that I would not be able to handle being alone. Upon leaving, I gave my grandma a big hug, kissed her on the cheek, and told her that I loved her as she helped me put on the kids' coats and they began saying bye to her. As I looked at my grandma, I could see tears running down her face as she kissed the kids, but she never said goodbye. That was something I have never ever heard her say. That was something she didn't do. At that moment, I began to cry because I was leaving my support and my champion.

First Day Home

As I drove home, sadness engulfed me because I was going home without Lionel. I kept telling myself, "It's going to be okay." I knew that I had to accept the reality that Lionel was gone, but it was hard. When we arrived home, I pulled into the driveway and told Deshone and Ginneria to watch Michelle and Lionel until I brought our things inside the house. Once I put everything inside and went back to the car, I told Deshone to look after Lionel, and I got Ginneria and Michelle out of the car and brought them inside the house. As soon as we all were inside, Ginneria asked me when her daddy was coming home. I was a little taken back by that question, and I couldn't say anything. During the time we stayed with my grandmother, she and I both talked with the girls about their dad. I explained to them that he would not be coming home because he had died in a car accident and was in heaven with the angels. Although they were young, and I knew they didn't fully comprehend what had happened, it became even more evident that they didn't see death as permanent. The only thing I could say to Ginneria was, "Why don't you help Mommy put your things in your room?" Once I said that, the girls started helping me put things away. After we finished, I was hoping the girls would not ask me about their dad again. Deshone then asked if they could watch television in their room, and I was more than happy to tell them they could. A cautious relief came over me. I then changed Lionel, gave him a bottle, and then put him in his crib.

Finally, I had a moment to myself. I went into our bedroom, sat on the edge of the bed, and all I could do was cry. Bringing the children home for the first time, I was scared and a little nervous without Lionel being there. As much I wanted things to go back to the way they used to be, I knew nothing was ever going to be the same again. Life as I knew it changed forever, but my circumstances and responsibilities to my children did not. I had to be there for them and knew I had to get myself together and be strong for my babies. I promised myself at that moment that I would keep going even when it may feel impossible, and I would be the best mother and do my best to raise them.

Once I got myself together, I brought the girls a snack and stayed with them for a while as they watched television. While sitting there with them, I didn't know how I was going to have the conversation with them that their daddy was never coming home again. This was their first time being home since their father died. Although I talked to them about Lionel before and they saw him at the funeral, they still didn't understand. Upon leaving the girls' room, I went into Lionel's room and checked on him. As I watched my baby boy sleeping, I fell down on my knees by his crib and cried. I remembered the day he was born and how excited his dad was when he was told he had a son, and now he would never get the chance to see his son grow up. He would never get to do the things he wanted to do with him. I grieved deeply for my children for not having the opportunity to experience the love this man had for them. I also grieved the loss of the future we had planned, and the dreams we had for them that I thought would never materialize. My grief was also mingled with feelings of being inadequate to face the challenges ahead of me. I prayed and asked God to help me and give me the strength to be able to raise my children with the values, integrity, and respect Lionel and I were teaching them at an early age. After getting up, I leaned over into Lionel's crib and lightly kissed him, and I said to him, "I know you will make your dad proud."

Preparing Dinner

I started preparing dinner and decided to cook the kids their favorite meal, spaghetti. As I was preparing dinner, I called my grandmother and told her that we were settled in and the girls were watching television, and Lionel was asleep in his crib. She asked how I was feeling, and I told her that Ginneria was asking about her dad, and I couldn't bring myself to say anything. I also told her that I had a meltdown because coming back to the house was a little overwhelming. She told me that it was going to take some time to get adjusted, and she would call and check on us later. After hanging up the phone, I finished preparing dinner.

As I was preparing dinner, I started remembering every evening when Lionel came home from work, and upon entering the house, he would say, "Daddy's home." He was then greeted with a lot of leg hugs. He would pick up each of the girls and give them a kiss. Afterward, he would go to Lionel and give him a kiss on the forehead. He adored his children. We all sat down every evening for dinner around six-thirty. This was our time to connect (family time) and talk about our day, and the kids would tell him what they did. Having dinner in the house for the first time was the hardest time yet.

Having Family Dinner for the First Time Alone

While sitting down for dinner, I kept staring at the now empty chair Lionel sat in. Seeing that empty chair opened a floodgate of emotions. As I tried to contain myself, I began talking with the girls asking them to tell me what they enjoyed most while staying with their grandma for the last several months. Deshone started getting excited, saying, I liked it when Grandma let me help her bake cookies, and she always read us stories. I could see that Ginneria was not as excited to talk about that. The only thing she said was, "I miss Daddy." I told them that I missed him too, but everything was going to be okay, and together we were going to get through this. At that time, I asked if they wanted to go visit Dad and place flowers on his grave. I also asked them if they wanted to write their dad a letter and color him a picture. They always liked coloring and showing him what they had colored. That brought a smile to Ginneria's face, and they both said, yes, they wanted to go. I also told them that we were going to visit Grandma so she could make them their favorite cookies. My grandmother loved to bake, and when we lived with her, she always baked them cookies and cupcakes. Once we finished dinner, I asked them to help me clear the table. They were laughing and playing around as they took turns spinning Michelle around in her walker while Lionel watched in his highchair. I was so happy to have some laugher in the house, and this made me feel better. After playing, I had the girls write their dad a letter and color him a picture. Once they completed coloring their picture and writing their letters, I placed them in an envelope and sealed it up. They were so excited and said they could not wait to give it to Daddy. I thought it was important to let them go back to the place where, only five months ago, we placed their father's body in the ground. I didn't want it to be a scary place. I wanted it to be a place where we could remember their dad together and aid them in their understanding that he was not coming home.

About an hour later, I started getting the children ready for bed. I ran them a warm bubble bath and let them play in the tub for a while. I then got Lionel's baby tub, gave him his bath, and laid him down in his crib. After the girls finished their bath, I put them on their pajamas and Michelle in her crib. I told Deshone and Ginneria they could watch television while I took my bath. After we all were set for bed, I decided we were all going to sleep together. I went and got Michelle and Lionel and laid all of my babies in bed with me. Once we were in bed, we just loved on each other and played around. I started tickling them, which brought laugher again in the house. After a few minutes, all of a sudden, Ginneria got up, went into their room, and came back with one of their storybooks so I could read them a story. This was what their dad did every night. Since we were back home, this is what she wanted me to do. From the day our children were born, Lionel embraced being a dad, and he loved doing things with them. He was always calm and was never rattled when the girls had disagreements or when things just weren't going right between them. He showed them self-control even at a young age. I loved watching him be a father. I saw how he responded calmly to our children, and because of this, they knew how to self-regulate their emotions. What a valuable lesson he taught them, and I was so grateful for how he set those examples. We both tried to be a positive example for them. I thought about what a good match Lionel and I were. We were a pretty good team, and now I had to build a team with my children.

Learning How to Cope with My Pain and Emotions

Lionel's death shook the foundation of my existence and affected me physically, emotionally, and mentally. With us returning home, I became preoccupied with my thoughts, memories, and images, which made it difficult for me to accept the finality of his death. This brought back tremendous feelings and a longing for his presence. In the midst of trying to deal with my grief, I was concerned about providing my children a sense of normalcy (when everything around me felt "un-normal") and how I was going to assure them and make them feel safe. I was giving them extra cuddling and hugs to help them manage their fears, as well as trying to guide them through their own grief so that they would be able to recover in a healthy way. I also knew I had to be okay with allowing my children to see me cry when I was sad and when I was not having a good day. I felt it was important to let them know it was okay to cry when they, too, were sad. This helped me to allow myself to grieve and not shut down and to accept it was going to take time to fully absorb the impact of Lionel's death.

As I laid in bed after the kids had fallen asleep, I struggled with being back home and in my bed for the first time since Lionel's death. I began contemplating being a solo parent and wondering if I was equipped for the biggest challenge of my life, raising our four children and pregnant with my fifth child on my own. I felt the weight of everyday tasks might feel overwhelming as I tried to make it through each day of solo decision-making and parenting. With those thoughts, I fell asleep.

The next morning, I awakened just before six o'clock and was careful not to wake the children. I sat in the kitchen thinking about what my mornings used to be like, but I quickly turned my focus on making breakfast so that we could get our day started. Again, I made one of the girls' favorite meals, pancakes and sausages. Once they were up and about, Deshone and Ginneria went into the bathroom to brush their teeth, and I took care of Michelle and Lionel. During breakfast, I told the girls that I had a surprise for them after we visited their dad. After getting dressed, we headed out to the cemetery. On our way to the cemetery, I stopped and picked out a bouquet of roses. As we were driving into the cemetery, Ginneria said, Is this where Daddy's at?" I said, 'Yes, this is where your Daddy is." After getting the girls out of the car, I got Lionel out. Both Deshone and Ginneria held onto Michelle's hands. We all slowly walked over to where Lionel's grave was, and Ginneria immediately said, "Daddy, me, and Deshone wrote you a letter and colored you a picture." As I stood there, tears filled my eyes, and my heart ached watching my children. As the girls placed their envelope on his grave, they started crying, saying, "Daddy, we want you to come home. We miss you." At that moment, I broke down, and we all were crying. Before leaving, I told him I was taking care of the children and our unborn child and that I was also taking care of myself. I also told him that we returned home yesterday, but the house felt so empty without him. I then gave each one of the girls, and even Lionel, a rose so they could place it on his grave. After we placed the roses, we left. As we were leaving, they turned and said, "Bye, Daddy. We will come back and write you another letter."

Once we were in the car, I reminded them of the surprise I told them about at breakfast. I said the surprise was that we were going to lunch and to the mall. Ginneria said, "Can we have McDonald's?" I replied, "Sure, whatever you want to eat." When we arrived at the mall, it seemed like hundreds of families were there, and all I seemed to notice were fathers with their children. I couldn't help but be sad after just leaving the cemetery, and I tried to escape the constant visual picture of happy fathers and mothers going into stores. This made me feel so sad that my children didn't have their father and that I wouldn't experience the joy of parenthood with my husband. In that moment, I told myself I was not going to allow myself to feel this way because I wanted to have fun and enjoy myself with the children. I told them that we were going to have lunch first and then do some shopping. This was something we often did as a family on Saturdays, and I wanted to maintain their routine as much as possible. Amid the changes they had experienced and all they had been through, it was vital for my kids that we get back to our family traditions. I believed that the continuous routines would reassure that their lives would be okay and normal again. I knew we might have to establish new routines, but I wanted to stick to the same family rules like before, such as mealtime and bedtimes. My children needed to have a sense of normalcy, enjoy themselves and play. That's what I wanted them to do. After lunch, I told them that we were going to go to Grandma's house tomorrow, which was Sunday.

Once we got home, I put them down for a nap, and that night after dinner, we watch television. As we were sitting there, I had a flashback. I remembered when we all watched television; Lionel would have Deshone on one side, Ginneria on the other, and Michelle on his lap while I held Lionel. I also started reflecting on the way he played with them. I would listen to their giggles as he bounced them on his knee or swung them through the air. Memories… memories… and more memories. I remember watching both his and their smiles as they colored and how we all put puzzles together. They soaked up and loved all the attention given to them like a sponge, and it filled them to the brim with joy and love. I'm so grateful that he took time for them and us. Even after a long and stressful day at work, instead of Lionel unwinding and relaxing, when he walked through the door, he was ready for his children. Our children were learning that family matters and that relationships take top priority because he always took time to bond with them.

Beginning to Feel Abandoned

Eventually, friends started drifting away, and they got on with their lives, thinking that the worst was over for me. I presumed they thought I was coping much better. I guess there's a belief that because you're young, you'll get over a death much faster and move on with your life. However, the biggest struggle I had wasn't that people started drifting away, but that they were uncomfortable being around me, so they avoided me. I was surprised at how a friendship could change so quickly for no apparent reason. Most friends left, and some stayed. The ones who stayed continued helping and supporting me throughout the first few months, and I was grateful for their continued support, but I lost friends who I assumed would be there to support my children and me as we struggled to regain some normalcy in our lives. Friendships, I learned, are not immune to grief. I was disappointed in them, but I understood that they perhaps didn't know what to say or how to act around me, or maybe they were terrified that widowhood might be contagious and it could happen to them. I really could not settle on the reason why this was happening, but I felt abandoned by all of them, and it hurt.

I Realized That I Was Not Alone—It Was Hard on My Children Too

After the kids and I were home for a couple of months, I continued to be filled with emotional pain being in the house alone. I missed my husband, and I had moments when I was sad and frustrated that he wasn't there in the house with us. My kids also missed their daddy. They could feel the difference, and they recognized the structure of our family had changed. In the beginning, there were moments when they, like me, didn't handle their dad's death very well, and at times, we all fell apart. In addition, our son turned one year old just after we moved back home. This was the first of our children's birthdays that we would celebrate without him. The pain was so great I cried out to God with intense agony and sought His presence. I was thankful that His Word showed me that I was not alone in my suffering and that even the greatest of saints I read about in the Bible struggled with despair. I knew I was not the only one who had ever lost a spouse, and I knew I wouldn't be the last, but it's hard when you're going through heartache and struggling with trying to move on with your life. I knew that things would have to be adjusted, and we would find our new normal without their daddy. Eventually, we did.

Bittersweet Moments

Being pregnant was always a happy and exciting time for me. However, now having to grieve during the course of my pregnancy was something I never imagined I would be going through. This was a bittersweet moment for me. Facing grief and death is hard, especially combined with the heightened emotions, which were sometimes agonizing. Grieving is so demanding, and taking care of my children at the same time, I had to learn how to manage and try to keep myself calm and focused on my unborn baby to make sure he or she was healthy. What I know now is that grief never goes away, no matter how long ago you may have lost a loved one. Although grief may ease over time, it lingers in the back of your mind and can come rushing back at the slightest memory. After Lionel's death, it brought me back to the loss of my brother as if it had just happened. Sometimes, it felt like I was on a roller coaster ride full of twists and turns and ups and downs. It also was bittersweet with every kick from the baby. During those times, all I could think of was that Lionel wasn't there to feel our baby's movement like the other times. I struggled even more with the fact that my baby would never be held by his or her father and would never get to know the man he was. I remember doing a lot of crying during my weekly doctor's appointments. One day, the doctor told me my blood pressure was slightly elevated. He instructed me to get some rest and to try to relax. I tried, but it was hard.

As I waited for the arrival of our new baby, Lionel was on my mind more than ever before. I was thankful for the support of my family and Lionel's family in helping me, but during my final weeks of pregnancy, it consumed me that I was going to be alone. I felt like I was pregnant forever, and I'm not sure how I got through those last few weeks. I began my day making sure I had everything in place. I set up the baby's crib in my bedroom, cleaned the kids' room, organized all their toys, and washed, folded, and iron all their clothes just as I had done before each of the children's birth.

Moving Forward to Make Sure I Had a Healthy Pregnancy

After my life started to smooth out a bit from the turbulence of the first several months, I knew I had to take care of myself and our unborn baby. So, each day I began to do something special for me. I quickly realized that I didn't have to do anything big. I asked my sister, Eloise, to come over a couple times a week, and I started taking short walks around the block. I listened to music that made me feel relaxed. These little "me" moments kept my spirit afloat during times when I wanted to drown in my sorrow. I learned over those seven months that a huge part of my grief was learning how to cope with what's going on inside of me. As I took time for myself while walking, listening to music, and even having quiet time, I realized that I was avoiding the pain by bottling up my emotions and rejecting the true feelings I was experiencing. The only way I was going to move forward and make sure I stayed healthy during my pregnancy was to move through the grieving process. It was impossible to escape the pain connected with my mourning. I felt that if I let go of my pain and allowed myself to release my emotions, I would be disloyal and unfaithful to Lionel. I realized that there was no way I could grieve without leaning into my pain. I also had to draw on my God-given strength to get me through this. Thus, I had to give myself permission to feel, learn, and live again.

Beginning of Labor

It was particularly overwhelming when I went into labor and knew that Lionel wouldn't take me to the hospital or be with me during labor and delivery. However, I was so blessed to have my best friends, Lillie Mae and Preston, who lived across the street from us, offer to take me to the hospital months earlier. During the early morning hours, I started to have mild contractions that were strong enough to wake me up. The contractions continued throughout the day. As the day wore on, the contractions stayed with the same intensity, but my lower back began to get achy. I called my neighbor and gave her the heads up that tonight might be the night since she and her husband were going to take me to the hospital. I also gave my sister, Eloise, a call for her to come over to the house (as she faithfully and always did). Later that evening, my contractions began picking up with intensity, and I had a small amount of spotting. After cleaning the kitchen and getting the children ready for bed, I took my shower and laid on the couch while my sister watched television.

Two hours earlier, I had been having regular and intense contractions. However, they weren't as close as I'd thought they should be for me to go to the hospital. I remembered my contractions with Lionel were intense but not very close together. Even though they weren't, I told my sister to call Lillie Mae to let them know I was ready to go to the hospital. On my way to the hospital, I began to cry because this would be the first time Lionel was not by my side. Lionel had always been there with me every step of the way with our other babies. I wanted him to be there to witness yet another miracle that he and I created together. My heart began to break again on the ride to the hospital.

Arrival at the Hospital

When we arrived at the hospital, and I was checked in, Lillie Mae called my mother, who lived a short distance away, to tell her that we had arrived and the doctor was in with me. They prepared to move me to the delivery room and then called my doctor. The nurse proceeded to put me on a hospital gown and took my blood pressure. At that time, they strapped a monitor around my stomach and placed the blood pressure cuff around my arm. I was told that I was in active labor, about five centimeters dilated, and my blood pressure was slightly elevated, but the baby was fine. Before my doctor arrived, I felt myself getting a little nervous, and I began to shiver so bad that my teeth began chattering. I kept telling myself, "Just stay calm. Everything is going to be okay," but it kept getting worse. The nurse then took my blood pressure again, and I heard her tell the doctor that my blood pressure was getting higher, which made me more nervous. I was already feeling a certain kind of way. I had such a terrible headache. I thought the trembling, blood pressure, and headache were connected. When my mom arrived, I was so happy to see her. I recalled the doctor pulling my mom aside to talk with her. My mom informed my doctor that I had been under a lot of stress for the past several weeks. My doctor mentioned to Mom that she noticed that my pressure was slightly elevated on my last visit, and she instructed me to get some rest and to try to keep myself calm. My doctor knew that Lionel had been killed, so she would always remind me to do something to relax myself and to take some "me time."

I remembered my mom returning to my side and suggesting I use visualization. I tried to put all my energy into picturing the times when Lionel was with the children and me, and although it helped to calm me, it was temporary and did not last long. I was so tired. I had been in active labor now for about ten hours and was already given an epidural to ease my contractions. The doctors also hoped this would lower my blood pressure. But this was to no avail, so the doctor told me she had to start an IV to try to lower my blood pressure. Although I am terrified of needles, at that point, I wasn't concerned about it. I just wanted my baby to be okay. Along with the epidural and the medication they gave me through the IV, I began to notice that my headache had subsided a bit, and I was thirsty. Because the doctor did not want to give me water, I was given a small number of ice chips, and slowly my blood pressure began to go down.

Final Gift of Love

Twenty-four hours later, my baby girl was born (ironically, on the same day my brother's body was found in the canal almost twenty years earlier), and she was in perfect health. Yes, I had just lost a life, but I was also blessed with another life. When I heard my baby crying, I cried too, realizing that this child was Lionel's last gift to me. As she was placed on my chest, I whispered to Lionel, "It's a girl," and to her," Your daddy loves you too." I named her Kim. I often laugh when people ask how I decided to name her Kim instead of Kimberly. There's really no special explanation behind it. The truth is, after already giving birth to four other girls, I simply ran out of names. When I looked at her, she just looked like a Kim to me, and that was that. Besides, I didn't want to name her Kimberly. She was my Kim. This was the moment I had been waiting for—to hold our beautiful baby girl. She was absolutely beautiful. The first thing I noticed about her was her gorgeous eyes. To me, they were just like her daddy's. I fell in love all over again with this five and a half pound bundle of joy. It was truly a bittersweet moment. Lionel never got to see her or even know whether the baby was a boy or girl. A wave of sadness and feelings of guilt overtook me because it didn't seem right for me to feel so happy when he wasn't there to share it with me.

My Fifth Baby—Bringing Kim Home

Coming home from the hospital was again another experience of mixed emotions. Lionel was always there to take me home with each one of our bundles of joy, and this time, even though my mom was with me, I still felt alone. When Kim and I walked into the house, the house was full of family, which put a smile on my face and welcomed us. It was a total surprise. It was like a party, with food and all. Kim was passed from arm to arm. She was held from the time we arrived home, and the girls were so excited to meet their baby sister. I remember them sitting on the sofa on each side of Alice, Lionel's cousin, and as she held Kim, the girls were learning to kiss her and rub her head. I could hear them telling my cousin, "Kim is so small." My grandmother was holding Lionel, as usual, and feeding him. He wanted no one else but my grandmother.

As I watched everyone enjoying themselves and making a fuss over Kim, I started crying. My sister, Eloise, came over and said, "I know this is an emotional time for you." I told her it was and that Lionel should be here and enjoying this special time with us. I told her I missed him so much and that I was tired and wanted to lie down and get some rest. She helped me to my bedroom, and Alice brought Kim in so that I could change her clothes and put her in her crib, which was in the bedroom. As she proceeded to leave the room, she started closing the door, but before she could completely shut the door, Michelle came running in to see Kim. Michelle jumped in the bed, and as we cuddled up together, she said, "I missed you, Mommy, and I'm glad that you are home."

Once everyone left, my faithful sister stayed with me. After she gave the children their bath, they wanted to come and get in the bed with me. I told them they could for just a little while because Mommy was tired. Once they were in bed, they began telling me everything that happened while I was gone. Even though I was tired, I listened to everything they had to say. Ginneria and Deshone then said, "Mommy, we really missed you, and we are glad you are home." At that time, my sister came into the room and told them I was tired and needed to get some rest. She added that it was also bedtime. They all gave me a kiss, and they wanted to kiss Kim too. During Kim's early morning feedings, I remember just sitting on the side of the bed after feeding her and sometimes feeling a cloud of sadness engulfing me. The tears would start streaming down my face as I thought how Lionel and I used to share these special moments together with our other children.

During one of Kim's early morning feedings, I was feeling a little overwhelmed because I was feeling sad and missing Lionel deeply. It had been only a couple of days since bringing Kim home. I thought this might be postpartum depression that was making me feel the way I was feeling. After putting Kim back into her crib, for some reason, I laid at the bottom of the bed. As I was lying there, it felt like I had a cloud come over me, and I could not move. Suddenly, it felt like someone was in the room and sat down on the bed next to me. I then felt someone leaning over me and kissing me softly on my lips. I still could not move or open my eyes. However, I was not afraid. I didn't know what was happening to me. It seemed as if I was in a trance at that moment. I finally opened my eyes and saw someone leaning over Kim's crib and kissing her. The cloud then lifted, and I was able to move. I had such a peace—a peace that I had not felt in nearly a year. I truly believe God allowed Lionel's spirit to come to see his baby girl and to say goodbye to me. The next several minutes were amazing. All I wanted was to stay in that moment.

The next several months were truly a blessing, and I knew that my children and I were going to be okay. There was peace and laughter, the kids were happy, and joy was in my spirit. The girls, especially Deshone and Ginneria, were great baby watchers.

As Kim got closer to being one year old, I started feeling anxious and sad as I always was with every milestone of my children's lives because their dad was not there to witness and experience the wonderful things they were doing. He was not there to see Kim or Lionel's first steps or hear their first words. Even though I would tell my family that Kim took her first steps or said her first words, etc., it never measured up to the excitement of Lionel and me witnessing it together. Not to mention, she would never know firsthand the depth of her dad's love for her. She would never feel his touch, kiss, or the security of knowing that her dad would have done anything for her. Although Deshone, Ginneria, Michelle, and Lionel were young, they had the opportunity to feel their dad's embrace and his love. This made me hypersensitive and overwhelmingly sad for her.

Adapting to Being Widowed and a Solo Parent

Being a solo parent is exhausting on so many levels. The weight of every decision is strictly on you. Parenting while grieving is so hard and emotionally draining. The good times hurt, and the bad times hurt more. I've learned that parenting is the hardest job in the world, especially if you are a widow. So much rides on everything you do, every decision you make. The pressure was insurmountable. Lionel and I were a great team. We shared the same parenting philosophy and agreed on just about everything, including how we wanted to raise our children. I had confidence in my parenting abilities with my even-keeled cohort by my side. After he died, my confidence was a little shaken. It was not easy, but I managed. I had to figure out how to live on my own, and manage my grief, my home, take care of my children, and keep up with the children's activities as well.

Reflection
Being Widowed

The death of a spouse is devastating and requires one of the biggest life changes you'll ever have to make, no matter what age you are. Your world will be turned upside down, and it will not be easy to come to grips with the many emotions you will inevitably feel. One day you are married, and then the next day, you are widowed and grieving. Between the intense emotions, the role and lifestyle changes and the many everyday matters that you have to take care of can be challenging and overwhelming. There may be concerns on how to cope mentally, physically, and financially. These are just some of the challenges you may have to face being a single parent. This task will be essential for you to take on, and no one else will be able to do it for you. Yes, you might have support from family and friends during this difficult period. However, in the end, it's about you.

When I reflect now on the feelings that went through me when Lionel first died, I felt alone, afraid, broken, hurt, and angry. It was hard, and at times unbearable. However, I had to work at getting through those feelings. I mistakenly felt I had to be strong for those around me, especially my children and his mother, by putting my feelings on the back burner and pretending they didn't exist. I thought this was what strong looked like. However, being strong is allowing yourself to feel your feelings and express them in a way you want to without being apologetic or having to defend them.

As a young widow and sole provider, not only was it a challenge, but a life adjustment for my children and me to make. I could not change what had happened, so I was determined to thrive, not just survive. But, for the most part, I had no idea what to expect or how to deal with certain problems that arose. I knew I needed to prioritize my life, which was going to be a process. However, I initially did not have a clear path forward. Therefore, I decided my first step would be to spend my time nurturing my children, proving comfort, and reestablishing a new life for us. I had to remember, as I hope you will, that grief is a process, and as time goes on, you will have to adjust to your new norm, and as you do, your grief will not feel as intense. This does not mean you will forget it; it only means that you have accepted the death and can begin to live in the present, savoring the memories you have as part of your past as you begin a new journey forward.

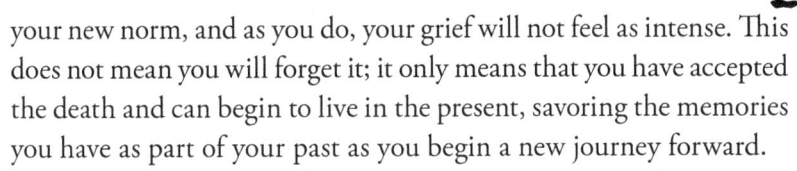

Lionel's death was devastating and one of the biggest life adjustments I ever had to make. This was a new beginning of a long and, at times, lonely journey in my life that was often frightening because I had to adjust as a single parent with four children and pregnant with my fifth. I went from being a stay-at-home mother and wife to being a single parent and a widow in need of employment. Lionel's death was unexpected, sudden, and tragic. It was emotionally devastating. The pain was physical and constant, but I knew I had to be strong for my babies and take it one day at a time. I learned later that I was emotionally and spiritually stronger than I ever imagined I was. Although I went through a roller coaster of feelings, I was assured in God's words that tell us, "Blessed are those that mourn. They shall be comforted" Mathew 5:4 (NIV). Jesus is saying to us grieving is nature's way of healing a broken heart. But the world's way is telling us to "get over it" even before we have started to grieve. As I allowed myself to take a day at a time, He began the process of healing me. I realized that there was life after Lionel's death, and I had moved forward for my children.

Therefore, we must all move forward no matter how slow the steps may be, how painful the days may get, or how overwhelmed we feel during this grieving process. I had to move forward. I had a purpose, and my purpose was my children. What's your purpose? Whatever it is, embrace it.

CHAPTER 5
Navigating Through the First Year

> "See, I am doing a new thing! Now it springs up;
> do you not perceive it? I am making a way in the
> wilderness and stream in the wasteland."
> Isaiah 43:19 (NIV)

Making My Way Through

It was extremely challenging navigating through the first year after Lionel died. Becoming a widow at such a young age was an experience that completely altered my life and turned it completely around. Everything that once made sense no longer did. I was suddenly thrust into unfamiliar territory. It felt like I was on an emotional roller coaster ride. As a result, I was feeling alone, afraid, hurt, angry, and even guilty. With Lionel gone, I was instantly and solely in charge of our home, children, and finances. I was faced with the shifting of my position and taking on the role of both mother and father. Furthermore, having to deal with the added responsibilities, I had no rest. Daily tasks such as making dinner, taking care of the children, bathing and putting them to bed were a challenge, especially when I was grieving and experiencing many different emotions at the same time while pregnant.

No doubt, Lionel's death was devastating. Even though I was heartbroken, I had to begin to navigate through life and a future without him in it. I also knew this was going to be a long and lonely journey and a frightening one with four little ones and pregnant with my fifth.

Lionel's death left a void in my life and feelings of abandonment, isolation, loneliness, frustration, hurt, and anger. It was hard trying to push my feelings aside so I could be "strong" for my children. I held ambivalence at times, being a Christian woman and a grieving woman. This, too, was a roller coaster ride, as part of me was confident in God's word that tells us: "Blessed are those that mourn, they shall be comforted" Matthew 5:4 (NIV). His words told me that grieving is nature's way of healing a broken heart. But the world's way tells us to "move on" even before we have started to grieve. It was hard for me to allow myself to grieve so he could begin the healing process.

Adjusting and Readjusting

The first year was a time of learning, adjusting, readjusting, and surviving. The first year naturally brought the first of everything! First Christmas, New Year, birthdays, and the first anniversary of Lionel's death. Facing these events was excruciating, emotionally, physically, psychologically, and spiritually. However, my faith and a caring family and friends helped sustain me as they cried with me, laughed with me, and prayed for me and with me. This helped cushion me during the most difficult times. The challenge I had to face was not only with raising my five children but struggling to rebuild our lives. In the beginning, I truly felt as though I didn't have much time to grieve. My thought was I certainly could not put my children on hold while I sorted out my own feelings of sadness, pain, and loneliness. In light of this, it was, life does go on, and my children needed stability. I was solely responsible for helping them deal with the loss of their dad. I won't lie. This mindset was incredibly difficult.

Grieving in Different Ways

Each one of my children responded differently to their dad's death. My babies didn't understand what was happening, and they could not comprehend that their dad was not coming back home. Hearing them constantly say how they missed their dad and asking when he was coming home during the course of that year was heartbreaking. What broke my heart most was seeing my eldest daughter, Deshone, having continual nightmares and crying uncontrollably. This was hard for me to witness her go through this. The only comfort I knew how to provide was to sit with her, hold her, and tell her that Mommy was there for her and that I loved her very much, and so did her daddy. I would also assure her that everything was going to be all right. After I would pray with her, I would stay until she fell asleep. Ginneria mainly expressed herself by drawing pictures of the family the way she did when her dad was alive. Whenever he came home, she would show him a picture she drew or one she colored. So, whenever she drew something or colored a picture, she would say, "Look, Mommy," and I would tell her that her picture was beautiful. She would then say, "Daddy would like it too." There was not a day that went by that she didn't say, "I miss my dad" when we were having dinner. The only thing I'd say was, "I miss him too. We all do." Sometimes, Michelle would say when it was time for bed that I wasn't her daddy, and because Lionel was only nine months, it lessened the weight of having to respond to him as well. Nonetheless, I didn't know much how to respond to grief, but I knew I had to be flexible in how I responded to meet their grief needs as I was mindful of my own. Aside from this, I also knew I didn't want my children to grow up in a house full of sadness and unhappiness.

Sharing Their Memories

My children and I talked about Lionel almost daily. As a result of me allowing them to talk about their dad, this brought them comfort even though they could not fully put their feelings and emotions into words. They shared so many stories about their dad. They talked about how they liked the way he tickled them and blew on their stomachs. They talked about how he would be in bed pretending to be asleep with the cover over his head, and they would climb upon the bed, and he would pull the cover from over his head and say, "I got you," and start tickling them. They also talked about how he gave great horsey rides and nose-to-nose rubs. For the most part, they talked about how much they missed him. With the children and me talking about Lionel, it helped them process their feelings, and in turn, it helped me to be able to talk about him too, which prevented me from falling into a depressive state.

Overtaken at Times

During the day when Deshone, Ginneria, and Michelle were at play school, and Lionel and Kim were asleep, I would wander around the house like a zombie trying to make sense of everything. I constantly would ruminate over the last week Lionel was alive and what we did together. In an attempt to try to lessen the pain, my mind would go to thoughts of whether Lionel was a person who was mean spirited, didn't provide or care for his family, wasn't supportive, hard to get along with, maybe it wouldn't be so hard, but he wasn't, and that's why it hurt so much. I honestly cherished every day I experienced life with him from the beginning when we first met to the end of his life.

I missed the intimacy we shared. When he came home and once inside the house, he would say, "I'm home." Upon going to bed, he would say to the kids and me, "I love you." It was so comforting to snuggle with the kids. Sharing a good night's sleep and upon waking up beside him in the morning and having that quiet time and a moment of closeness together before starting our day was priceless. I longed for the closeness of being together each day, planning for the future of our children, and telling each other about the dreams we had for them.

Sometimes, I would sit and wonder what I could do to overcome the overwhelming sadness that had overtaken me since his death and how I could move forward into the next journey of my life. I felt like the world was going on around me, but my life seemed to be standing still. The constant thought going on in my head was, "Lionel is dead." It was my first thought each morning and my last thought at night. There were days when all I would do was think about him and long to see his loving smile and feel his warm embrace one more time. I also reflected on the unspoken bond that held us to each other, even in the tough times we had and on the many fond memories we shared and cherished, and when the children had their sad days, I shared those memories with them and how proud their father truly was to be their dad and how present he was in their life from the beginning of their births.

Unbearable Loneliness

There was emptiness all throughout the house that could not be filled. There were always reminders in the house that he was gone. It was hard not having anyone with whom to share all the things that went on during the day with the kids like, what they did or said. Although it was hard, sometimes my kids kept me laughing by doing silly things. They kept me busy, and it kept me from wallowing in self-pity. I found strength in loving these incredible children of mine, who needed me, and I needed them even more. The return of their love was healing. I just kept telling myself to keep moving—keep moving, and doing what needed to be done.

I'm Stronger Than I Thought

After that first year, I learned that I was emotionally and spiritually stronger than I ever imagined. As I reflected on Lionel and our marriage, I reached a point where I could remember without experiencing intense grief. I focused on the fact that we had a happy marriage, and together we had five awesome children. I did not want to forget the good times or the exciting life events we had shared. As I moved forward, I held tight to the thought that Lionel left behind a wonderful legacy for his children to cherish. Ultimately, his greatest legacy was his children. Lionel loved being a father, he was a natural, and his children adored him. Also, he inspired everyone he came in contact with. I celebrated in my heart that I was so blessed to have shared so much with him in such a short period and experienced how good it felt to be truly and completely loved and that he would do anything and everything for his family. We were always first in his life. His love was so pure and real, an experience almost too good to be true. Although we would not grow old together like we had planned, I cherished the time we did share. Therefore, I decided that the best thing I could do for my children and myself was to choose a life of meaning and happiness. Lionel's death took my life in a very unexpected direction. I learned so much about myself while surviving that first year, and I felt like now it was time for me to thrive.

With each passing day, Lionel's presence was becoming less sharp and less fresh. My sister helped to redecorate the house, and my brother-in-law painted. In my bedroom, I bought a new headboard, hung new drapes and a bedspread. I even had the girls help with redecorating their room. They helped pick out their bedding, curtains, and new pictures for the wall. They were so excited. I just wanted to feel different and not continue to live in the past, and I felt like this was one way to do that. Although I made those changes, it was evident I could not wipe away the past.

Approaching the Second Year

As I reflected on the woman I'd become after surviving such a tragic death of the man I loved deeply, I realized I was a survivor, and I had not lost my faith. I also was at peace and had more joy and laughter. I showed my children how to survive in the face of adversity, and I recognized that it was time for me to get my life on track and move toward reestablishing a future for my children and me. Deep down in my spirit, I knew that I would eventually find love and happiness again in someone else, and I knew that transition would be a totally different journey.

Transitioning from a Stay-at-Home Mom

When Kim turned six months old, I decided to go to work. I enrolled Deshone
and Ginneria in preschool and Michelle in playtime for half a day so she could have playmates her age. Fortunately, I had the support of my family, and they were willing to help me take care of the children. At first, I was a little concerned and wondered how they would adjust to me not being home with them during the day. Since Lionel's death, their world has been centered on me. I wanted to let them know before I started working so they could have time to adjust. I began by talking to Deshone, Ginneria, and Michelle. I did my best to explain to them that I decided to start looking for a job. Once I started working, I was going to be dropping them off at school, and Grandma Mildred was going to pick them up. Their grandma Mildred was Lionel's mother, and she stayed across the street from us. She agreed to watch them until I got home from work and took care of Lionel and Kim.

Stepping Out into the Workforce

I knew I needed to start looking for a job, but I did not want to make a hasty decision and just accept any job. I wanted to be selective in my employment opportunities, and I wanted a job that allowed me to be off on weekends because that was important to me.

Those six months after Kim's birth gave me time to emotionally recuperate and think about what I really wanted to do. Shortly after Kim turned six months old, the perfect job opportunity became available. I started working at a blood bank as a technician. Since I had been a stay-at-home Mom for years, it was hard for me to leave my children. I knew leaving them was going to be tough, and truth be told, I found myself unprepared with the thought of leaving them. But I knew I had to do this to provide for my family. It helped that I was comfortable with Lionel's mother and their grandmother taking care of them.

It Was Harder Than I Expected

Once I started working, I didn't realize how hard the transition was going to be. Working a full-time job and taking care of five young children, one an infant, was exhausting. I struggled to keep up. Working full-time, getting my children ready for and taking them to school, and running a household were exhausting. At times, I would say to myself, "I just can't do this." I know single parents have been doing this for years, and I applaud them. My mother did it, and my appreciation for what she went through became more heartfelt. What I regretted was having limited time with my children, especially during the week. Even though I had limited time and was tired, my guilt made it more important for them to know I was there for them.

I often wondered if I made the right decision to go to work so soon. I constantly thought if I should've waited until Kim was one year old to work full-time. With not having the financial stability I had before, my mind said it was necessary, but my heart refused to agree. Family and friends often would say, "You're so strong." My response to them was, "Truly, it's not that I'm strong. I don't have a choice. No one is going to pay my bills or put food on the table. So no, I don't think I'm strong. I'm surviving."

Reflection
Supporting Children After a Parent Dies

Losing a parent is difficult at any age, but the loss can seem almost unbearable for children. The grieving process is quite different for children than it is for adults. They grieve differently. Although they may not always outwardly express how they feel, it doesn't mean they are not grieving. It is important for children to know that they are not alone and have someone to confide in and someone who will listen. As a parent, we are responsible for providing as much support as we can and walking alongside them as they go through their journey through grief. These are some suggestions to help your child cope with the loss of a parent:

- ❖ **Acknowledge their feelings.** Children deal with many of the same emotions as adults do. They get angry and sad but often do not have the words to talk about how they are feeling. Instead, they sometimes act out these emotions in unbecoming ways.
- ❖ **Encourage them to express what and how they are feeling.** Children may not recognize how they are feeling or how to communicate what they are feeling. However, they need to grieve in healthy ways and be allowed the opportunity to talk about their feelings, whatever they may be. While death brings many uncomfortable feelings, try not to avoid talking with your child/children about how you're feeling. Talking and crying with them is much healthier and allows you and them to heal over time.
- ❖ **Be empathic.** Show your child/children understanding by demonstrating that you empathize with what they are feeling. Also, provide plenty of love and give a lot of hugs.
- ❖ **Be honest.** Explain in simple language what happened to their mom or dad. You don't need to go into specific details, but you do need to tell them something for them to be able to process their loss.

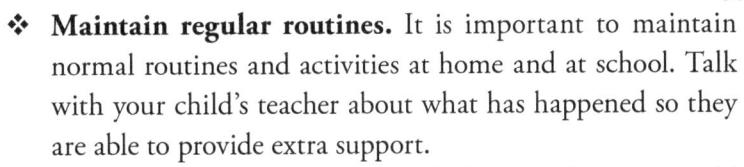

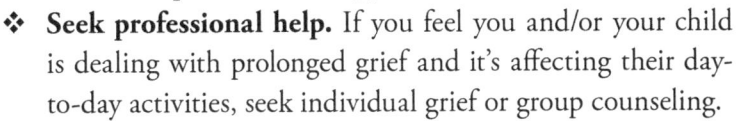

- ❖ **Maintain regular routines.** It is important to maintain normal routines and activities at home and at school. Talk with your child's teacher about what has happened so they are able to provide extra support.
- ❖ **Seek professional help.** If you feel you and/or your child is dealing with prolonged grief and it's affecting their day-to-day activities, seek individual grief or group counseling.

CHAPTER 6

One More Chance at Love

> "There is no fear in love. But perfect love drives out fear because fear has to do with punishment. The one who fears is not made perfect in love. We love because he first loved us."
> 1 John 4:18-19 (NIV)

An Admirer

I personally never thought I would ever date again and considered remaining single forever. I felt guilty even thinking about the possibility of dating and could not see myself with anyone else. As I reflect on one particular time when my sister-in-law, Gerri, who was married to Lionel's brother (he was killed one year prior by a hit-and-run driver), were out shopping, I noticed a man watching me while smiling. He was a very attractive man, and to my surprise, I found myself attracted to him. As I continued to walk past him, he asked me how my day was going. I then told him my day was going well. As I turned around, he was still watching me and then smiled and waved. At that point, I didn't know what to do. I felt totally uncomfortable about how I found this stranger attractive to me. As I caught up with my sister-in-law, I told her what had just happened and what I was experiencing. She said that I was only human and I shouldn't feel ashamed of those feelings.

Seeking Guidance

After that experience, I revisited the idea of dating and thought it best to talk to my grandmother to get her opinion about me dating and giving someone access to my children. What was more important to me was if she thought it would be a betrayal to Lionel. Grandma told me she didn't see anything wrong with me wanting to start seeing someone but for me to be mindful of whom I dated. Furthermore, she said that she didn't see it as a betrayal to Lionel, and she only wanted me to be happy and thought Lionel did too.

A Lot to Think About

As I thought about my conversation with my grandmother, I then decided I would seriously think about it. I didn't want to be dating just to fill a void and have different men in and out of my life. I wanted a committed relationship, and if I dated, I wanted it to lead to marriage. I had to further remember that I was a single mom with five children, and my options for meeting men were pretty limited—so I told myself. Nevertheless, I knew it would come a time where I would have to work on moving forward to the future. I also knew I had to get to a place where I was ready for male companionship. Even so, I wrestled about the impact dating might have on my young children and if dating was worth jeopardizing my children's peace and stability. I became conflicted. I wanted to establish a new life, but I was still in the process of restructuring myself as a person, which became instrumental in that rebuilding process. The reality was, the thought of opening my heart to another person was a bit scary. I felt maybe it might be unfair to the person coming into my life, especially if I wasn't truly ready. All these thoughts were going through my head, and time organically made a way of making room for change.

Embracing the Change

Five months later, I started dating, and I had to become okay with the new and uncharted waters that I was about to embark on. My first hurdle was acknowledging that I was ready for a committed relationship and accepting that moving forward with my life was not a betrayal to Lionel or that I was leaving my love for him. I still loved and continue to love him deeply. I also knew that in two years, I wasn't fully over his death, and I still mourned for him as I entered into this relationship. I mourned the loss of our future dreams and plans that would go unfulfilled. Although I knew this was true, I still felt that I wanted to dip my foot in the water of dating, open myself up to a new life, and potentially try again at marriage. I was willing to risk the inevitable pain, the loss, and the grief, all in the name of unforeseen happiness. I didn't know if I could fall in love again, yet, then again, I just didn't want to be settling. As the intense grief lessened over the months, it became painfully aware that loving an absence was something quite different from loving in the present. In the beginning, I couldn't imagine ever loving anyone else again, and then I moved into the possibility. I did not know what this possibility would look like, but I knew that I did not want to try to love again in the same way. Although this felt strange, and I was not quite sure what this meant, I just knew it was important to me and helped me move forward. With that, I decided I was willing to open myself up to a new life and a "new love."

It All Started

On one particular day, a donor named Malcolm came into the blood bank where I worked as a lab technician extracting plasma. Malcolm would come into the lab at least three times a week to donate plasma, and immediately he struck up a conversation with me. I asked him why he was there since he had already been there earlier in the day. He said he just brought his friend, James from Chicago, to show him where he hung out and where they had some attractive ladies. James pulled him to the side to inquire about me. "Who is that?" James asked. "Oh, that's Betty," Malcolm replied. I had never seen James around the lab before because I would have remembered if I had. Malcolm then introduced James to me, and we briefly talked before he and Malcolm left. I later learned from Malcolm that James was in town for a few days to attend the Bayou Classic, an annual college football game held between Grambling State University and Southern University, two of Louisiana's largest historically Black colleges and universities. Attending the Classic was a family tradition for him. Although James' dad was from Chicago, his mother lived in New Orleans.

Invited to Lunch

A couple of days later, James came by the blood bank and invited me to lunch. At first, I was reluctant and told him I wasn't sure because I really didn't know him. He said Malcolm could vouch for him, but I responded that Malcolm wasn't there, so how could he do that. He kept insisting and added that we could get to know each other. He then said, "It's only lunch, and you have to eat, so let me take you to lunch, I'm not going to bite" With that, I agreed. During lunch, we had small talk. He shared with me that he and Malcolm went to school together and his many experiences attending the Bayou Classic every year in November. After lunch, he asked if he could call me sometime. Naturally, I was a bit skeptical about giving him my phone number, but something told me to go ahead and see where things would go. We had several more lunch dates, and during them, James talked about him living in Chicago and the reason for him moving there. I shared with him that my sister-in-law lived in Chicago, and she had been asking me after Lionel died if the children and I would come and visit her. I also told him that I might consider visiting the windy city now, and we both laughed. James was completely different from Lionel—no similarities, no reminders—which is probably what attracted me to him. James definitely embodied the phrase "tall, dark, and handsome." He was 6'1"; he had an afro and often wore bell-bottom pants to complement his athletic build.

Dating Challenges

Even though I was thinking about dating, dating was not something that was pressing on my mind. I wasn't quite sure how to date since I had been with Lionel since I was a teenager. It was also difficult for me to consider dating because it could bring up complicated feelings, not just for me but also for my children, who were beginning to adjust to their dad not being there. Despite my wish for a personal life, my children have always been and were going to remain, my number one priority. I wasn't going to compromise their emotional security.

I was scared and unsure about getting involved with someone. I wasn't sure how I would balance the challenges of working a full-time job, taking care of my household while raising five small children, and finding the energy to date. On top of that, I was not confident I knew how to navigate dating. I was concerned about every what if. What if my children are affected? What if they are further hurt or disappointed by my choice to date? What if people talk about and judge me? What if this doesn't work out? What if this is a waste of my time? And on, and on. The insecurities I felt about myself bubbled up to the surface. Am I good enough? Why would someone want to be with a widow with FIVE little children? What I was certain about was that this was going to open up a new dimension that I never experienced before, and I had to battle through to resist living in fear and move toward happiness.

Getting Acquainted

During our initial phone conversation, it didn't take long for us to discover that James and I were from two different worlds. We were complete opposites. He was more into the fast lifestyle, while I was more comfortable with a slower way of life with my family. As quickly as I was getting to know him, James was learning more and more about me as well. He too quickly discovered that he was dealing with someone totally different from what he was used to, and I think that is why he found me to be so intriguing.

He often talked about his time in the United States Army as a paratrooper and how he was discharged only a few years prior to our chance encounter. After seeing James for several weeks, I decided to share with him during one of our phone conversations that I was the mother of five small children. I explained that my husband was killed in a horrific car accident, and it's just been my children and me ever since. After "breaking" the news to him, I waited for a response. I really didn't know what to expect, as I had never been in a situation like this before. I wasn't sure if he'd immediately hang up the phone and disappear for good or tell me how upset he was that I hadn't bothered telling him the moment we met. To my surprise, he didn't react that way at all. In fact, he really didn't have a reaction. He told me that at that point, his main priority was just getting to know the real Betty first and for me to get to know him. He added that having children certainly wasn't going to be a deal-breaker, and he wanted to get to know them as well. He then said, "You come with a package, and it's okay with me." So, me having children really didn't make any difference. I eventually introduced James to my children, and he quickly grew fond of them. This was critical because I was concerned about what impact dating would have on them. I was apprehensive because this person could eventually develop a relationship with them, and if it did not work out, I could potentially be jeopardizing their peace and stability. After all, I can't say it enough (I sure told myself this all the time). My children have always been my top priority and the most important part of my life. Notwithstanding, James' plan was to stay in New Orleans for only a week, but it lasted for a little over five months, and we spend a lot of time together.

Guilt, Shame, and Betrayal

Dating for me was an awkward experience because it brought out feelings of guilt and betrayal. I was risking opening myself up to another person, knowing that sometimes a relationship might not last and then the possibility of experiencing another loss. It also brought out feelings of embarrassment because I recognized that I had not been with anyone other than my husband. I was certainly concerned about my in-laws, mainly my mother-in-law, and what they would say given they lived across the street from me.

Feeling Guilty

I felt guilty and ashamed that I was attracted to someone other than my husband because I wondered what his family, my family, and our friends would think since I started dating. Then it was my children. I worried about how my little ones would feel if they saw me with someone other than their daddy. I told myself often and frequently, "It's too soon. I haven't had enough time to work through my grief over Lionel." I knew on some level this was my way of trying to avoid the drama of dating again and dating as a widow. I hoped I was misreading his interest in me. I hoped I'd find some flaw in him that would make him less appealing. I really, really wanted to talk about all this with someone, but I assumed my friends and family would be as shocked as I was by the idea of my dating. My challenge as a survivor was to expand my new life beyond that life, to make room for new experiences and new people. But no one told me how this would create such fear and ambivalent feelings. I asked myself what a normal single woman would do if she were attracted to an available man, and I decided to go for it. So, after weeks of angst, I relaxed and let myself enjoy the feelings I had.

Progressing in Our Relationship

During this time, we talked about how our relationship had progressed. We also discussed where we wanted to go and what the future held for us. James and I cared for each other deeply, and he displayed to me he cared for my children, which was important to me. I had begun to embrace the fact that I was starting to find happiness with James being in my life. I was very satisfied to have met such a man who had become very special to me. Of course, as time went on, I honestly didn't think that we thought things would go as far as they had between us. After all, his initial reason for even being in New Orleans was to simply have fun with friends and family, but obviously, he acquired way more than he anticipated.

Revealing My Relationship

James and I had been dating for a few months, and I'll never forget the day I told my mother-in-law that I had started seeing someone. I hid it from her for a few weeks, not because I thought I was doing anything wrong, but because I was married to her son. I knew it would be a sensitive and emotional topic for her and her picturing me with someone else. I knew it would only be a matter of time before she found out that I was seeing someone because, as I said, we lived across the street from each other. Furthermore, I wanted to be the one who told her that I was seeing someone. The last thing I wanted to do was hurt my mother-in-law since we had always had a special relationship. Surprisingly, she took the news very well. After Lionel was killed, I promised myself that I would always stay close with his family because of the children. Upon hearing the news, she just stared at me for a second, then reached over and hugged me, then said that she understood. It was a bittersweet moment for both of us. I left her house feeling much better that I told her, and she accepted it.

Returned to Chicago

Shortly after Mardi Gras, James returned to Chicago. During that time, I realized that James and I began to have strong feelings for each other, and I was open to continuing our relationship, not to mention there was definitely something that attracted me to him. We had enjoyed the time we spent together, and yes, we agreed to continue our newfound relationship. We decided that we were going to try to have a long-distance relationship and would visit back and forth. The plan sounded great in theory, but it didn't take long for us to realize that we wanted more than just a visit and random phone call. After about a month, I called my sister-in-law, Rose (Lionel's oldest brother's wife), who lived in Chicago, and told her that I was going to come there for a visit. After Lionel died, she had been asking if the kids and I could come to visit her and to see if I would consider eventually moving there. So, this was a great opportunity for me to go and check out the city because this was where James lived. Rose said OKAY and that she was looking forward to seeing me. She then asked me what changed my mind about coming because she had been asking for quite some time. I told her we would talk about it when I saw her.

Chicago Here I Come

Upon arriving in Chicago, it was cold and snowing, something I wasn't used to. The snow was absolutely beautiful. I had never seen that amount of snow before, and I was unprepared—I didn't even have a coat. When I arrived in Chicago, I didn't call to let James know that I was in town until I was approaching the end of my visit. Of course, he was completely surprised that I was even in Chicago since I never mentioned that I would be coming to visit my sister-in-law. During my visit, Rose showed me around the city. Downtown was beautiful. I saw the most amazing architecture and Navy Pier. We pretty much stayed in the downtown area, and I was in awe. In a matter of days, Chicago stole my heart just the way James did. After that experience, we talked about the possibility of my children and me relocating. I also informed her that I had met someone and that he lived in Chicago and that our relationship was pretty serious. I then asked her what her feelings were about the situation. Rose said she only wanted the kids and me to be happy. The longer we talked about moving to Chicago, it didn't seem like such a bad idea. She told me that the kids and I could stay with her and my nieces and nephews. I told her I would consider it and would let her know. James had gotten to know me and knew I wasn't a spur-of-the-moment kind of person.

Taking Everything into Consideration

The more I entertained the thought, the more I began to believe that the change might be good for the children and me. It would be a different environment for all of us, and I believed that I needed something different. The thought of this caused emotions to well up once again. I lived with ambivalence. It became my friend, my other relationship. I felt strange thinking about how I could even consider being with someone else and making plans to move forward when I still felt like I was someone else's wife. Most importantly, I wondered whether I should move and whether it was fair to Lionel to enter into a relationship when I was still torn and vulnerable. Equally important, I was filled with mixed emotions laced with confusion. I called and shared with my family and Lionel's family that I was contemplating relocating to Chicago and received nothing but reassurance from them. I think Lionel's family didn't have any problems with me relocating because I was going to be with my sister-in-law. I decided to move. Now, there's one thing I haven't mentioned about me that is important. I've always been the kind of person who had to have things planned out, and everything had to be in order. I was not one who made hasty decisions. In the end, I think my final decision to move to Chicago was a combination of my love for the city and my love for James; I just needed validation. Before leaving Chicago, I shared my thoughts with James, and he immediately replied, "Uh oh, what's going to happen next?" After laughing a little, I let him in on my plan to go back home to New Orleans just long enough to get the kids and return back to Chicago to stay with my sister-in-law for a while, and then ultimately begin a new life with him.

Headed Back to Chicago

A few days later, I headed back to New Orleans to get the kids, and within several weeks all six of us were on our way to Chicago to begin our new adventure. The kids were too young to really understand what was going on. As far as they were concerned, we were taking a trip on a plane, and that was all the excitement they needed. I was taking an enormous risk by moving so far away from all of our loved ones, but to me, it was worth a try. Of course, I was extremely skeptical about jumping into something so serious so quickly. Although James never questioned his love for me, I thought, "Was he really ready to set aside his old ways to be with me? Was he willing to leave his fast lifestyle behind for a life of stability and security?" Well, at that point, I believed he was certainly willing to try. Upon returning to Chicago, the kids and I moved in with my sister-in-law on the Southside of Chicago in the South Shore area. After several months, James and I found an apartment on the far north side of Chicago.

Took the Chance at Love and Marriage Again

We later married after James re-enlisted in the United States Army. When I married James, it was really hard to understand sometimes how I could go from tears for my late husband into happiness and thinking of my new husband. I reconciled within myself that I would always love and cherish my late husband. I thought, "I love both of them, one here and one gone." No one could ever replace Lionel, but James was a man I felt I could love. I was willing to risk the inevitable pain, the loss, and the grief, all in the name of unforeseen happiness for an unknown number of years.

During my first year of marriage, it provided yet again many "firsts" that provided rich experiences, but in a different way. There is that word again—different. I remember thinking that I may have rushed into this marriage. I was ready, but I now know James wasn't. As I reflected on my "new normal," I thought, "How could I have put my family in such a predicament?" For a while, these thoughts were part of my new normal. Marriage can be one of life's most beautiful experiences or one of life's most miserable experiences. I've experienced both. The silver lining is that the anguish I had gone through in life ultimately led to joy and happiness.

Once I patiently trusted and waited on God, He showed me how to use those adversities to make me stronger and to endure.

Choices and Decisions We Make

Life is about choices, and the decisions we make can lead to happiness or to sadness. I remember reflecting back on the anguish that I endured during the early years of my marriage with James. Perhaps the most perplexing for me was thinking I put my children and myself in such a vulnerable place. I quickly realized I rushed into marriage, knowing James wasn't really ready. I thought he would give up his fast lifestyle, but he didn't. I found myself living a life that I was not comfortable with. I was infatuated with a bad and edgy boy; however, I didn't know the extent of how edgy James was. I had no clue the magnitude of his problem with substance abuse and alcohol. Unfortunately, it had gone undetected for more than a year because he was pretty good at hiding it. Sadly, I've watched one person close to me battle with addiction, my sister, Eloise. She lost her life to alcohol addiction, and I didn't want to lose another person I loved to an addiction.

Stay or Run?

When I found out James had an addiction, I probably should have turned and run right then and there, but I didn't. I took a vow for better or worse so, I stayed, hoping he would change. I had faith in him even when he had no faith in himself. I had faith that he could come out of all this and be a changed person, a new and improved version of himself (soon). Boy, a wishful thinker and naïve. This began my journey of being a holder of secrets, first, with my children. It took a lot of energy for me to keep James' addiction a secret from them. They knew something was wrong, but they don't know what it was. Even when they got older, I still tried to keep his addiction a secret, so I thought.

Since James was in a lifestyle that I didn't approve of, in an attempt to protect my children, I decided that I would be their sole caretaker just as I did after their dad's death. Even though James was physically present in our home, I continued to do everything on my own. Sheltering them was the best way I knew how to keep them safe, and their well-being was my main concern. I guess you could say that keeping my relationship with James and my relationship with my children separate was intentional. Maybe it wasn't the right thing to do, but it was my way and my vow when Lionel died. Now, I would have loved for them to establish a close relationship with James in their earlier years, but I was convinced this was the soundest way, and it was also a way of trying to keep a more positive image of him in their minds.

Periods of Abstinence

With me trying to keep James' addiction a secret, it only perpetuated denial, and nothing was ever addressed. The road to lasting sobriety was just as fragile as my hope. There one minute and gone the next. During times of James' sobriety, everything went smoothly. It was as if his addiction were a small part of his past that we could forget. However, it was not for long periods. I was naïve too many times to count, believing that he had stopped, and then he would relapse again. Living in stress, fear, and dread was like being on a roller coaster ride of emotions, and it became a normal pattern. When he relapsed, the roller coaster ride of emotions would start again. If you have ever been on a roller coaster ride, you get a feeling in your stomach when the ride starts climbing upward. You have this mounting feel, anticipating when it will get to the top, and you know what's coming next. You then start to take that long deep breath and hold it, and as you descend downward, you hold on tight until there is a release—until that long horrible sinking feeling mounts up again because you know that roller coaster is going to take off again. It's a moment of suspense and fear as you peer over the edge, waiting to see what is going to happen next. Living with James during this time was quite similar. I had the "climbing upward," the pain, lies, inconsistency, cover-ups, pretending, and justification. I would be lying if I said that my compassion had been never-ending. It was exhausting. I felt as though I had nothing else left to give him.

Co-dependency

There were so many times I was on the verge of walking away, but I didn't because as much as he needed me, I needed him too. There is a term I learned when I reached out for support with Al-Anon, a program offering support to families on how to cope with a family member with an addiction; it's called co-dependency. Co-dependency is just as bad as addiction. I didn't think it was so bad until one day, I realized that I was co-dependent. At that moment, I thought the most loving thing I could do for myself, my children, and my husband was to leave. I felt if I kept making it easy for him to spin this cycle again and again, it wouldn't be good for any of us. I was tired of this balancing act between being blind with hope and having a firm grip on reality, and that reality was that James really needed professional help. It was a balance between being a helping hand when he needed it and being a crutch as well. I had to choose to put myself and the children second or first because they were my priority. They have always been my priority. I had to understand that his addiction didn't have to define me. I also realized that others' addictions can take over and control your life if you let them. I knew both of us needed to let it go for a while.

Grieving Once More

The situation with James was causing me to grieve all over again. I was grieving over the loss of my marriage, grieving over losing my husband and grieving for my children. It often made me feel like my heart was disintegrating into tiny pieces. I had to put on a happy face for my children during the day, but at night when they were asleep, I found myself lying in bed with tears streaming down my face and the weight of the hurt heavily weighted on my chest. I wondered if I'd ever make it through the pain, and worst of all, feeling completely alone in this situation. The biggest challenge for me was dealing with the fear of being widowed again. I know what "Till death do us part" really means, and I didn't want to go through it again. I also didn't want my children to have to endure another loss. I began having nightmares. In my dreams, I would see James' body in a casket, and at times, light and love pouring out of him. I was totally disappointed that James failed to take his place as head of our home. It was a challenge trying to replace those pictures with the James I first met.

Concealing the Truth

One thing I became good at was hiding the fact that James was an alcoholic. I made excuses for why he was not home or didn't come on family outings like going to the zoo, the movies, school performances, even graduations with us. I made excuses to my family and friends; I even made excuses to myself. The lies and how his actions were affecting my children hurt me beyond words. At times, during our communication or disagreements, I often had a picture in my mind of how Lionel would handle the same problem or situation, and it was in a different way. When James became upset, I'd imagine Lionel's calm demeanor. You get the picture. After my brain followed this exercise a few dozen times, I felt great shame and anger. I didn't want to disrespect James, but I felt deceived. I was so broken, and I was stressed and worried all the time.

When I looked at the person I loved struggling with addiction, it was hard not to take it personally. For the most part, I had to understand that the battle he was fighting was within himself. I also had to understand that addiction and co-dependency often go hand-in-hand, and since discovering my husband was an alcoholic, I learned a lot about the two. I knew I could not force James to get help if he was not willing; he had to make that decision on his own. I knew James loved my children and me, and my struggle led me to have faith and trust God that eventually, James could and would change his lifestyle. I also came to the realization that James' drinking problem had nothing to do with me, and this, in a way, set me free in my heart and mind.

For Worse for Sure

Eventually, I decided that I was not going to tolerate James' behavior, especially if it was affecting me mentally, emotionally, and psychologically. I can remember staying in the hospital many times with James due to his body not being able to tolerate the abuse. When I made the decision to leave, James hadn't changed and wasn't willing to change. But what had changed was my attitude. I stopped asking him to stop drinking and taking drugs or asking why he didn't want to stop. I kept my expectations low so I wouldn't feel disappointed. It was a relief for me (I guess for him too). I finally reached out to my best friend, Vera, and my doctor and started talking with them. During that time, I was able to release all the bottled-up frustration I had and then wondered what the hell took me so long. It wasn't that I was in denial, but I was trying to love away the hate I thought he had toward himself and the shame and guilt he may have been carrying. I wanted to be there for my husband and to honor the vows I made, vows to love him through sickness and in health till death do us part. Only his sickness was addiction laced with denial, deception, and manipulation. I learned that addiction is a disease, and over time, this sickness changed my husband into a complete stranger that I didn't want to know. I prayed for God to give me wisdom and understanding on how to help him and how to deal with him and his addiction. I couldn't go on with the heartaches that were suffocating me. I would ask, "Why me, God? What did I do to deserve this? Did I not wait on your instruction and guidance before we got married?" After year upon year of trying to change James and encourage him to stop doing the things he was doing in my own strength, with nothing happening, I then knew what I had to do. I had to totally give everything over to God and take myself out of it. I couldn't go on feeling vulnerable, anxious, and depressed indefinitely. So, I took the following steps to begin to move my life forward. I had to live what I knew. I've always considered myself to be a person of faith. Now I had to go to the only source that I knew, and that was God. I had to stop doing things on my own. When I got out of the way, I started clinging to scriptures for my comfort and praying for James in a different way. God gave me peace that surpasses all my understanding. Believe me, prayer and faith truly do work. So, I had to stand on God's promise. The Bible says, lay all of our hurt on the shoulders of our heavenly Father 1 Peter 5:7 (NIV), and I did. There is nothing that God cannot do. I knew how consuming grief can be and is. He healed my grieving heart and the pain I was going through. As I stated early, not only was I grieving for my marriage, but also for my husband and for how he was destroying his body and his life. Not only did God heal me and help me work through my hurt and pain. He also showed me how to pick up the pieces of my life and live again. He shielded my children, and He changed my husband and completely turned him around. But know this—there was a reason for James to be still alive today. God was not finished with him yet and spared his life because, by all accounts, the alcohol and drug abuse could have been his demise long ago. Once I took myself out of God's way, He did what He needed to do with James.

Subsequently, James entered a detox program at Haymarket Center in Chicago. The guys working at the center were all recovering substance abusers. They started talking with James and encouraging him, telling him that he could change his life around the way they did. James went through the program, and what those individuals talked with him about really stuck. Once he completed the program, he applied for a position at Haymarket Center and was eventually hired. James later enrolled in school and obtained his counseling certification, counseling individuals dealing with alcoholism and substance abuse. James was promoted supervisor and later manager of the program. Unfortunately, James relapsed after Ginneria was murdered. Eventually, he got back on track and has been alcohol and drug-free for over thirty-five years. He also continued to counsel individuals for over twenty-five years.

Experienced Family Life Differently

I remember having a conversation with James where he shared that he realized that I was someone he really needed. He said I brought a sense of stability, balance, and security to his life. As I stated, we were complete opposites. He liked the fast life, and while he frequently went out, he never brought what he was doing in the streets into our home. It was as if, when he came home, he would close the front door leaving everything where it belonged—the street life in the streets. He, too, learned to cover up pretty well and had a level of respect that he was determined to maintain for our home. Then, of course, there was James' relationship with the children. Because of his lifestyle, he hasn't always been what you would consider a typical "father," but later, as they became adults, their relationships changed. He was part of various milestones in their lives, but the reality was that although I kept a certain boundary between them, James was not in a place as the children were growing up to be the father figure in their lives. Now that he is in a different place, he can't do enough for them. With all of them being adults with children of their own, it has created opportunities for open dialogue on why there was never really a solid relationship among them, and James is more present with our grandchildren. I believe it is a way for him to make up for lost time and make meaningful connections.

Turbulent Ride

Alcohol abuse and alcoholism within a family is a problem that can destroy a marriage, and it almost did. I married a good person who suffered from addiction; I tried everything to get him sober during this process. I found myself lost, alone, depressed, and searching for answers I couldn't find. Moreover, shame and helplessness were challenges for me but nothing compared with the guilt that I had. Although we had a turbulent ride during the course, truth be told, there have been moments when I wondered whether we would survive. I am not ignorant to the fact that if it hadn't been for the vows I made, and his love for me and my children, as well as his commitment to our marriage, even in the face of his addiction and other issues, we may not be celebrating forty-eight years together.

The Question Is Why

Those who know me sometimes ask, "Why?" Why have I chosen to stay in my marriage despite all he put me through? I jokingly say, "It's because I couldn't pay anyone to take him." But the truth is simple. It's love. When I give all my stress, frustration, and concerns over to God, and after realizing I can't handle the situation I was in, I let it go and put it in His hands, completely. Whatever God does, I know it'll be done well. So, whenever I'm going through anything, I know that when I give it over to Him and leave it there, He will see me through. Eventually, that fast lifestyle changed, and James settled down. He is now retired and, unfortunately, was diagnosed with cancer in 2017. This was the beginning of being thrust into new, unfamiliar territory, but I know that God will see us through this as well.

After many years of living with James' addiction, I've learned that there was absolutely nothing I could do to change him. I realized that I couldn't ride in the passenger seat any longer with someone at the wheel who was on such a relentless path to self-destruction. It took many years, a lot of sadness, and a lot of pain to come to that decision. I also decided that when he was ready to change his direction, I would be there for him with love, compassion, and a fierce commitment to stand beside him in whatever way he needed me during his time in recovery.

CHAPTER 7

The Strength of a Woman

> "She speaks with wisdom, and faithful
> instruction is on her tongue."
> **Proverbs 31:26 (NIV)**

What exactly does it mean to be strong? More importantly, what does it mean to be a woman of strength? Being a strong woman means taking the stones that life has thrown your way and build something amazing with them. It is developing a sense of perseverance despite all you've been through. It means having the courage to continue living, even when you feel like life is too hard, and you reached a point where you're ready to give up. Being a strong woman is to be deeply rooted in your faith in God and knowing that all things will work together for your good. A strong woman has a strong sense of who she is; therefore, she will not be swayed by anyone else's opinion. She stands up for what is right, even if she has to stand alone. She doesn't pretend to be strong but actually is strong and lives a life of balance while maintaining a peaceful home environment where her children and her family feel safe. She's capable of doing a lot but not foolish enough to do more than she's able to handle.

Women like these make the day-to-day challenges of life a bit easier when faced with adversities. For me, this woman of strength was my grandmother, or as I liked to call her, Mama. Mama certainly did not have an easy life, and she suffered through a lot of tragedy. She was an incredible survivor, always passing through each trial, not without scars, but always in wholeness. Mama was a schoolteacher in Carriere, Mississippi, and like many people in the South, she was of African, French, and Indian descent.

My mother and grandmother were the most influential women in my life, and I am fortunate to have come from a family of strong women. They both raised me to be the person I am today. My mother provided for my physical needs and taught me how to be a strong independent woman, while my grandmother cultivated and nurtured my spiritual needs. Although both my mother and my grandmother impacted my life greatly, the person who made the strongest impact on my life was my grandmother. She demonstrated the strength of a strong woman. I truly admired my grandmother's strength and tenacity. There was no one like her, and I pray that I can pass along everything she has taught me to my children and grandchildren so they too can be strong and independent.

She was an absolutely phenomenal woman. Not only was she wise, but incredibly humble. Mama had a quiet and humble spirit and always had a welcoming and pleasant smile on her face. Even though she had a tough life with my grandfather (she suffered from domestic abuse), she stayed in an effort to try to make it work for the sake of her family. (Sounds like someone familiar?) After trying time and time again, she eventually tapped into her God-given strength and began to put a plan into action that would change her life and the life of her children, including my mom, forever. One day, when my mother was still very young, Mama ran away to try to start a new life for her and her family. Through those tough obstacles she went through, she came out with a sense of grace and dignity. She settled in New Orleans and eventually came back for her children when it was safe. When I find myself in a dark place, I always remind myself of Mama's story and how she was able to find her inner strength to continue pressing on for her family. Mama's independence became my inspiration. Her life lessons, will power, and determination to succeed through every battle she fought encouraged me during my darkest times. She drew a blueprint that showed me how to find strength in struggles and to handle them with grace.

Mama was an amazing woman of God, and she loved Jesus. She relied on prayer and the Holy Spirit to get her through tough times, and she never wavered in prayer. Mama diligently prayed for her family and others on a daily basis. She always looked for the good in everyone, no matter who they were or what they may have done. Not only did she have an impact on my life, but on the lives of all those she touched. I truly believe that one of her callings in life was prayer. I remember when my children and I stayed with her after my husband died; she would sit on the side of the bed and pray for us. I thank God for her faith and prayers that helped me draw closer to God during my most difficult time.

There were so many things I learned from my grandmother that have and continues to impact my life. Some things were humorous, and some were profound. My grandmother taught me the importance of family. She was always there for my mother and my siblings. There was never a more important priority than being there for her family. She was the backbone. Mama was the glue that held our family together. When Sonnyboy died, it was her who was there to provide strength for the entire family. She always made time to be with me and made sure that she knew what was going on with my siblings and me. My mama inspired me to be the best person I can be. She was my teacher, my role model, and my inspiration. She taught me what it means to stand up for what you believe in, even when you're standing alone. At a young age, she taught me that nothing comes easy. You have to work hard for whatever you are striving to accomplish, and you will have to make sacrifices. I learned not only to strive for my goals but to accomplish them. Mama would say, "When situations become challenging, keep moving and don't give up." She had the strength and the determination never to give up, and she pushed me to do the same. Mama also taught me the basic fundamentals in life, such as honesty and integrity, which I have carried with me throughout my life. They steered me in the right direction. Mama's never-ending support helped shape my confidence and reminded me that whatever I set out to do, do my best to accomplish it. I will always cherish the moments and memories we shared, and I will hold them close to my heart. I thank God for her being the rock that held our family together.

My grandmother died on October 8, 1980, at the age of eighty. She was still energetic, and in fact, she would walk at least two miles every other day. Mama was diagnosed with colon cancer and one day was admitted into the hospital due to complications. Somehow in my mind, I just figured she would fight through this challenge like she had done so many times before in her life. Only this time, it was different. I was at work when I received a phone call from my mother. All I could hear was her screaming and saying, "Mama is dead. Mama is dead." I just stood there with the phone in my hand and started crying. After a brief moment, there were those words again, "Mama is dead." I could not believe what I had just heard. I was devastated. I had just talked with her about two hours before receiving the call. I called her to see how she was feeling, and she said she was waiting for the doctor to come into her room so he could discharge her from the hospital. She also said she couldn't wait to lie down in her own bed. I then told her that I'd call her tomorrow and before she hung up, she told me she loved me, and I told her I loved her too. We talked for about fifteen to twenty minutes, and a little over an hour later, she was dead. I thought my head and heart were going to explode. After I hung up from my mom, I ran into one of the empty exam rooms (at this time, I was at work) and just cried. The strongest woman I had ever known was gone after battling cancer. We later learned she died of a stroke. It was definitely a hard pill to swallow for all of us, especially my sister, Eloise, who just absolutely adored Mama.

A relationship with a grandparent is unlike any other. Losing such a special person in my life was difficult. The hardest part of my grandma's death was learning to live without her and constantly trying to fill the void that was missing in my life. For the first time in my life since I was a little girl, I would not be able to talk to her. I remember one day, after feeling tired and in need of encouragement, I reached for my phone to call her. Without thinking, I stared at her number, and a wave of disbelief overcame me because I couldn't call her. Time and time again, I wanted to ask her, "How can I do what you did so well?" "How do I make this? ... my life? my work?" I didn't know what to do anymore. There would be no warm and compassionate voice at the other end of the line saying "Hello." I remember never wanting to forget the way her voice sounded. Just thinking of her filled my heart with sadness because she was my rock and the person I could confide in about every aspect of my life.

I was able to cope with her death by simply reminding myself of all the wonderful times we had, the things we shared, and the things she had done for me throughout my life. Recalling as I grew into being a wife and a mother, my grandmother started relating to me more as a woman than a little girl. She began to share stories and experiences I had never heard before. She encouraged me, and she believed in me. Her death was a life-changing moment for me. I cried, and then I prayed for the strength she had shown.

Today, I take my grandmother's strength and tenacity along with me everywhere I go. My grandmother expected a lot from me. She wanted me to be a complete woman, one who could hold her head up in pride over her accomplishments. My grandmother showed me the importance of living my life with dignity and self-respect. What I learned from her continues to motivate me every single day. By emulating her, I was able to find my own strength to overcome some of life's biggest challenges and adversities. I was certain that I had already experienced enough pain and heartache to last a lifetime, and I thanked God for giving me the kind of grandmother who was my anchor when I needed it most. When she made her transition, naturally, I was devastated, but because of her, I knew how to, once again, pick up the pieces of my life and continue to live on like she would've wanted for my family and me. At least, that is how I felt until a few years later, when I experienced the greatest heartache and tragedy of my life.

CHAPTER 8

Her Name Was Ginneria

> "Children are a heritage from the Lord, offspring a reward from him. Like arrows in the hands of a warrior are children born in one's youth."
> **Psalm 127:3-4 (NIV)**

By now, I'm sure you've probably figured out that my children are the beat of my heart. I am extremely close to each one of them and love them more than life itself. Looking back over my life, I sometimes wonder how I was able to raise five amazing and incredible children with all that I had experienced so early on in my life. No matter what struggles or challenges I've faced, whether they were large or small, I still had to trust God and hold onto my faith. However, in the blink of an eye, God allowed my family to plunge into a deep, dark, and unimaginably painful pit as we experienced so many unexpected deaths. Then there was the ultimate tragedy that had me on a downward spiral that took a while for me to deal with. Still, I had to continue to trust Him, even when it was extremely difficult while trying to cope. This was not easy because of the anger, bitterness, sadness, and grief I was experiencing. But God used all this to produce more strength, faith, and perseverance in me once I surrendered everything I was dealing with to Him. I had to continually trust in God no matter how I was feeling or what was going on around me. I had to hold onto the word of God, which tells me in Proverbs 3:5-6 (NIV), "Trust in the Lord with all your heart, and lean not on your own understanding; in all your ways submit to him, and he will make your paths straight." I thank

God every day for walking with me through my darkest hours and those challenging times, which gave me the strength and hope that I needed to hold on. He never let go of me even when I felt alone and thought I couldn't go on. I had to learn that the struggles and challenges I endured were part of a greater plan that ultimately helped increase my faith and trust in God even more.

The Unimaginable

In an instant, my family's lives changed. On Wednesday, December 7, 1983, two and a half weeks before Christmas, I experienced every parent's worst nightmare; Ginneria, my seventeen-year-old daughter, was murdered in Chicago, Illinois. This was something I often saw reported on television, or I read in the newspapers, and my heart ached for those families. I, myself, never imagined I would be one of those families experiencing such horrendous pain, but I was. Ginneria's death was a pain like no other I had ever experienced, even though I have grieved for many family members over the years. Ginneria's death was the ultimate heartbreak for me. Not only did I lose my child, but also the hopes, dreams, and aspirations I had for her future. During this tragedy, I wasn't able to immediately see that God was there with us, leading us in so many ways. Ginneria's death catapulted our lives into a world we never would have imagined. Fortunately, I was able to see Ginneria's dreams and aspirations become a reality through two of her siblings.

One of Ginneria's aspirations was to enter the United States Army and become a military police officer. She had just talked with a recruiting officer two weeks prior. In an attempt to make one of her dreams a reality, her sister Deshone joined the United States Army in Ginneria's memory. While in the military, she obtained her Master's Degree in Psychology and became a family and couples counselor. After twenty years of service, she retired. Her brother, Lionel, fulfilled her other goal, and he became a police officer working with the Chicago Police Department. Her sister, Michelle, worked as a family educator, working with women dealing with substance abuse, and later became an entrepreneur. Her youngest sister, Kim, earned her Doctorate in Clinical Psychology and partnered with me in providing grief counseling to families of homicide/violent crime victims.

As for me, I began working with the Cook County State's Attorney's Office as a Victim Witness Advocate in homicide two years after Ginneria's death, and I've dedicated my life to families who have experienced a violent death due to murder. I later founded a not-for-profit organization providing grief counseling to families of homicide/violent crime victims and have been doing so for over thirty-five years.

It's hard to acknowledge that anything positive can possibly come out of a tragic loss for the families left behind. In the face of Ginneria's death, we wanted to do something that was going to make an impact and difference in the lives of other families who were experiencing a tragic and violent death. Each one of my children has made great accomplishments, and I love them dearly, but it was Ginneria's death that changed the entire trajectory of each one of our lives.

Who was Ginneria?

Ginneria was my second oldest. She was born July 12, 1966. Almost immediately after giving birth to her, I was flooded with such a rush of emotions. It was all so surreal as the doctor placed her in my arms for the first time just minutes after she took her first breath. Even though she was only a few minutes old, I knew right away that she would be special. I just couldn't believe how beautiful she was and how much love I instantly felt for her. She had a beautiful caramel complexion with long curly dark brown hair and deep brown eyes. As I looked down at her little body and her sweet face, I was filled with joy. My newest little girl weighed six pounds eight ounces, and she was absolutely flawless. After staring at her for a few moments, I looked at my tiny little girl and whispered, "I love you" for the first time.

After having Deshone, I honestly didn't think it was possible to love another child as much as I loved her, but I did all over again. I just could not believe how I could so quickly and instinctively feel such a strong bond with another child. I can still remember the day I brought Ginneria home from the hospital; she was dressed in a pink and white onesie and wrapped in a white crochet blanket. As we drove home, I just could not stop looking at her. She was so beautiful. I could not stop telling her how much she was loved. I can still feel that same love I had for her fifty-five years later. She was a perfect and cheerful baby. I thanked God for entrusting me with not just one child but now two beautiful daughters to care for and to love.

Ginneria was a genuinely happy person from the moment she was born. In fact, she would often wake up happy just because! As an infant, there were times when the only way I knew she was awake was because I would hear her cooing in her crib. She was a very calm baby, which was a trait that would carry on throughout the rest of her life. She made having two young children extremely easy for me. As I watched Ginneria grow, my heart would just burst with joy with each new step and every milestone. Every time she fell, I felt her pain in ways only a mother could understand. I remember spending hours just watching her sleep and the joy she brought into my life. I relished every phase of her growth, and everything she did practically blew my mind. As a toddler, when she began to speak, I was constantly taken aback by the things she said. I would think, "Where did she hear that?" or "Where did she learn that?" I recognized she had her own unique individuality as a person, even as a child. Children grow so quickly, which is why it is so important to cherish every moment and every day you have and store those memories because you don't know when it will be your last. One of my fondest memories was when Ginneria was around two years old, and almost every Sunday, Lionel and I would take her and Deshone to Audubon Park Zoo in New Orleans. Like many children, my girls enjoyed playing on the playground, climbing on the slides, and swinging on the swings. They also liked playing and watching the animals.

We Called Her Toby

I still remember the first time Ginneria saw this big gorilla. The gorilla had intense, passionate eyes and seemed to connect with her. He was drawn to her, and she immediately was drawn to him. She fell in love with him. The gorilla seemed to sense Ginneria's compassion and the love that was within her, and he completely trusted her. Ginneria's compassion was a quality that she has always possessed throughout her short life. We later learned that the gorilla's name was Toby. He was playful, and when we would approach the front of his cage, Ginneria would call out his name, and he would instantly come over as if greeting his friend. Because of their connection, we nicknamed her Toby. I would give anything to go back to those days when we would tell Ginneria to say "Hi" to Toby as he would just sit and stare at her. My heart yearns for the days when my little girl would notice that Toby was responding to her by stopping in his tracks to see what she wanted as she continued to smile and point at him. I have so many memories like this, and today, they are more precious than ever before.

Another fond memory of Ginneria was her first day of kindergarten. I remember her being so excited to be there. I can still see her with a huge smile anxiously waiting for me to open the door that stood between her years of being a toddler and her new life as a big girl ready to learn all about what the world has to offer. Despite my resistance and slight anxiety, Ginneria walked into her classroom and immediately took claim to her very first cubby with such confidence. As I stood there and watched my little girl, I knew she was ready, and all was well.

Ginneria would later go on to carry that same confidence throughout elementary school and high school. She definitely had a presence about her that demanded respect and attention. She wasn't exactly quiet, but if she had something to say, she would speak her mind, and that was it. She just had that type of demeanor. As a teen, she stood about 5'6" and was probably what people would consider a "tom-boy." She enjoyed the outdoors and was very athletic. In fact, she was the first and only girl on an all-boys Chicago basketball team. I remember attending one of her games, and there was such anticipation from the crowd to see Ginneria play. After three-quarters of the game, the coach finally called Ginneria to enter the game. When her name was called, and she stood up, the crowd instantly stood up almost in unison and started chanting her name, "Toby! Toby!" Wow! We were all so proud of her that day. Ginneria ran to the court with such confidence, just as she did on her first day of kindergarten. Her confidence was underscored when she began to dribble the ball gracefully and effortlessly down the court, void of intimidation by the opponents. While the crowd stared in amazement, she maneuvered around several defenders before releasing a jump shot that would rain down, hitting all net causing the entire gym to erupt in applause, exploding with cheers and whistles. To this day, I cannot watch the WNBA games because of Ginneria's passion and love for basketball and the idea that she may have grown up to be one of those players, and maybe even a coach.

She was a Go-Getter

Ginneria was a go-getter. She was strong-willed and not easily overlooked or forgotten. She was compassionate and had a humble spirit, but she had no problem making sure everyone knew where she stood. Ginneria left nothing to chance, and she didn't let anyone or anything stand in her way. In some ways, her spunk and her fierce independence were my favorites of all her qualities. She didn't let anyone push her around, and she made sure her voice was always heard, but she was always very respectful. Ginneria stood up for anything she was passionate about, and she didn't let adversity hold her back. I admired her determination and her zeal.

Ginneria got her first job at the age of fifteen as a babysitter, and she took that job very seriously. She made sure that she was on time and hardly asked me to drive her to work. Instead, she would gladly ride her bike to and from work. When she got paid, she would treat her siblings. Before I knew it, Ginneria had grown into such an incredible young woman both inside and out. As I sit and reflect on my daughter, I don't think she even realized the impact she had on the lives of her family and friends. She literally personified humility by appreciating the smallest and seemingly insignificant things with thoughtfulness. Even with a personality as big as hers, she never shied away from the unconditional love that she had for her family. Her respect for me as her mother was something that I deeply appreciate to this day.

The Call that Changed Our Lives Forever

> "Come to me, all you who are weary and burdened, and I will give you rest. Take my yoke upon you and learn from me, for I am gentle and humble in heart, and you will find rest for your souls. For My yoke is easy, and my burden is light."
> **Matthew 11:28-30 (NIV)**

On Monday, December 6, Deshone and Kim were scheduled to tape a McDonald's commercial at nine o'clock that evening in the northwest suburbs of Chicago. They had recently taken up modeling and booked commercials. The taping of the commercial didn't finish up until early Tuesday morning, around two o'clock. I was concerned about the time because the girls had an appointment later that morning at ten o'clock with their agent

We arrived home about 3:00 a.m. and were able to get a few hours of sleep before making our appointment on time. Once we finished the meeting, we made it home around one o'clock that afternoon. After returning home, I planned on taking a nap because I didn't get much sleep, and I was really tired. As I was on my way to lie down, Ginneria came into my room and asked me for money to go buy "some goods," meaning candy. At the time, I told her "No," because I didn't see the need since we had plenty of snacks in the house already. But now, in retrospect, I wish I had responded differently to her simple request. It seemed so small at the time, but it was this moment that has stuck with me after all these years.

After my nap, I started preparing dinner a little earlier because I had a scheduled parent-teacher conference and report card pickup for Kim. Ironically, I decided on making Ginneria's favorite dish, which was spaghetti and meatballs with cornbread. After preparing dinner, I started getting ready for the meeting. As I was walking out the door, Ginneria told Kim she better hope her grades were good on her report card. Once I returned home from the parent-teacher conference, we all had dinner. Shortly after dinner, Deshone asked if she could go out for a while to hang out with her girlfriends, and Ginneria decided that she would stay in and watch television with Kim. She later put on her light-blue pajamas, and she and Kim watched television. Later, Ginneria's friend, Stacey, called to see if she wanted to hang out for a while. Initially, Ginneria said no and that she was going to stay in for the evening. Stacey called back a bit later, and this time Kim answered the phone. After a short conversation, Ginneria decided that she would go hang out with Stacey for a while. Ginneria then told Kim that she would be back and they could continue watching television. Kim remembered Ginneria putting on a pair of jeans over her powder blue pajamas, and then she left. To this day, Kim regrets ever handing Ginneria the phone, thinking that perhaps, by not handing her the phone, Ginneria may still be here today.

When my children were younger, they knew that they had to be in the house once the streetlights came on, but as they grew older, I allowed them to stay out a little longer to hang out with their friends. When Deshone and Ginneria entered their final years of high school, I extended their time even longer. They were allowed to stay out until nine o'clock on school nights and eleven o'clock on weekends. I guess I was trying to give them a little more freedom. However, on this particular night, I started to feel a little strange and uneasy about them being out.

When they were out, I never went to sleep until they were in the house. I remember, on this particular night, the news was just about to come on when I heard Deshone come in. I heard her voice, but I noticed that I did not hear Ginneria. I immediately asked Deshone where Ginneria was. Deshone was shocked because I always called her Toby. She immediately said that she was unsure of Ginneria's whereabouts, and suddenly, I become anxious. She further stated that she last saw Ginneria earlier standing outside the neighborhood grocery store located about half a block from the house, talking with her friends, Stacey, Juan, and Jason. She also told me that she noticed two other individuals were standing there among them that she had never seen before. As she was talking, I grew even more anxious than before, and I don't know why, but I began to panic. Deshone went on to say that she talked with Ginneria, Stacey, Juan, and Jason for a few minutes but never engaged in any conversation with the two other individuals. After engaging in small talk, Deshone said she proceeded to leave and told Ginneria that she would see her when she got home. As she crossed the street, she turned around and looked back at Ginneria. In that moment, Deshone felt somewhat uncomfortable about the two individuals who were standing in the group. She further said that something in her was urging her to call out to Ginneria to tell her to come with her because she was a bit apprehensive about leaving her. Deshone shared that she did not act on her instinct, and it was probably overridden by the fact that she didn't want Stacey to come along.

The Call

I'm not sure how much time passed after Deshone came home; I think it was no more than half an hour or forty-five minutes. I was in my bedroom watching the news and waiting for Ginneria to come home. After the news went off at eleven o'clock, Ginneria still had not made it home, and this was not like her. At that time, I went downstairs and asked Deshone if she heard from Ginneria, and she said no. Immediately, my anxiety level heightened. I went back upstairs to my room, and around eleven-thirty, the telephone rang. I quickly answered the phone, hoping it was Ginneria calling to apologize for missing curfew or to let me know where she was and that she was on her way home. I swiftly answered, "Hello." The person on the other end of the line said, "This is Augustana Hospital calling." At that moment, I froze, and my heart sank. The person on the other end of the line told me that they had a patient there by the name of Ginneria Major and that they needed to speak with Ms. Major. I said I was Ms. Major. I was then told that I needed to get to the hospital right away. Even though I was afraid to hear, I asked if Ginneria was all right and what happened. Without providing any answers, the person simply repeated that I needed to get to the hospital right away and hung up without giving me an opportunity to respond. In that moment, the room started to spin, and my body felt really strange, a feeling that was foreign to me. The throbbing in my head was so hard I could hear it, and I just stood there frozen, with the phone in my hand in a daze. I stood there clutching the phone in my hand as if the intensity of my grip would bring clarity to the words coming from the voice I just heard. I was unsure if I heard correctly. After the daze came the thoughts. I began to think that maybe someone was just playing a horrible joke, but why would they do that? My mind began to replay the conversation, and immediately my stomach dropped because the tone of the person didn't sound like they were joking. In confusion and disbelief, I called the hospital to confirm if it was really the hospital that called, but I was unable to reach anyone. The phone just rang and rang with no answer—and that is what I was left with, no answers.

Panicked, I ran over to James to wake him up. I told him about the call as I was frantically getting dressed. As I was making my way downstairs, I heard the phone ring again, and seconds later, I heard my children screaming. Upon hearing those screams, fear gripped my heart. Unbeknownst to me, Ginneria's friend, Jason, was with her that evening, calling to say we needed to come to the hospital because Toby was shot. As soon as I made my way downstairs, I saw the children running around the living and dining room screaming, "Toby got shot. Toby got shot." "No, no, not Toby, not Toby!" At this point, the house was in chaos. As I stood at the bottom of the stairs, I was unable to move. I didn't know what to do. I just stood there crying as I watched my kids in a state of hysteria. A few minutes later, the phone rang again, and it was Juan, the other person who was with Ginneria, calling to talk with Deshone. Juan told her that he was at the hospital and he was in the car with Ginneria when she was shot. As Deshone repeated those words to me, I began to hyperventilate. I could hardly breathe. It felt like I was having a heart attack. The overwhelming pain overtook me, and I began crying hysterically. James calmed me down enough so that we could get to the hospital. Once calm enough, I ran out of the house to the car. It wasn't until I approached the car that I heard footsteps behind me. It was James and Deshone. Once we were in the car, James said he told Michelle, Lionel, and Kim that we would call them once we knew what happened to Toby.

The Ride to the Hospital

Driving to the hospital was the longest ride ever, even though the hospital was only ten minutes away. It felt like we would never get there. As I sat in the car, there was a deafening silence. I was left with my thoughts, which were running wild. I sat quietly, looking out the window as my heart throbbed. I felt totally helpless, and I couldn't stop wondering. The questions began to roll. "Where is she shot?" "What is her condition?" "Are her injuries life-threatening?" "Is she in pain and calling for me?" I started thinking that she must be asking why it's taking me so long to get there. The thought of her being really scared and alone overwhelmed my heart. The more I thought about it, the more anxious I became. All I wanted was to be there by her side to comfort her and tell her that everything was going to be all right. In my helplessness, I called on God to please be with my child and let her feel His presence. I wanted Him to let her know that everything was going to be all right. I reminded myself that God brought her through when a car struck her and when she broke her leg while roller-skating. I prayed and asked Him to get her through this injury like he did before, no matter how serious it might be.

As we were approaching the hospital, fear tightened its grip on me again. My anxiety began to intensify, and I couldn't breathe. I was beginning to have a panic attack. I remember James pulling up to the hospital emergency room entrance, and before the car came to a complete stop, without any thought, I immediately opened the door, jumped out, and ran straight for the emergency room entrance. As I entered the waiting room area, it appeared to be empty, and all I saw was white. I had tunnel vision. My main focus was on getting the information I needed about my child. Once I spotted the check-in sign, I sprinted to it as if it was the finish line. I gave my name and told the person at the desk that I received a call informing me that my daughter, Ginneria Major, was being treated in the emergency room. I was then instructed to have a seat and that someone would come out shortly and speak with me about Ginneria's condition. The words "Have a seat" hit me like a cement wall representing those double doors that I couldn't break through to get to my child. As I tried to compose myself, I went to the waiting room area to wait to hear the news about Ginneria's condition. I was expecting the staff to tell me to come in and direct me to where she was. The thought of having to wait to see my child was becoming overwhelming. As soon as I was able to gather my thoughts, I called my mom, who lived in New Orleans. I told her that Ginneria had been shot and that James and Deshone were with me at the hospital. I also told her I had not been able to see Ginneria, and we were waiting for someone to come out to let us know about her condition. My mom told me that she would be there as soon as she could get a flight out. After talking to her, I began pacing up and down in the waiting room area, praying that Ginneria was going to be all right. I was also telling myself to be patient, convincing myself that the doctors were with her and taking care of her. I was trying to look past the fact that it was taking so long for someone to come out to let us know what was going on with Ginneria. I was becoming more anxious as time went by. I needed someone, anyone, to come out and tell us something.

Unsupportive and Un-Empathetic

After waiting for about twenty minutes or so, my anxiety was growing more intense. Since no one had come out to get me or give us any information, I went back to the check-in desk and asked what was taking so long for someone, anyone, to tell me what was going with Ginneria.

At that time, the person at the check-in desk told me to wait just one minute while she got someone. A few minutes later, a staff member came out and informed me that Ginneria was in surgery. I asked why I wasn't informed that she was in surgery earlier and was told they didn't know why I wasn't informed of this. I begin thinking that it had to be really serious for her to be in surgery. However, the fact that she was in surgery gave me a sense of hope that regardless of her condition, there was a good possibility that she would pull through this. I breathed a little sigh of relief and reminded myself that Ginneria has always been strong. I believed she would overcome just as she did when she was hit by a car several months earlier. Ironically, she was taken to this same hospital. As we continued to wait, the only thing I could do was pray that the surgery would be successful. But for some reason, reasons I couldn't explain, I became really anxious in that moment. Something just didn't feel right. I felt strange, and my spirit was uneasy.

Why the Deception?

After some time had passed, I became nervous, anxious, and confused all over again. I finally mustered up enough strength to walk up to the window and ask what was going on with Ginneria and if she was out of surgery. I became insistent. I asked to speak with a nurse and shared that I had been waiting way too long and that the doctor or someone should have been out by now to tell me about Ginneria's condition. I also asked if someone could take us to the surgical waiting room area. The nurse responded by saying, "Just one second." A few seconds later, the double doors opened, the nurse came out and asked us to come in. I became enveloped with relief. Finally, I would be able to see Ginneria. The nurse escorted us to an examination room and told us that the doctor would be in to talk with us. Shortly thereafter, a doctor entered the room and introduced himself. I remember him having a really strong accent, which made it difficult for me to understand what he was saying. As he began to talk with us, he called Ginneria by the name of the other female who was in the car, Stacey. We learned later that Stacey had also been shot. To add to the confusion, he was using medical jargon that we didn't understand. He then began to tell us that "Stacey" had been shot twice in the head and what procedures had been done. I finally interrupted him and said, "We're not here for Stacey. We're here for Ginneria." I added, "Ginneria is my daughter, not Stacey. I want to know what is going on with her." At that time, the doctor corrected his mistake and said, "There was nothing we could do. YOUR daughter, Ginneria, is dead!" Although he had a strong accent, I clearly understood those words, "YOUR daughter, Ginneria, is dead!" Hearing those words pierced my soul, and my heart split in two while my mind tried to process the words that my daughter was dead. That was the moment when we learned that Ginneria was not in surgery as the staff had previously mentioned. The truth is, Ginneria was dead upon her arrival at the hospital. Ginneria was already dead when I first received the call from the hospital. In actuality, when we arrived at the hospital, the staff was getting her cleaned up before we could see her. Questions flooded my mind. Why didn't anyone tell us this earlier? Why did they have us wait all that time and have us believe that she was alive? This was beyond my comprehension. They could have told us anything else other than she was in surgery because this gave us false hope. I felt betrayed and could not understand why anyone would deceive us by saying such a malicious thing, not realizing the effect such deception could (and did) have on the family.

As I sat there, I began to weep. I wept for my child and the thought of her being shot in the head. How am I supposed to accept this? My child is dead, and how am I supposed to even think about life without her? It wasn't fair! In an instant, with no warning, the day turned very dark, and everything in our lives changed. My faith, prayers, and hope were snatched from me, and my heart was ripped apart. I felt as if I was suffocating, and everything around was closing in on me. I recall Deshone falling to the floor and screaming and James taking hold of her to try to console her.

After the doctor gave us this gut-wrenching news, he showed no compassion, nor was he empathic. He immediately left the room without giving me a chance to ask him any questions. I know there was no easy way to give such hardening news, and there were no words that would have taken the sting out of it. But then again, the manner in which everything was done made a big difference in how we received it. This was the worst nightmare that I could ever possibly conceive. What was worse, my child died by the actions of another person. Her life was taken in an act of violence. Once the doctor left the room, we sat there trying to absorb what we had just heard. While sitting there, I couldn't take in what I just heard. I became really angry. The lies, the insensitivity, it was too much. Furthermore, I was angry because after the doctor left the room, no one came in to take us to see Ginneria. But, as soon as I was able to compose myself, I walked to the nurses' station and told them, "I want to see my daughter. Would someone please take me to see her?" I then went back to the room and waited for someone to come to take us to where Ginneria was. Soon thereafter, a nurse came into the room and said that she was there to take us to see Ginneria. As the nurse escorted us to where Ginneria was, Deshone held onto my arm. She held on so tight while leaning her head on my shoulder. I will never forget how the three of us followed the nurse in silence down this seemingly long and never-ending corridor. With each step I took, I never ever could have imagined I would ever be experiencing such a loss. As soon as we made it to the area where Ginneria was, the nurse drew back the curtain. As the curtain slid along the pole, it pierced my inside as it came to a sudden "pop!" I froze. The nurse then immediately left the room without saying a word.

Suddenly, Deshone rushed over to Ginneria and started calling out her name, "Toby, Toby," as she cried and kissed her all over her face. I stood there for several minutes in disbelief. I couldn't move. It was as if my feet were nailed to the floor. When I finally tried to lift one foot to take a step toward Ginneria, it felt like lead. Each step I took was extremely difficult, but I slowly and painfully made my way over to my baby girl. I just stood there looking at her lifeless body, lying on that gurney covered with a white sheet and a white towel wrapped around her head. The sight of her literally took my breath away. My breathing seemed to stop and time for me stood still. Everything around me disappeared, and it was as though I was there alone with her. I don't know how long I was in that state, but I snapped back at the sound of Deshone crying uncontrollably. Her cry for her sister pierced my heart. I then noticed James with his head down, and he, too, was crying. Up until this point, I had never seen James cry or show any form of real emotion. I know he was trying to be strong for us. However, this was a very emotional time for all of us. One minute, Ginneria was alive, and the next, she was dead. I kept saying to myself, "This isn't really happening. No. No. This is a nightmare. Can someone—anyone—please, please wake me up!"

As I continued looking at my beautiful daughter lying on that stretcher with that white towel wrapped around her head, she looked as if she was asleep. I went closer and began to shake her, trying to wake her up. I then noticed there was black and blue bruising above her left eye. I leaned over a little closer and kissed her where the bruising was. I eventually mustered up the strength to pull back the towel from her head, and my Lord, I saw the first bullet hole in my baby's head just above her eye. I was almost swept off my feet. I gazed into her slightly opened eyes, those same beautiful brown eyes I had fallen in love with seventeen years ago when she was only a few minutes old. At that moment, it was just she and I again, just like it was then. I rested my head on her chest, hoping that I could hear a faint heartbeat, but I wasn't able to. As I lifted my body off her chest, I begin kissing my precious little girl repeatedly. Even though I could not hear a heartbeat, I still tried over and over again to wake her up as disbelief took hold of me again. I still couldn't believe she was dead. I then leaned in and whispered in her ear, "I love you" for the last time. When I looked up, I noticed Deshone rubbing her cheek. She, too, leaned over and kissed her on her forehead. After about fifteen, maybe twenty minutes, the nurse returned and told us we had to leave because Ginneria had to be transported to the morgue. That word freaked me out. It felt cold, distant. Just then, I began to cling to Ginneria. As soon as the nurse noticed that I made no attempt to leave, she repeated herself, "It's time for you to leave." With those words, I clung even tighter to Ginneria and said, "I want to stay a little longer." By this time, James began to tug at my arm, telling me that we had to leave, but I didn't want to hear that. I wasn't ready. Eventually, James had to pry me off of Ginneria. Once he did, I stood there for a little while longer, unable to move. I didn't want to leave her there lying on that stretcher because that would make the separation final. At that point, James physically had to guide me out of the area and down the hall. As we began walking down the hall, I could feel my legs weakening, and it was hard for me to keep my balance. I felt myself beginning to fall. That's when James grabbed me around my waist to give me support. As we continued making our way through the emergency room, passing the room where the doctor informed us that Ginneria was dead, my heart started pounding. Once we went through those same doors we entered earlier, I just lost it. James sat there with me as I screamed. I remember saying, "I can't leave her here. I just can't leave her here." Deshone and James walked me over to a chair so that I could sit down. They sat there with me and tried to calm me down. After a while, James told us that he was going to get the car. While sitting there, this was the first time I thought about Michelle, Lionel, and Kim being at home alone, waiting on us to let them know what was going on with Ginneria and how she was doing. I began to feel really bad that we didn't get a chance to call them, and now we had to tell them that Ginneria was not coming home because she was dead. We left the hospital around two o'clock that morning. I was feeling broken, unsupported, and angry.

Having to Tell the Shocking News

The ride home seemed longer than going to the emergency room. Not a word was spoken. Deshone and I sat there crying, and again I was left with my thoughts. Several months before Ginneria's death, I had a horrifying dream. I dreamed that my eldest daughter, Deshone, was stabbed in the head. When I awakened from this dream, it seemed so real. I became petrified as I recalled having another disturbing dream just prior to my first husband, Lionel, being killed. I became discombobulated and frightened at the same time. Besides, I could not shake this feeling I had. It stayed with me for days. It had gotten so bad that I called my mom to share the details of this dream and how it affected me. As I reflected on that dream of Deshone being stabbed in her head, I was faced with Ginneria being shot in the head. I knew I had to pull myself together at least long enough to tell my other children that their sister was dead.

Once we made it home, we sat in the car for a few minutes because it was hard to go inside the house. I knew that on the other side of that door were my children waiting for me, and Michelle, Lionel, and Kim were about to receive news that was going to be devastating. This was the second hardest thing I ever had to do. The first time was telling the three oldest, Deshone, Ginneria, and Michelle, that their dad had been killed. Lionel was too young to understand, and Kim wasn't born yet. My heart was heavy because moms are supposed to protect their children from pain to help alleviate the bumps and the bruises that the world throws at them. I was not prepared, nor was I able to prevent the pain they were about to experience.

Once we finally got out of the car and walked into the house, I saw all three of my children anxiously waiting for information on their big sister's condition. Almost in unison, they asked if Ginneria was okay, and before I had the chance to say a word, I started crying. All of a sudden, Deshone dropped to her knees and said, "Toby is dead." The words barely left Deshone's mouth before Michelle put her hand over her face and screamed. I've never heard anyone scream like that in my life. It was a gut-wrenching scream that pierced my soul, and I will never forget it. As she was screaming, she started saying, "No, not Toby! No, not my sister, Toby!" over and over again while rocking back and forth as she sat on the edge of the sofa. Lionel and Kim were crying hysterically. Lionel then got off the sofa where he was sitting with Michelle and began walking back and forth, calling out Toby's name. Kim ran upstairs screaming, and Deshone was still on the floor on her knees. The house was in total pandemonium.

As we sat there in the early morning hours trying to make sense of what happened, we wondered why she was murdered. As I watched my children, they began hugging and comforting each other while saying this couldn't be true. Toby couldn't be dead. Trying to come to grips with the fact that she was gone and she would never be physically a part of our lives was hard for us to comprehend.

Since we were unable to sleep, we just sat there comforting each other and trying to share happy memories in the midst of such loss. As I sat there watching my children struggling to console each other, my heart ached seeing the tremendous and agonizing pain on each one of their faces. Their pain penetrated the very core of my being, and there was nothing I could do to take the pain away. It was an absolutely heartbreaking scene that no parent should ever have to witness. As a parent, I always tried to fix things or make things better for them. But I could not fix this one. I could not make it better, and neither could I soothe their pain nor make it all go away. I felt helpless. The only comfort I was able to give them at that moment, in the midst of our excruciating pain, was to sit there with them as we all cried together. I was drowning in so much pain. As we all sat there, my mind went back to my brother's death and my first husband. Seeing my children comforting each other brought back memories of when their dad was killed, and Deshone and Ginneria would comfort Michelle while they watched television because that's how they shared that special time with him before he was killed.

Lingering Regrets

Even after many years, there were unclosed wounds that were still unhealed inside of me. Ginneria's death only reopened those wounds, and everything came rushing back. My brother's death was over sixty-two years ago, and Lionel's was fifty-one years ago. A great deal had changed, but some things remain the same. What was so hard for me was that their death, like Ginneria's, was traumatic, and as I looked at my children, they too were experiencing similar pain.

After my brother, Sunnyboy's death, I went into a state of shock followed by deep, persistent sadness. As a child, I only associated death with mostly older people, and grieving was not encouraged or talked about. After someone died, you just had to "let go and move on" with your life, especially for children. I remember my mom's friends continually coming over to express their condolences to her. My siblings and I were pushed aside. This caused us to believe that the pain and grief we were experiencing didn't matter. This left me alone and confused, and I struggled to understand why I was having perplexing thoughts and feelings. Part of my grief was guilt. I felt extremely guilty after his death because I wasn't there to protect and keep him from drowning. I didn't know how to process the intense feelings I was experiencing, and therefore, I dealt with them in silence, which really scared me. His death also provided me with some insights into what losing a sibling feels like. His death felt as if I had a double loss. Not only did I feel the loss of my brother, but also the loss of my mom. I witnessed my mom being deeply caught up in her grief, and she wasn't in the right frame of mind to comfort my sibling and me. We were left to deal with our pain and hurt the best way we knew how. Now, I felt that my children might be feeling the same way, and I didn't want them to feel that they lost me. I didn't want my children to fall into that same pattern of guilt. My girls felt guilt and struggled with it for many years. Kim regretted ever handing Ginneria the phone, thinking that perhaps, had she not given her the phone, she may still be alive today. Deshone felt that Ginneria would still be alive if she would have only had her come with her that night. Knowing they felt this way affected me terribly. I felt lost and alone for years. Now, my own children are grieving the death of their sibling and experiencing a tremendous amount of pain, sadness, and guilt, and I wanted to make sure they didn't experience isolation the way I did. I realized and recognized that I had to try to find a way to comfort them.

Dreading What's Ahead

In those early morning hours, we weren't able to sleep, and nothing seemed real. Eventually, I went to my room to try to get some sleep, but sleep evaded me. The only thing I could do was replay over and over again in my mind being at the hospital and seeing Ginneria lying on that stretcher. I was also visualizing moment-by-moment when she was in that car and when the bullet actually entered her head. I also was unable to wrap my brain around the fact that the bullets shattered my child's brain. What was so strange was that my body felt as if I was there when the bullet penetrated her head. Since I was unable to sleep, I got up—unwilling— even though I was exhausted. Once I got up, it was hard facing the first day without her, and I dreaded needing to make funeral arrangements. So, I just sat on the edge of the bed and began to cry. I kept saying to myself, "This just can't be happening," "This is not happening," "They made a mistake. Ginneria is not dead."

To comfort myself, I began to reflect on how I loved being Ginneria's mom and the love I had for all my children. When my children were young, I loved the sweetness of it, even when I was worn out from all the motherly duties. Lionel and I always made sure that we had a major impact on their lives. We had strong family values, and we cultivated a very strong family bond. Spending time with the children was our greatest joy. We did everything with them. We put Deshone and Ginneria in half-day preschool to be around other kids their age, and they really enjoyed it. Michelle was too young to attend, and Lionel was a baby. We would talk, laugh, and spend quality time together, helping with all their school activities and doing things they enjoyed. At a young age, they learned the importance of creating a good sibling relationship and establishing a strong sibling bond. Even though they were young, we had family meetings with them to air their grievances or share what was on their minds. This was a time we allowed them to express their disagreements with each other. My children spent most of their time together. As they grew older, their relationship grew even stronger. I'm so thankful that God placed on our heart to lay that foundation years earlier for such a time as this. Thinking about those bonding moments with them gave me great comfort. I believe that sibling bonds are some of the strongest connections we can make in our lives. In each person's life, much of the joy and sorrow revolves around attachments or affectionate relationships—making them, breaking them, preparing for them, and adjusting to them even in their loss by death. The closeness they had with each other brought me great comfort, knowing that they were going to draw strength from that close sibling bond they established early on.

Not Looking Forward to the Days Ahead

"Praise the Lord; praise God our savior! For
each day, he carries us in his arms."
Psalm 68:19 (NLT)

Something I Was Not Looking Forward To…

The morning of Thursday, December 8, was the most agonizing morning I ever had to endure in my entire life. I had to come to the realization that several hours earlier, my child was murdered. Besides that, I was particularly concerned about Deshone and Kim, and I needed to know who murdered my child and if that individual had been apprehended and charged. If that was not enough, I had to start making funeral arrangements, which I was not looking forward to doing. I knew this was going to be a difficult task, and I had to get myself mentally and emotionally prepared.

Once everyone had gotten up, I noticed they were all downstairs. When I finally was able to pull myself together, I got up to take a shower. On my way to the bathroom, I glanced at the open door of Ginneria's room. I stood there for a moment, and then I slowly started walking toward her room. As soon as I made my way to the doorway, I stood there while looking at her empty bed. When I entered her room, I walked over toward her bed and stood there for a few seconds. I gently sat down on her bed. At that time, I took her bed, covering and cuddled myself in it while smelling the scent from her body. As I wrapped myself in her bed covering, I started crying while my heart ached. I missed her so. As I laid there crying, I didn't feel that I was strong enough to get through this. I just couldn't imagine never seeing my child's face, never hearing her voice, never hearing her laugh, never seeing her smile, and never hearing her say, "Oh Mother!" I would never again be able to watch her sleep. The pain of my child being murdered was hard for me to accept. I just wanted to stay there in her bed, smelling her scent, and never getting up. I don't know how long I was in her room before hearing one of my children calling me. At that point, I was so disoriented I wasn't sure which child it was or was it all of them. I pulled myself up from her bed and began straightening the covering. As soon as I walked out of her room to make my way downstairs, I heard someone talking. I then realized the voices I heard were coming from the television. As soon as I made my way down the stairs and into the living room, the children started telling me that Ginneria was on the news and the newscaster was talking about her death. I was already an emotional wreck from being in Ginneria's room. I just sat on the couch, overwhelmed, and began to cry again. I didn't want her to make the news this way. I sat there living every parent's nightmare, and I became angry with the person for taking my child's life and angry that she was dead. I was just angry. Ginneria was so young. She was only seventeen years old and had her whole life ahead of her. The question, "Why did this happen?" invaded my mind constantly. All the while, I thought of the things she wanted to accomplish, like entering the military and so many other things that she would never have the opportunity to do or share with us. Thinking about this just made me even angrier. My heart was so heavy, and the pain was so deep. I felt as if someone had reached inside of me and ripped my heart right out of my chest. While I was still sitting there, my children came over and began to comfort me. We all just cried together. We sat there, and even though no one said a word, the closeness of our bodies felt so comforting.

After some time, I began thinking about needing to make funeral arrangements for their sister, and thoughts began rushing through my mind of the first funeral I ever had to plan, their dad's. Even though it was difficult, I did it. However, this time it was my child's funeral, and that made it much more challenging. Where would I have it? The funeral home that came to mind was Johnson Funeral Home. It was just two blocks from where we lived, and on the very corner where, two years prior, Ginneria was struck by a car while riding on her bike and taken to the same hospital where she was just pronounced dead. The thought was too much to take in and process. As my thoughts returned to the present, we got up to get dressed and start our day, which was really hard without Ginneria being a part of it. As soon as I got dressed, I made a few calls before calling the funeral home. I tried everything to avoid making that call. I finally mustered up enough courage and strength to call to make an appointment. Mr. Johnson, the funeral director, answered, and as I began to explain what happened to Ginneria, I became so overwhelmed I sobbed. This was the first time sharing what happened with someone outside of the family, and the words were painful. Mr. Johnson listened, and he explained to me that Ginneria's death would possibly be ruled as a homicide. He went on to state that she would have to have an autopsy, and once the autopsy was completed, her body would be transported to the funeral home of my choosing. Mr. Johnson then asked if I wanted to use their services and if so, they would pick up Ginneria's body from the medical examiner's office. I agreed to use their services, and he shared that, under the circumstance, he thought it would be best if he came to our home to complete the paperwork. I was grateful for his sensitivity and act of compassion because I truly did not want to go to a funeral home.

Mr. Johnson arrived later that morning to talk about the funeral arrangements. We decided to have the funeral service that Saturday and then arrange for Ginneria to be transported to New Orleans the following day because I wanted to have another funeral the following week for my family. I also wanted her to be buried in the same cemetery as her father. Once the funeral arrangements were completed, Mr. Johnson had me sign a release form giving the medical examiner permission for Johnson Funeral Home to gain custody of Ginneria's body. He added that, before this could be done, someone had to go to the medical examiner's office to identify her body. After finalizing the arrangements and signing the necessary paperwork, I was told that there was still one more thing I needed to do—select Ginneria's casket. That was something I did not want to hear. I wasn't ready to look at caskets, and making the funeral arrangements was emotionally and physically exhausting. I thought it might be a bit more bearable if I looked at a catalog of caskets, but I was told the caskets were stored about forty-five minutes to an hour away at a warehouse located on the west side of Chicago.

During the drive to the warehouse, I laid my head back and closed my eyes to find a place in my mind to escape, so I didn't have to think about where I was going. It took about an hour to get there, and when the car stopped, I began to panic. I then heard Mr. Johnson say, "We're here." As I opened my eyes, I saw this huge gray building, a place where I didn't want to be. I could not bring myself to get out of the car and go inside. James saw my hesitation and extended his hand for me to grab hold of it. As he was helping me out of the car, he told me that it was going to be difficult, but he knew I could do it. Once I got out of the car, James literally had to forcefully lead me into the building. Upon entering the building, I suddenly froze, and I couldn't move. As I stood there, all I could see were rows and rows of caskets, and some were mounted on the walls. As I looked and walked around, the walls began to close in on me. In that moment, I felt a cold feeling engulf me, but at the same time, I began to sweat. The thought of my baby girl being placed inside one of those boxes caused me to become panicky. I began to imagine her in one of those caskets with no ventilation and unable to breathe, crying out for me to get her out of there. Fear gripped my heart. I then placed my hands over my face and began to weep because I knew this was final, and I didn't want to accept the fact that Ginneria was dead. At that moment, James reached out, put his arms around me, then he held me as he assured me that it was going to be all right. Somehow, I managed to pull myself together so that I could make a decision and get out of that cold place. After looking at several caskets, I selected a sapphire light-blue casket with a hint of white. Blue was Ginneria's favorite color. After choosing the casket, a deep sadness overcame me because I knew she was going to be placed inside, and it was going to be sealed forever. On our way home, I felt numb and just sat there in silence. Disbelief overtook me again. This could not be happening. Once we arrived home, and just before exiting the car, Mr. Johnson asked us to drop off an outfit to the funeral home for Ginneria so that he could dress her for the viewing. I paused for a moment and whispered that I would take care of it. A whisper is all the energy I had.

Once we were inside the house, James told me that he was going to go to the medical examiner's office to identify Ginneria's body and sign the release forms that would allow Mr. Johnson to pick her up. All of a sudden, Lionel asked if he could go along with him. After James and Lionel left, I tried to keep myself busy around the house so I wouldn't think about everything going on. However, that was impossible because the phone was continually ringing. The news of Ginneria's death had gotten around so fast it surprised me. I had always known she was popular and well-liked, but I didn't know to what extent. Some people I knew and some I didn't were calling to express their condolences. Some were coming over to see if they could do anything or if we needed anything. It blessed my heart to see how much she was loved in the community. I was also touched by the love her friends had for her. As Ginneria's friends continued coming to the house to pay their respects, I saw their faces, but I didn't really see them. Although I felt as though I was walking around in a fog and paralyzed with grief, it was comforting to know that everyone was trying to show their support.

The media was an element I was not prepared for, and it overwhelmed me. Newspaper reporters were calling wanting to talk with me about what happened to Ginneria. I told them I wasn't ready to be interviewed, and I didn't want any cameras. One newspaper asked if someone could stop by to pick up a picture of Ginneria and then call me later to see if I was willing to talk then. I told them that would be okay. Everything was moving faster than I could keep up with, and it was becoming more than I could manage. I still had not called my job to notify them that Ginneria had been killed, and I would not be returning to work for some time. Once things had quieted down, I sat in the living room and stared at the front door hoping Ginneria would walk through it, but she didn't. As I continued staring at the door, I started crying again. It seemed as though that was all I was (or could do). It hurt so much knowing that I would never see her walk through that door ever again. One minute she was alive, and the next she had died. One minute I'm making funeral arrangements, and the next, picking out a casket. Now, I had to choose an outfit for her to wear. My thoughts were all over the place. I thought to myself, stop, stop, wait. Give me some time for my mind to process all of this. I didn't want to think about Ginneria and her not being here. I just wanted to remember her smiling and being happy. I was trying really, really hard to keep it together, but increasingly it was becoming too much for me to handle. I still kept hoping that this was some awful nightmare and that I would wake up from it all. But then again, I knew that was not going to happen. I just couldn't believe that my baby girl's life was taken in a split second in an act of violence.

After I finished making my calls, I went upstairs to look through some outfits so I could decide on one for Ginneria to wear. It was painful knowing that this would be the last outfit she would ever wear and the last one I would ever have to choose for her. I finally decided on the royal blue dress that she wore almost one year to the date—October 9, 1982. This was the date that James and I remarried. I remember Ginneria coming into my room looking beautiful in that dress and shared with me that she was so happy we were getting married again. Reflecting on that moment was bittersweet because she was so happy to share that special moment with me. So, I thought it was fitting for her to wear that dress.

Once I made the decision, I went to my bedroom, sat on the edge of the bed, and asked God, why? Why did this have to happen to her? I wasn't ready to accept and face the reality that she was no more. I prayed and asked God to help me walk through this path because I knew I couldn't walk it alone. It was too painful. We don't always know why things happen, especially in times like this, but I desperately needed the peace and strength of God during this time. As I sat on the bed, I thought I heard Ginneria's voice calling me from downstairs. It was so instinctual that I got up and was headed toward the stairs. As I was facing the top of the stairs, my mouth instinctively opened with the words coming out of my mouth, asking, "What is it? What do you want?" Still standing at the top of the stairs, I looked down toward the bottom and realized she was not there. At that moment, I was taken aback. I began questioning what was going on with me. Was I beginning to hallucinate? I didn't know how to deal with that. A few minutes later, James and Lionel returned home from identifying Ginneria's body. I immediately asked if they were able to see her. James answered and said they were only able to view and identify her from a television type of screen. I knew it must have been really hard for Lionel to see his sister for the first time after her death, and having to see her that way was painful. He didn't say a word; he just went straight to his room.

Murderer in Custody

Later that afternoon, two detectives came to the house to talk about Ginneria's death. The detectives informed us that all the individuals in the vehicle the night Ginneria was killed were taken to the police station for questioning, with the exception of Stacey. They also informed us that Stacey had been shot, but it was not life-threatening. We were also informed that two individuals, David and Marvin Gladney, were brothers and that charges were being filed against David Gladney because he was the shooter. The detectives further informed us that the witnesses stated that Ginneria and Stacey were seated in the front seat of the vehicle, and Juan, Jason, and David were seated in the back seat. The detectives shared that David and his brother, Marvin, got into an argument over eighty-five cents that belonged to Stacey. Marvin told David to get out of the car, and they continued to argue. The argument began to escalate. At that time, Marvin tried to search David's pockets to retrieve the eighty-five cents. Marvin then got back into the car, and before he could drive away, David opened the driver's side door where Marvin was seated. As the door opened, everyone turned to see what was happening, and seconds later, there were several gunshots striking Ginneria twice in the head and Stacey in her wrist. The detectives also informed me that the other two occupants, Juan and Jason, were not injured. I was furious that my child's life was taken over eighty-five cents. However, I was relieved to hear that the person responsible for Ginneria's death was in custody. Later, I thought about how Stacey was shot once in her wrist, and Ginneria was shot twice in the head. I began to wonder, was this a setup by Stacey, and if so, why?

Walking Around in a Fog

After the detectives left and hearing what led up to Ginneria's death, I told James that I needed to get out of the house for a while to be alone. I couldn't believe what I had just heard; my child was killed over eighty-five cents! After leaving the house, I found myself walking back and forth down North Avenue Street. Down one way and then back on the opposite side of the street where Johnson's funeral home was located. I had no idea why, but I walked for about an hour. I began to feel the way I did earlier, in a fog. I don't remember seeing anyone or anything. It was just me. At times, I would stop directly in front of the funeral home and just stare at the building, crying and thinking that Ginneria was going to be in that place alone and she was going to be cold. Everything seemed so unreal. It seemed as if the world was a distant and unfamiliar place, and I was just not part of it. My brain was preoccupied with the "What ifs" and "if only." I felt like I was going crazy. I thought if I could continue walking, I could walk away from what was happening.

Losing a child was the most painful trauma I ever experienced. There was nothing that could be compared to it. It is something parents pray they would never have to face. For those of us who lived this fate and have other children, it can be a battle between coping with your own devastating grief and the struggle to know how best to deal with your surviving children. Her death was a pain like no other. I cannot describe it or put it into words except to say that it is unbearable. It was especially difficult because she died a violent death. My heart felt like it had exploded, and I could feel the warm blood rushing through my body. I was also feeling so overwhelmed that my other children were grieving, and they needed me, but I didn't know how to comfort them and deal with my hurt at the same time. I tried extremely hard to see their suffering. However, it gave me great comfort knowing that my mom was on her way. I knew they were going to be receiving the support and attention they so desperately needed.

After returning home, I tried to take a nap, but sleep escaped me because of the thoughts running wild in my head. My every thought was laced with agonizing pictures of Ginneria in that car and if she knew she had been shot. I finally got up because the phone was continually ringing, and Ginneria's friends and neighbors were still coming over to extend their condolences. Later that evening, a minister from my church came over to pray with my family. After everyone left, we sat around for a while, still trying to process what happened. This was the first full day since Ginneria's death, and I was experiencing even more anxiety, which left me feeling mentally and physically depleted. After getting in bed, it was hard for me to fall asleep and stay asleep, even though I was exhausted.

Support is on the Way

The next morning was so hard getting up without my child not being there. It was hard for me to function because I had no energy, and my ability to focus was becoming increasingly difficult. The only excitement I had to look forward to was that my mom would be arriving later that day. My mom arrived around midday, and I was so happy to see her. I really needed her more than ever. She was the only one in the family who came since we decided to have a funeral service for the rest of the family in New Orleans the following week. I knew my mom would help bring a little normalcy back into the house, and she would be instrumental in getting us all through the coming days ahead. Also, she would help me do what needed to be done as well as be there for her grandchildren. Once my mom settled in, we all sat around and talked. I told her it had been really hard for me to focus, and I was concerned about my children. I expressed that I didn't know how to comfort them, let alone help them deal with their feelings and mine at the same time. As we sat there, it brought me back to when Lionel died. My mom and my sister, Eloise, were there supporting and helping me with Deshone, Ginneria, Michelle, and Lionel through the loss of their dad, which was tremendously hard for them. Mom told me to give myself some time because it was hard on everyone. She also reminded me that I got my children and myself through a tragic loss once, and I would be able to get them through it again. I told her that the way I was feeling now, I couldn't see it. Ginneria's death was much harder, and when Lionel died, they were much younger. She said, "Yes, even though they were young, it was a challenging time for them after their dad died, but eventually, we all got through it together." She also assured me that we would eventually be able to get through Toby's death as well.

My mom and Grandma always had a way of making me feel better, even when I was in pain. I recall both of them always saying, "This too shall pass." They didn't mean that the problem, feelings, or circumstances would magically disappear, but rather it could lead you to have reflective thoughts to help you process what was happening and find the strength to process the challenges you were faced with. You had to simply continue to put one foot in front of the other and let God direct the path he wanted you to take.

An Uncomfortable Moment

Later that evening, my mom and I were sitting downstairs in the dining room talking, and we noticed James walking toward us. At that time, he asked what we were having for dinner. I don't know why but it made me so angry to think that he was thinking about food at a time like this. I knew we all had to eat, but it made me angry. I was not in a good place, and although my mom was there and she was planning to prepare dinner (which everybody loved and was looking forward to) before she could say anything, I told her I would prepare dinner. I wanted to do it because I needed something to do; I needed some type of distraction. I decided to cook Ginneria's favorite meal, spaghetti with meatballs and cornbread. This was the last meal we had together the night she was killed.

As I started cooking, I began to reflect on the last day Ginneria was alive and her enjoying her last meal that evening. This brought a smile to my face. Once I finished cooking, I called everyone and told them that dinner was ready. My mom said that she would prepare their plates. I told her that I would make James' plate, and as I was dishing the meal, I became angry all over again. I started thinking that Ginneria was not there to eat with the family. I began to think about when James came downstairs earlier, asking what we're going to eat. I thought again, "Why is he thinking about food at a time like this?" and that it wasn't the first time he had done this. That's when I became infuriated. Once his plate was ready, I called him down. As he entered the kitchen, I had the plate in my hand, and as I looked at him, I said sarcastically, "Now you can eat since you are so hungry and thinking about food so much." In that moment, I thought of him eating and Ginneria not, and I started screaming, saying that she would never have the opportunity to ever eat again. Before I knew it, I threw the plate I had in my hand up in the air and all the food splattered onto the kitchen ceiling. I continued screaming and crying as James, my mom, and the children looked at me with shocked faces. I was also upset with James because he had done the same thing the night before. He wanted to know what he was going to eat, and I think this is why I exploded. I felt that he was more concerned with eating, which was the last thing on my mind. After this, I immediately ran out of the kitchen, grabbed my keys, and ran out of the house. I didn't know where I was going; I just needed to get out of the house.

After standing in front of the house for a while, I got in my car and sat there. While sitting in the car, I was able to calm myself down, and I began to recognize that I overreacted. With everything going on, I was angry and didn't know how to express what and how I was feeling. While sitting in the car, my heart ached, and I was worn out from crying. There is nothing like physical and emotional pain to drive you to your knees in prayer. Even though I wasn't on my knees, I started praying. I asked God to help me release all my anger, bitterness, hurt, and pain and to give me His peace. I so desperately needed peace because anything would set me off. I also asked for him to protect my heart, and keep me from going into the depressive state that was looming over me.

On Friday, December 9, the day before the funeral, my mom and my daughter, Kim, dropped off Ginneria's clothes at the funeral home. After they returned, my mom and Kim shared with me that they were able to see Ginneria. They told me that Ginneria was lying on a silver table that looked like a slab, with a white cloth draped over her, where only her face and neck were uncovered, and it was up to her neck. Kim shared that there was a sink-type bowl positioned under her head, and when they pulled the cloth back, they saw a "Y" shaped stitching across her chest and down to her abdomen. After hearing that, I thought not only was my child shot in the head but she was also spilled open when they did the postmortem examination. Thinking of that just devastated me. I started thinking about the endless night at the hospital, the return home, the hours that passed, and the collective silence as we all gathered in the living room.

My family and I still couldn't accept the fact that she was gone forever. We were all a little uneasy knowing that the funeral would be the next day, especially Michelle since she had not seen Ginneria since the night she died. During dinner that evening, there was a strange silence in the house. To break the quietness, I believe it might have been James or my mom. I wasn't sure who, but we started talking about Ginneria. I can't remember all that we were talking about, but it brought a little laughter and smiles. Once we finished dinner, everyone headed upstairs to get ready for the next day, which no one was looking forward to. After going to bed, I still was unable to sleep. As a matter of fact, I had not been able to sleep more than two or three hours since Ginneria's death, and when I did fall asleep, I had awful nightmares of Ginneria trying to get out of the car after hearing the gunshots being fired. This began to take a toll on me. This night was the hardest, and I actually fought going to sleep because I knew the morning would bring a fresh wave of pain. I wasn't ready to see my child's lifeless body in a casket. I never could have imagined going to any one of my children's funerals.

The Visitation/Funeral

"So do not fear, for I am with you; do not be dismayed,
for I am your God. I will strengthen you and help you.
I will uphold you with my righteous right hand."
Isaiah 41:10 (NIV)

I Wasn't Ready

Saturday, December 10, was an unbelievably cold day, and all I wanted to do was stay in bed. Besides, I didn't want to think about this being the day of my child's funeral. After getting out of bed, it was hard for me to focus. It was as though I was moving in slow motion. I then became aware that everyone was already up and moving around. There was this overwhelming calmness in the house, but I began to feel anxious in the midst of this calmness. My mom was making breakfast. I became so nervous that my anxiety level heightened, and I started feeling knots in the pit of my stomach. My mind began to wander again, and once again, I began thinking about how she died and why this didn't have to happen to her. My child's life was taken because of one person's anger, stupidity, and senselessness. The more I thought about how she died in that moment, the angrier I was becoming. I started weeping, knowing that in a few hours, I would be going to my child's funeral, and I would see her lying in that casket. I knew I had to face the reality that she was dead and we would not be the same without her, but I couldn't. As tears rolled down my face, I began to cry out to the Lord. I asked Him to give me the strength to get through this night. As I continued praying, these words came in my spirit, "The Lord himself goes before you and will be with you; he will never leave you nor forsake you" Deuteronomy 31:8 (NIV). He was saying to me, you're not going through this alone. Hearing those words in my spirit gave me such an overwhelming peace. The only thing I could do was praise Him. Praising God in that moment didn't minimize the heaviness of my heart, but it had me redirect my focus on Him and His promises and knowing that He never changes. He promised never to leave me or abandon me. Later that morning, as my mom and I talked, I told her about how I was feeling and how anxious I was to see Ginneria lying in that casket. Talking to her about my feelings and fears helped take some of my stress and anxiety go away, but as I started getting dressed, my anxiety was beginning to intensify again. The thought of seeing my child lying in that casket was heightening my anxiety even more. I sat on the edge of the bed, and tears started streaming down my face. I just sat there. I had to keep reaffirming God's word that He would never leave me or abandon me because the weight of the day, the heaviness of my broken heart and pain, and the anxiety I couldn't shake was a lot to bear. I felt like I was in a battle. I knew I had to pull myself together for the sake of my children because I didn't want them to know that I was experiencing any distress. This was the only reason I was able to stand. Once I was able to compose myself and put on my I am okay mask, I went downstairs to let everyone know that I was ready and we could leave.

Once we arrived at the funeral home, I started having a weird feeling inside my stomach. Before we got out of the car, I noticed there were so many people standing outside and wondered why. After everyone got out of the car, they were waiting on me to get out. Once I got out of the car, it took every ounce of strength I had for me to walk toward the entrance of the funeral home. As we made our way to the lobby, it was completely full. I then understood why all those people were standing outside. When we made it into the chapel, I noticed that it too was filled to capacity, and there was standing room only. People were standing alongside the walls. As we walked toward the front of the chapel where we would be seated, it felt like all eyes were on us. Despite my initial feelings, all the people who came out were not curiosity seekers but people who loved Ginneria and wanted to say their final goodbyes. I remember seeing so much sadness on all their faces. After we made it to our seats, I stood there, pain-stricken, and instead of taking my seat, I slowly walked toward the casket. It was really hard for me as anxiety began to take over my body again. As I looked at her, I have to admit that I was momentarily startled to see her lying there. She looked as though she was asleep. I'm not sure what I was expecting, but it was a relief not to see the bruising over her eye. While looking upon my child's face, I began to have that strange feeling in my stomach equal to the feeling I had when we were approaching the funeral home. I also recall having those similar feelings when I saw my first husband, Lionel, while standing at his casket, looking at him as blood was oozing out the side of his mouth. In that moment, I began to perspire, and my knees started to tremor. Standing there looking at her sweet, beautiful face, I couldn't help but wonder, "What am I doing here? Why am I here? I'm not supposed to be here. We all should be home, not at a funeral." As these questions surfaced, I believe my mom took me by my arm and led me to my seat next to my children. When I sat down, all of a sudden, someone leaned down toward me and told me that they were so sorry for my loss and that Toby was such a wonderful young lady and that she was well-liked. Then countless other people started coming up to me to express their condolences. I don't remember who they were, neither do I remember their faces; all I remember was that there were so many hands patting me on the shoulder. I couldn't tell you who those hands belonged to as they whispered in my ear, "I'm so sorry for your loss." There were also hands reaching out to shake my hand and leaning down to hug me. There were so many people, and although I didn't remember their faces, I remember how they made me feel. I was so thankful for their kindness.

Before the service started, the funeral director closed the casket. As the lid was being closed, I thought that she was not going to be able to breathe. It was overwhelming knowing that she was inside there with no air, and during the service, I just sat there and stared at it with tears streaming down my face. I couldn't help but thank God; He gave me seventeen wonderful years with her. Though I wanted more time with her, I couldn't have been prouder of the way she touched and changed so many people's lives. As I withdrew within myself again and blocked out everything around me, I begin to think about her and the last minutes of her life and when the bullets entered her head. I also prayed that she wasn't in any pain and that she didn't feel the bullets when they entered her head. My thoughts were all over the place. I started reflecting on her as a child, her first words, and her first steps. I couldn't help but note at that moment that in a few short months, she would have been preparing for her high school graduation. Instead of us seeing her walking down the aisle of the school's auditorium, we were walking down the aisle of a funeral home and looking down at her lifeless body in a casket. During the service, I continued to have similar thoughts of so many potential memories that would never come about. All of those precious moments would never happen for her, and we would not have the opportunity to share those wonderful moments with her. I knew I had to face the reality that she was dead and we would not be the same without her, but I couldn't.

I don't recall all that took place during the service, but I do recall Pastor Milton talking about Ginneria and the kind of person she was. He talked about how she showed kindness and compassion toward others. Although life had stopped for her, it was a transition, passing from this world into eternity. Pastor Milton also went on to quote the psalmist, saying, "Surely goodness and mercy shall follow me all the days of my life; and I shall dwell in the house of the Lord forever" Psalm 22:6 (NIV). I begin to ponder on what he said Ginneria passed from—this world and into eternity. This brought me back to when Ginneria had accepted Christ early on in her life. I remember the day she was baptized; it was exciting, and when I witnessed her being lowered into the water, that was a memorable day. Yes, she will be spending eternity with Him. My only other clear recollection was of my children sitting there staring at their sister's casket and crying. It broke my heart watching them experiencing so much emotional pain. After the service, Ginneria's body was then transported to O'Hare Airport to be flown to New Orleans.

Once we made it home, I was exhausted. However, my mom wanted me to eat something, but I couldn't. Once we undressed, we sat around for a while and talked. After going to bed, I still was unable to sleep. I kept thinking about Ginneria. I could not wait to get on that plane and get to New Orleans so I could see my little girl's face one more time. My emotions transitioned from fear to anticipation, which surprised me. I actually had something to look forward to.

Sunday, December 11, my family flew to New Orleans for the second funeral and burial. As soon as we arrived, we went to my mom's house. After settling in, my family came over for Sunday dinner, and we just hung out for the rest of the day. That evening, my sister, Eloise, did her usual pep talk, encouraging and trying to comfort me. She was assuring me that everything was going to be all right and that she was there for me the way she had always been. I was so grateful for her.

Finalizing Arrangements for Burial

Monday, December 12, my mom drove James and me to Glapion Funeral Home to finalize the arrangement for Ginneria. What was most challenging for me was walking through those doors; it brought back so many memories and so much pain. Over the years, Glapion Funeral Home has handled funeral arrangements for most of the family, on both sides, including my husband, Lionel's funeral. Once inside the funeral home, the funeral director informed me that Ginneria's body had been picked up from the airport Sunday morning. I was also told that her makeup had been redone per my request. At that time, I asked if I could see her. I was then escorted by an assistant to the chapel where Ginneria was. I was also informed that the chapel she was in would be the chapel where the services were going to be held. After entering the chapel, I told the assistant that I wanted some time alone. I had not had an opportunity to be alone and spend some time with her without someone being around. When I was finally alone, I looked at my baby girl as she laid there so motionless. It was as if she was asleep. At that moment, it was just she and I. I then rested my body across hers and laid my head on her chest, and wept. I began kissing her on her lips and then all over her face. Her body was warm and soft, and that made me feel good. I began telling her how much we loved her, how much we were going to miss her, and that we would forever treasure every moment we had together. I also told her that I was immensely proud of her and that her life had touched so many people. Once I finally pulled myself up, I noticed a kneeling bench near where her casket was. I moved the bench over to the casket and kneeled on it. I began praying, asking God to give me, and especially my children, the strength and the peace we needed and not to let us go. I expressed to Him that I didn't understand why this had to happen to Ginneria and that I also needed Him to help me come to terms with her death. Even though I knew I would never completely get over losing her, I needed Him to get me through it. I also asked God to please comfort my children because they were so overwhelmed with pain and grief over the death of their sister. I could feel tears begin streaming down my face as I pulled myself up and started kissing her again and again, telling her how much I loved her.

When I was leaving the chapel, I noticed that my movements were becoming restricted, and my breathing was becoming labored. I started feeling lightheaded. I stood there for a few minutes to gain my composure before going back to the office. While standing there, I stared back at the casket. If I could, I would have stayed there all day. Once I made it back to the office, I told the funeral director that they had done a great job of softening up her makeup, and she looked absolutely gorgeous. She looked like herself, more natural.

After leaving the funeral home, our final stop was Providence Memorial Park Cemetery, where so many family members are buried. I had not been to this cemetery since my ex-mother-in-law, Lionel's mother, died three years after his death. On the ride to the cemetery, I don't remember saying much. I just sat quietly in the back seat, trying to process everything that was taking place. Upon arriving at the cemetery, I didn't want to get out of the car and go inside the office. I knew I was going to have to pick out a gravesite and that soon I would have to leave Ginneria here and my ability to touch her and see her would end. Once James and my mom got out of the car, I sat there for a few minutes, hesitating to get out of the car but eventually forcing myself to do so. As soon as I got out, my eyes became fixated on all the surrounding gravesites and then on the mausoleums. I couldn't imagine Ginneria being placed in a deep hole. Being there brought back so many memories and such pain that I had been suppressing for so many years. After we entered the office, my mom informed one of the staff that we were there to choose a gravesite for "Ginneria Major." The staff person responded that they were expecting us, as they received a call from Glapion Funeral Home. The conversation sounded so formal, and before I could process it, it hit me, this was going to be the last decision I would be making for her. The reality of this surfacing to my consciousness was hard for me to take in. How do I process this in this moment? Before I could really grasp that fact, I was handed a map showing me the available areas. This snapped me back and grounded me in the room. After reviewing the map, I chose an area with several oak trees surrounding the burial site, which I felt would be a good marker for us to identify where she was. Also, it was several yards from where her dad, grandmothers, great-grandmothers, and grandfather were buried. Once everything was finalized, we left the cemetery. On the ride back, I resumed my thoughts that in a few days, my baby girl was going to be placed in a hollow hole that I had just chosen for her. I wasn't ready to accept that.

Once we made it back to my mom's house, she called the family to come over for dinner. I knew having my family around during this time was going to be a great comfort for us. When they all arrived, I was still having feelings of sadness and emptiness. While having dinner, we talked about Ginneria and our grandma. I recall my sister, Eloise, out of the blue, saying she didn't think Mama (that's what we called our grandmother) would want to go to Ginneria's funeral. As she said that, I remember that whenever we visited my grandma, it was always hard for her to see us go and to say goodbye. Whenever we came for a visit and got ready to leave, she would never say goodbye. She always said, "See you later." I agreed with my sister. Although she loved Ginneria dearly, Mama would not have gone to her funeral. She would not have wanted to see her laying in a casket, and she would not want to say goodbye to her.

Our Final Goodbye

Tuesday, December 14, was the final service. When I woke up that morning, I felt as if someone has sucked every ounce of strength out of me. As I sat in the living room, I started thinking that this would be the last time I would be seeing Ginneria, and this would be the final goodbye to my baby girl. I then noticed my mom looking intently at me. As I looked up at her, I realized that she was the only one who truly understood how I felt and what I was going through because she, too, lost a child tragically. I told her that saying goodbye to Ginneria and burying her today would be the hardest day of my life. As I expressed this, my mom held me in her arms and said, "I know. I know how you feel. You will get through this." Our hearts connected in that moment. This gave me such comfort because my mom wasn't a touchy-feely type of person.

Upon arriving at the funeral home and walking toward the building, it was extremely hard for me to go inside. Many memories started rushing back. As I began making my way toward the door, James and I believe it was Lionel, they both took me by my hand, and we slowly walked inside. As we entered the lobby area, I noticed some family and friends standing in the lobby that I hadn't seen in years. Seeing all of them there to celebrate Ginneria's life added another level of sadness. When we made our way to the chapel, I saw more people, some I knew and some I didn't, standing together talking, while others sitting crying and consoling each other. Then I noticed people standing at Ginneria's casket crying. My uncle Herman then came over to me, hugged me, and said, "You have been through so much." He then gently kissed me on the forehead as he wept. That was the first time in my life I had ever seen my uncle showing any kind of emotion. I remember him being there for my children and me after Lionel was killed, but he never once expressed any emotions. He then led me to Ginneria's casket.

As I approached the casket, I leaned over and began kissing Ginneria on the lips. They were still so soft. She was also warm to the touch, which gave me some comfort (I didn't want her cold and hard). As I looked at her, she looked so beautiful. I knew this was going to be the last time that I would be able to look upon my baby's face, and I wanted to take it all in. I placed my hand on her hands and again prayed and asked God to strengthen us because I knew how heavy this would soon become. My legs began to buckle, and my hands began to tremble. My uncle then led me to a chair to keep me from falling. I remember sitting down, and everything after that was a blur. I blocked out almost everything and everyone around me throughout the majority of the service. It was again as if Ginneria and I were the only ones in the room, the way it was when I was with her in the hospital while seeing her lying on the hospital gurney. When the service came to an end, the only thing I remember was the funeral director telling everyone that it was time to close the casket. I suddenly gasped for air, thinking, "This is it!" I wasn't ready! I cried out in the depth of my soul, "Oh Lord, help me." I wasn't not ready to look upon her face for the last time and say goodbye to my baby.

The funeral director directed everyone to come up for the final viewing. At this point, the room felt like it was closing in on me, and all of a sudden, I felt myself getting hot. Pain started tugging at my heart, and I was gasping for air as I began to say repeatedly, "This is it." As I sat and watched with dread as family and friends passed by Ginneria's casket, I tried to brace myself to say my final goodbye. When my turn came, I wasn't ready to let her go. I wasn't ready for them to close the casket for the last time, never to be opened again. I remember telling the funeral director that he couldn't close her in that box. I kept thinking, she's still alive. She is still warm. You can't close her in; she won't be able to breathe. It felt as though my heart burst open, and I could feel the blood rushing inside of me. Nothing could change the wretchedness I felt. Nothing and no one could say or do anything that would take away the horrific pain I felt. My baby, my baby, I will never see her sweet face again. As they were closing the casket, I just lost it, and the room became hot, and everything went dark. The only thing I remember was James, and I believe my sister, Eloise, walking me to the limousine and helping me inside. Once inside, they tried to give me some water. As I climbed into the family limousine, my eyes were fixed upon Ginneria's casket as it was being placed inside the hearse.

Once we departed the funeral home heading to the cemetery, I laid my head back and reflected on the time I was pregnant with her and throughout the seventeen years, I had her with me. I just wanted to relive all those precious memories and every moment we had. No matter how hard I tried to focus on the memorable times, my mind kept going back to seeing Ginneria lying on the gurney in the hospital with her eyes half-opened and having to leave her there. I was stuck with the thought that now I was going to have to leave her in hollow, cold ground. As we made our way to the entrance of the cemetery, I raised my head and looked out the window at the giant old oak trees surrounding all the graves. This was a place I didn't want to be because it made the day a little more real and final.

The thought of burying your child is one of the most agonizing experiences a parent will ever have to face. If you've never had to bury a child, there is nothing I can say that will give you even the slightest understanding of the utter helplessness and anguish that accompanies it. The death of a child at any age is a deep and painful experience. It was so hard knowing that we were never going to see Ginneria again was incomprehensible for me to process. My heart grew weak even as I tried to see how my family was going to survive the days, months, and years to come.

The minute the cars made their way to the gravesite and finally stopped,

I began to panic. James helped me out because I couldn't do it alone. My mind and my body were in agreement. They both said no. We were then escorted to where chairs were placed for the family. Deshone, Michelle, Lionel, Kim, and my mom were seated together, while James stood behind me, as other family members and friends all gathered around us.

The Burial

Once we were seated, my eyes immediately were fixated on the hole that had been excavated to place Ginneria's body in. I then noticed that my brother and cousins were position near the hearse to pick up the casket and placed it over the open hole. I remember saying, "I can't do this. I can't do this. I can't bury my baby. I'm not ready to let her go." I just sat there paralyzed during the gravesite prayers as I watched Ginneria being lowered beneath the earth. It was as if a part of me was being buried along with her. I could not believe that I was sitting in front of her grave trying to embrace the reality that this child I bore, and held, and loved would never be in my arms ever again on this side of heaven. I began to wonder how much more pain my heart could endure. This couldn't possibly be the journey God had for me to walk, but now I see it was.

When you lose a child, you walk through a kind of darkness, everything changes, and the world looks so much different. As parents, we cannot imagine a more traumatic experience than the death of a child. Parents naturally expect their children to outlive them, but what happens when this isn't the case? This unnatural, life-altering experience presents a unique challenge, rebuilding your life without your child. This is what I had to learn how to do, how to live without Ginneria, and how to rebuild my family's lives.

After the funeral, we gathered at my sister, Doris' house. I recall everyone sitting around eating and talking about Ginneria. However, all I wanted to do was lay down because I wasn't in the mood to laugh and talk. While I was lying across the bed, I noticed my sister, Eloise, coming into the room with a plate of food in her hand. She then walked over to the bed and told me she wanted me to eat something because she didn't want me to get sick. I told her I wasn't hungry, but she insisted that I take a few bites for her and for Toby. As I lay there, I heard the family talking and laughing, and I became so angry that I felt as though they should be feeling the way I was. I remained in the room by myself for the remainder of the time to process the day. As we prepared to leave, my mom told me that she wanted us to stay a few more days before returning to Chicago because my birthday was coming up, and she felt that we needed to be around family. I agreed with her and told her that it was a good idea for us to stay a while longer. I really needed to be around my family during this time.

December 15 was my birthday, and I was not looking forward to celebrating, especially since I had just buried my child. However, my sister, Eloise, thought it might make me feel better. She had one of my sisters, I believe it was Dooley, get me my favorite birthday cake from my favorite bakery, McKenzie Bakery. They had the best pineapple filled birthday cakes. My sister, Eloise, did everything she could to make that day special for me. Everyone sang happy birthday with all the best intentions and effort, but this birthday wasn't the same because Ginneria was not there to share it. It was hard for me to be happy. I remember Eloise insisted that I eat a slice of my favorite cake, but it, too, didn't taste the same. All I could think about was Ginneria and her being in that deep dark hole in a sealed box.

Not Looking Forward to Returning or Looking Forward to Christmas

On December 19, my family and I returned to Chicago six days before Christmas. After a few days of settling in, my children noticed there was no Christmas tree, and I hadn't even attempted to put up any decorations. I really wasn't looking forward to celebrating Christmas without Ginneria, and it was a struggle getting myself mentally prepared to do so. I used to look forward to and cherish those moments of decorating the Christmas tree with my children. In fact, I had already completed my Christmas shopping at the end of November, and the gifts were already wrapped and waiting to be put under the tree before Ginneria was killed. But this year, there was no joy to be found. I literally thought that there was absolutely nothing to celebrate, and putting up a tree didn't feel right to me.

The memories of past Christmases became bittersweet. Growing up as a little girl, I enjoyed Christmas. Christmas was always my favorite holiday, and every Christmas season was magical for me. It felt like my own personal holiday. My mom always made it special for us. I really enjoyed decorating the Christmas tree with my sisters Eloise, Doris, Edna, and my brother, Sonnyboy. We spend hours decorating the tree and the entire house, and making our Christmas list was a major event. Once our lists were completed, Mom would take us downtown to Maison Blanche Department Store to see Mr. Bingle, who was Santa's helper. Each of us would give Mr. Bingle our Christmas gift list (one year we made the local newspaper, which published our picture in line as we waited), and then after visiting him and Santa, we would walk down Canal Street to look at all the beautiful decorations in the store windows; they were all so magical. A few days before Christmas, my siblings and I would then spend the day baking cookies with my grandma while my mom was prepping for Christmas dinner. On Christmas day, my siblings and I would wake up early in the morning and look under the tree to see what presents Santa Clause brought us. Most of what we had on our list we got. We also enjoyed exchanging the gifts we had for each other. Later in the morning, we sat down and ate breakfast, and afterward, my mom and my grandma started finishing up Christmas dinner. The aroma throughout the house smelled so good. I can still smell Mom's famous cornbread dressing, turkey, and ham baking in the oven. Also, Mom made the best mac and cheese along with her delicious yams and greens with smoked ham hocks. They were the best. We also had gumbo, which was a tradition. I almost forgot my grandma's favorite jelly cake. The table would be covered with nothing but food. These are just a few of my many wonderful Christmas memories.

I so looked forward to the time when I had my own children to make Christmas as magical as I experienced. I wanted them to have those special memories to hold onto the way that I had. I continued many of these traditions with my own family. When we moved to Chicago, I would take my children to the Christmas Parade. The parade was filled with pageantry, and they had such amazing floats. After the parade, we would walk down State Street to look at the beautiful Christmas window displays at Marshall Field's and Carson Pirie Scott, which had various animated themes. Afterward, we went to lunch, and then they shopped for their Christmas gifts for each other. Once we were in the store, they would all scatter throughout the store, trying to hide from each other so they would not see what the other person was buying. Once we got home, each of them found a corner in the house to wrap their gifts. They really enjoyed the tradition of exchanging gifts with each other, and it was exciting seeing them so happy. Seeing this always led me down the memory lane of my own childhood.

We also had several other traditions. We went to church on Christmas Eve for midnight service, and afterward, I prepared a huge breakfast that included grits, eggs, bacon, biscuits, and various juices and fruits. After breakfast, they were allowed to open one gift from under the Christmas tree and the gift from each other. They would stay up until three or four o'clock in the morning enjoying themselves. With all these wonderful memories, I was faced with the reality that Christmas would never be the same, especially this one, because eighteen days before it, Ginneria was murdered. In light of her death, I had no intention of putting up a tree, let alone decorating one. In fact, I didn't want to celebrate Christmas at all. The only thing I wanted to do was be alone and try to process why this happened to Ginneria.

Three days before Christmas, Kim, my youngest, approached me and said, "Mama, why we don't have a tree up yet? We always have a Christmas tree." What she said next shocked me to my core and brought me back to reality. She said, "Toby is gone, but we're still here. We want to celebrate Christmas." She also said, "And I want a Christmas tree." I had not taken into consideration that my children needed to keep our traditions, and I knew I had to since she was the youngest. Before she got ready for bed, I told her that I would get a tree and we were going to celebrate Christmas. When I got ready for bed, I prayed and asked God to help me to make this Christmas special for them because it wasn't all about my feelings only. It was about theirs's as well.

The next day we went out to find a Christmas tree. We usually got a fresh tree, which was hard to find since it was two days before Christmas. After going to several tree lots, we finally found a place that only had two trees left. The man who ran the tree lot told us since he only had two trees left to take the one we wanted at no cost. Once we got home, we untied the tree and placed it into a base with water to let it set and fall into place. Later that evening, we began decorating the tree, and it brought smiles to their faces. I then placed their gifts underneath the tree. It was very emotional for all of us that night because Ginneria was not there to help decorate and celebrate that moment with us. Christmas Eve was different because we didn't go to church, but we opened our gifts. On Christmas day, we had our usual Christmas feast. We did our best as we held joy and sadness simultaneously, knowing that Ginneria was no longer there with us.

My one take away moving forward was that I knew I had to focus and remember that Christmas was about life and the birth of Christ. I needed to celebrate Christmas for my children and with them.

After Christmas, I went through the bag that contained Ginneria's belongings that she had on the night she was killed. The medical examiner's office had given the bag to the funeral home when they picked up her body. When I opened the bag, I saw her gray hooded jacket that was drenched with dry blood. There were also the light-blue pajamas that Kim said she had on under her jeans when she left to meet Stacey that night. There was also a white tee shirt, her jeans, and a pair of brown boots. I took the jacket out of the bag first. After taking it out, I began to cuddle her jacket and then buried my face into it. When I moved the jacket from my face, I noticed there were white-looking dried particles inside of the hood. I began picking up the particles, and at that moment, I remembered that she had been shot in the head, and the bullet shattered her brain. I then realized it was her brain particles that had oozed out of her head and onto the hood of her jacket. This hit me like a ton of bricks. I sat down and began weeping. I kept repeating to myself, "My baby's brains were blown out." I then put her hood against my face again and placed the brain particles toward my lips, and held it there for a few minutes. While weeping, I then cuddled her jacket in my arms close to my heart as if I were cuddling her. I then began picking my child's brain particles out of the hood and placed them in tissue, and later placed them in my Bible between the folds of the page of the 23rd Psalm:

> The Lord is my shepherd; I shall not want. He makes me to lie down in green pastures; He leads me beside the still waters. He restores my soul; He leads me in the paths of righteousness for His name's sake. Yea, though I walk through the valley of the shadow of death, I will fear no

evil; For You are with me; Your rod and Your staff, they comfort me You prepare a table before me in the presence of my enemies; You anoint my head with oil; My cup runs over. Surely goodness and mercy shall follow me All the days of my life; And I will dwell in the house of the Lord Forever. (NKJV)

Then and there, it came to me that even though she was in the valley of death…I believed that God surrounded her, and she was not fearful. Her brain particles are still in my Bible to this day.

Navigating Through the First Several Months After Ginneria's Death

As we were approaching the New Year, our lives had been changed so dramatically that I sometimes wonder if I was still the same person. I began to see things through a different lens. I used to hear stories of awful tragedies and never thought it would happen to my family. I found out that the unthinkable could happen, and it did happen to us. Ginneria's death shattered the very fabric of our being, but I had to trust that God was going to see us through. Three months after her death, I could not have foreseen that I would experience another devastating loss, but I did. My eldest sister, Eloise, died suddenly. I didn't believe that I had any more tears left in me. I remember being at work when my Mom called. I answered the phone, and the first thing she said was, "She's dead. Eloise, is dead." I responded by saying, "Eloise is dead." I began to shake. As I began shaking, one of my co-workers stood by my side, and another had their hand under my armpit. My legs wobbled, and they helped me sit down. I wanted to say, "I'm okay," but I couldn't speak. After a moment, I told them that I was okay, but they continued to stand by my side. Still holding the phone, I continue to say, "My sister is dead." No one knew what to say. They just stood there. I sat there trying to process what I had just heard. I just couldn't believe my sister was dead. I tried to keep myself calm because I knew I had to drive home.

I pulled myself together for as long as I could to make it home, or maybe I was just numb and in shock. This wasn't happening again! The pain felt as though someone had put a knife in the pit of my stomach while my heart was being crushed at the same time. I began to experience a tidal wave of different emotions. I didn't know how I was going to handle both my sister's death and Ginneria's at the same time. I felt completely unable to imagine a future without both of them. Eloise had always been there for me, my rock, my comfort, my sister! She was not only my sister; she was also my best friend and confidant. Eloise played an important part in my life. She practically helped raise my siblings and me. She taught me so much, and I respected her and looked up to her. She was also one of my strongest supporters. My sister was always there for me in good times and bad times. Eloise saw me through a lot of heartache. We may have had our disagreements at times, but she always had my back when I needed her, and she knew she could always count on me. She was a person you could trust, someone you could relate to, and, in my eyes, the best sister anyone could ever have. I was angry. I was so angry that she was gone, and I became angry with myself because I wasn't there with her when she died. It wasn't fair. With my sister and my daughter gone in such a close period, what was I going to do now?

Processing the Unimaginable

I struggled to navigate through two traumatic losses in three months. It was inconceivable for me to do it. I was still in the infancy stage of my grief with Ginneria, and as I stumbled through that, I had no idea how to cope with her death and my sister's death at the same time. Do I grieve one then the other, or both at the same time? How do I do this? Will one death get more attention than the other, or does one need more attention? Their deaths were so different and brought up so many feelings, and I did not have any direction to lead me to the "right way." I was so overwhelmed and confused. I was left with one question and no answer, how do you multitask grief? I just cried until there were no more tears left in my body or any pain that was left in my soul. My mind literally had no room, my eyes had no more tears, and my body did not have any energy. I was left empty with no space trapped in my feelings. I became the container of pain.

Saying Goodbye to My Sister

I never imagined my sister dying, and saying goodbye to her, my best friend, was extremely hard. It was even harder standing at the foot of her grave and watching her being lowered into that hollow ground—the same ground Ginneria was buried in. It felt like I was in a daze, a bad blurry dream. The pain was overwhelming, and I was going to miss her more than words could express. I was going to miss how much she cared for those around her and her concern for everyone else's well-being more than her own. Who was I going to call? As I stood there, I reflected on her practically standing in that very spot just three months earlier, comforting and supporting me when Ginneria was buried. As I stood there, I told her how much I was going to miss her and that I always would. I just wanted to scream at everyone and say, "You just don't know how hard this is. I was just here burying my child, and now I'm here again burying my sister!" I had her buried in the same plot as Ginneria because she was so close to my children, and I didn't want her to be alone.

After my sister's funeral, I would just sit and wonder, "How do I walk a path, a path I've never walked before?" "How do I help my children deal with their grief?" How will my children be affected by the death of their sister, especially Deshone and Kim, because of the way they were feeling about how they thought they could have prevented what happened. How do we move forward without Ginneria in our lives?" So many hows.

Trying to handle all this was too much. Feelings of sadness, pain, and sluggishness became a part of my everyday life. Everything was becoming extremely intense, and I felt as though I was in a continuous battle to keep things going. My endurance was completely wiped out, and I was being depleted of all my energy. It was to the extent that the slightest tasks became monumental. What previously was easily achieved became insurmountable. At times, I had absolutely no concept of how to cope. The biggest hurdle for me to grasp was that Ginneria was alive several hours earlier, and then several hours later, she was dead.

In my heart, I knew that death was a part of life. Death gives meaning to our existence because it reminds us of how precious life is. Although I knew this, it was extremely hard for me to cope with it. Dealing with my current losses triggered and deepened my past experiences with loss—losses

I had not fully dealt with. Many of us are weighed down by a lifetime of losses, and we don't realize the impact it has on our lives and how some of those losses can affect us in many different ways. Some of those losses may have happened when we were young and others when we were older. There is the tendency to suppress feelings, to push them down so that we do not have to deal with the pain. Unfortunately for me, that's exactly what I did with mine. Now, the feelings that I had suppressed for so many years were coming back with an uncontained intensity.

Unsure of My Emotional State

My grief had engulfed me as well as impeded my ability to move forward. I was on an emotional roller coaster ride, having to learn how to ride out this unbearable nightmare. I was deliberately trying to avoid thinking about what happened, but my brain needed to reprocess every waking moment over and over again. Furthermore, I had no one to talk to, nor did I have anyone who really understood what I was experiencing. My feelings were deep and excruciating. I had a profound sadness that was a constant cloak around me. My grief was always there, festering beneath thin layers of denial that tried to cover my pain and leave me with a false acceptance. Trying to ignore and hide how I was feeling only made it worse. I went through the motions and put on an "I'm okay face" for days, weeks, and months, all the while hiding my pain despite that I was aching inside. I felt paralyzed by this word called "grief." I couldn't let myself express how I was really feeling, especially for the sake of my children. I realized that they were also experiencing enormous pain and grief in similar, but yet in a different way, and I didn't want to "bleed" my stuff on them, so I hid mine. My pain was reserved for the isolated moments. I was also afraid for their safety whenever they left the house, always thinking that something might happen to one of them. Hypervigilance became my new companion.

Ginneria's death took me to a dark place I've never been before. My whole entire world came to a halt. Nothing seemed real or fair anymore. As I watched the world around me, everyone was going on with their lives. I thought to myself, "How can they go on with their lives when I'm drowning in mine?" I resented everyone. Why did they get to be happy while my world was falling apart? As I struggled to dig myself out of this deep pit I was in, it was becoming increasingly more problematic to get out. The overwhelming deep emotional pain consumed me, and the only thing I kept hearing in my head over and over again was, "Your daughter Ginneria is dead. Your daughter Ginneria is dead." Those words consumed me. They were a part of me, and I couldn't get them out of my mind. My old life now became more and more of a distant memory that flooded my mind, which left me with feelings of emptiness and loneliness. It was even harder for me to go into Deshone and Ginneria's bedroom and having to look at Ginneria's empty bed. My heart ached deeply for Deshone and the pain she was going through because they were extremely close. I constantly thought about her having to experience that same emptiness and loneliness every night she went into their room to go to bed while trying to figure out how she was going to cope without her sister being there with her. I was also concerned about Deshone's mental health and wanted her to go to counseling, which she eventually did.

There were also times when I woke up during the night to go the bathroom, and when I got back to bed, it was hard for me to fall asleep again. Waves of sadness would surround me, and I would spend several hours crying until I cried myself back to sleep. After waking up and getting out of bed, sometimes my feet would hit the floor, and it would seem as if something was preventing them from moving. My feet would feel like they were fastened to the floor. As I would try to move them, my heart would begin to race, and I would feel a heaviness pressing on my chest where I couldn't breathe. It would be so intense it frightened me. I didn't know what was happening to me, and the only thing I could say was, "Lord help me. What's going on with me?" My heart ached so bad that it was beginning to affect my physical and mental state. Grief sometimes overtook me to the point that it pushed me into a depressive state that was becoming intensely overwhelming. I began to question my own sanity. I questioned if I could make it through another day because my grief was intensifying. I felt angrier than I thought I could ever possibly be. I was so angry with the murderer, David Gladney, for taking the life of my child, and I was angry that my children had to experience such a tragic loss, and I didn't know how or what to do to help them. As I shared earlier, I have lost loved ones in the past, and it was hard, but losing my daughter was the hardest for me to deal with. I found myself recreating scenarios of that fatal night, and this, coupled with constant dreams, was exhausting.

In one of my dreams, I was at the hospital after the doctor informed us that Ginneria was dead. After seeing her, they told us we had to leave, and then I heard Ginneria screaming. She was telling me not to leave her there because she wasn't dead. She was just in a deep sleep. The only thing that I needed to do was shake her a little harder to wake her up. In another dream, we were at the cemetery, and I could hear her beating on the casket, calling out for me to open the lid and get her out because she was beginning to suffocate. When I woke up, I felt myself pulling at something. Other times, I would hear the front door opening, and my heart would stop for a minute. I waited for a while, hoping to hear her voice saying, "Mom, I'm home," while the door slowly closed. My heart would be filled with joy at the thought that she was home, only to awaken and be forced back to reality. It had gotten so bad I didn't want to go to sleep because I was terrified of having those dreams.

My child was dead, and simply put, I just couldn't believe it. I didn't want to accept it because the feelings attached to it felt so overwhelming. The intensity of my grief was compounded by the traumatic and violent circumstances in which she died. These "night anxieties" I was experiencing, including the vision of Ginneria sitting in that car as the bullet entered her head and shattering her brain, was something that never escaped me. Losing her was the single worst thing that had happened to me, and there was a gaping hole in my heart that I just didn't know how to close or if it would ever close.

Encouraged to Move On

While the agonizing pain was diminishing in intensity over time, it wasn't gone completely. Although my friends, co-workers, and others were very supportive, they didn't understand the continued gravity and depth of my heartache and pain. Unfortunately, what everyone was doing, and some were Christians, they tried to make light of how I was feeling and did not really acknowledge that I was grieving or that I needed to grieve. The thought of moving on was frightening because it meant that I would have to leave Ginneria behind-so I thought. I didn't know how to live without her while establishing a life that she was not a part of. I didn't know how to live in both worlds. How could I move on with the thought of Ginneria being left behind? I didn't know how to come to terms with the fact that I had no closure. I felt "moving on" wasn't for me. It was for those around me. I realized that they were not encouraging me to grieve. They were trying to discourage me from grieving. In fact, everyone wanted me to stop crying and talking about what happened because it made *them* uncomfortable. As for me letting go, that was out of the question. That was never going to happen.

What really hurt me was when people would say to me, "She's in a better place," or "She's watching over you." I didn't want to hear that Ginneria was in a better place watching me. I wanted her with me. I heard others say, "I know how you feel because I have lost loved ones too." I would listen and think, "How can you possibly know how I feel?" "Do you really understand what I am feeling, to have had a child murdered?" Yes, some had experienced losses, but not one had experienced the murder of their child. They still had their children, so they couldn't possibly know how it felt despite that they had dealt with death. I also remember someone telling me that everything happens for a reason. Losing my daughter, having her brains blown out over eighty-five cents was not a good reason. I understood that things were said with the best intentions, and they meant well, but wow, some things were hard to hear, and it had such a negative impact on me. Each statement was minimizing my grief. If only people knew that every waking moment of every day, I replayed that dreadful night over and over again in my mind, and every morning when I woke up, it was a reminder that Ginneria wasn't there; she was dead. They just didn't understand. They didn't understand the depth of my pain and heartache or the traumatic stress I was dealing with. If only they knew. The most important thing I wanted was for those who were around to just listen, to be there and walk alongside me during this journey that I was on. I didn't need them to tell me what I should and shouldn't do; I just needed their presence to be there for me.

Felt Abandoned

Sadly, after a while, most of those individuals stepped back, and the support that I thought I had eventually faded away when I needed it the most. I realized that they couldn't handle the emotional stress I was dealing with. Fortunately for me, I had not completely lost my faith, which had a strong presence in my life. I had to remember who the source of my strength was. When most of them left, I had to remember that God was still there with me, and He never left me, even in my pain. He knew me so well. He created me. He knew the number of hairs on my head, and He even knew the thoughts I conceived in my heart before I ever vocalize them. I also had to remember that He told us to come to Him and ask for what we needed. I also had to remember Jesus was a man of sorrow and was acquainted with my grief. He understood my pain and my heartache. Therefore, I had to be honest and release my whole self and how I was truly feeling. When I did that, I began to feel the strength that I thought I didn't have. When I felt discouraged, I began to find hope. When I was feeling depressed, I knew I would have the ability to endure, the faith to overcome, and the determination to keep going. Even when I fell (and I fell many times) and when it was hard, I remembered that God was my strength and my true comforter. I knew I had to lean on Him to get my family and me through this traumatic and devastating loss we experienced.

The Rollercoaster Ride Continues

As I was battling with trying to become accustomed to Ginneria not being there in the house and becoming tolerant of my aching heart, I began to really push back at this notion of moving on. I felt like a failure because my grief was not matching up with the time constraints that others were placing on me. When you are in the midst of intense pain from grief, it seems as though things will never get better. At times, I would feel better for a few days, and something would trigger me, and I found myself overwhelmed with emotions, and then I was back at square one. At any given time, I could be completely thrown off guard by one single thought or reminder, such as the neighborhood grocery store where Deshone last saw Ginneria or the funeral home that was two blocks away from our home. Driving back and forth to work made it difficult because I had to cross the street where she was killed every day. Before coming to that corner, I would slow down, pull over, and look down the street, trying to visualize where the car was when the shots were fired. The thought brought on intense sadness and anger, and it would take several minutes until I was able to process my feelings and focus again.

A Spur-of-the-Moment Decision

Grief continued to be my partner on this rollercoaster. I remember one evening, I was pacing back and forth in my bedroom, feeling very alone and still somewhat isolated because my family was so far away. So, I decided to relocate back to New Orleans. I felt that we needed to be around family. I wanted to get away from everything and all the reminders of Ginneria's death. So, at the end of the school year, summer of 1984, we moved. After moving back, it initially was great. We were around family, which made grieving much easier for me. But I soon realized no matter how far of a distance I went, it was not going to erase what happened.

Moving back and being around my family didn't relieve me of what I was dealing with. In actuality, while on the surface I tried to escape the pain, I actually went back to where it all began. It was kind of full circle. New Orleans was where Ginneria was born, and it brought back all those early bittersweet memories of her young years. Not to mention, this was where she was buried, this was where my brother died, this was where my first husband died—this was where everyone that I loved died. Everywhere we went and everything we did, there were constant reminders with intense despondency because she (they) was not there with us as a family.

Approaching the First Year

Getting through the last six months of the first year was one of the hardest challenges we faced as a family. We survived, but I'm not really sure how. This time was filled with disbelief as we agonized over coming to terms with the reality and acceptance that Ginneria was no longer there with us anymore. We had to learn how to live and adjust without her, and it brought on sadness as longingness for her lingered in our lives. With months passed since Ginneria's death, I still wished I would wake up and have it all be a nightmare. I never thought I would make it through a month, much less make it through a year. But no matter how much time passed, it still felt like yesterday.

I couldn't believe we were approaching the first year of Ginneria's death. The first year was a year that made it possible for me to put one foot in front of the other, which then allowed me to move toward acceptance and healing. It was a year of reckoning and trying to make sense of what happened as well as make sense of this new reality my family and I were facing. I became better at allowing myself to feel whatever feelings I was experiencing and not bottle them up. I gave myself space and permission to work through my grief instead of holding it in. I also realized that grief was ongoing, and it wasn't going to stop at the end of the year or the second or third year, and so on.

As time went by, we learned to cope so that we could get through each day and deal with all of the "unpleasant firsts." During this journey of firsts, we didn't know what to expect, her graduation day and birthday. We just did the best we could as a family. We were also in New Orleans on the first anniversary of Ginneria's death. It was hard for all of us, especially for Deshone. On the evening of the seventh, Deshone experienced an intense panic attack where she had to be taken to the emergency room. She began to relive that dreadful night, and it came crashing down on her to where she was in an uncontrollable state.

During this time, we learned that over the course of the first year, there wasn't a secret formula that I used to survive. I had to trust God through this whole grieving process. We had to love each other more each and every day through every moment. We had to be patient. We had to embrace each other and give one another space to grieve. We had to trust and hold onto God over and over again. We also had to laugh more. As I slowly began to let go of my pain, I realized that it didn't mean that I was forgetting. Letting go of what used to be did not mean that I had forgotten. I had to realize that Ginneria would remain in my thoughts and heart forever. Letting go meant leaving behind the sorrow and pain and choosing to move forward. Moving on meant that I could take with me only those memories and experiences that enhanced my ability to grow and expand my capacity to help others.

Although the grieving process was beyond painful, I had to let myself feel the intense, unrelenting pain, accept the love and hugs from those around me, and fully embrace the process. This is how I slowly was able to move forward. Even though there were many ups and downs, there came a time where there were just as many good days as bad…until one day I realized that my bad days were fewer and farther between. This was scary in the early days of my grief because I missed Ginneria so much.

One thing that I would hear is that "time heals all wounds." I came to realize that time is not a healer. It does not heal pain. Personally, what time did for me was it allocated me the chance to process my thoughts and feelings and get to a place where I could give myself permission to grieve. Inevitably, the grieving process takes time, and healing comes gradually; it can't be forced or hurried, and there is no "normal" timetable for grieving. For me, time also made people stop talking and asking how I was doing, and they stopped mentioning Ginneria's name. What they didn't understand was that grief is never something you get over. You just don't wake up one morning and say, "I'm done with this pain, and I'm moving on." Grief is something that walks alongside you every day. There was never a day that went by that I didn't think about Ginneria and wished I had another opportunity to have one more moment, one more one-on-one with her, or one more hug. I had to learn how to live with those desires and to accept that they will never come to pass. In truth, over time, it did get easier for me to cope, but I was no less over my child's death. It is clearly apparent with the consequences of loss; the passing of time cannot heal your soul. Action taken to work through the pain will help to alleviate the pain for you to get to healing, but "time" itself does not heal a griever's heart.

Over time, the pain began to lessen, and even though I was encouraged by my faith in God and his help, there was still a battle. At times, I still felt isolated and felt somewhat alone, and not a day went by. I didn't think about my child. During those difficult times, I knew I had to survive not only for myself but for my four surviving children who were grieving and needed their mom more than ever. I was not willing to sacrifice my role in their lives by succumbing to the pain and grief that, at times, was trying to paralyze me. The pain of losing her was still extremely intense, and the realization of never seeing her again was painful for me to accept. Memories of her flooded my mind, and there was an unimaginable void with her not being there in our lives. Gradually acceptance was setting in, and I began to grasp that, yes, this is real, and there's nothing I can do to change it. Along the way, I was learning to process the changes that were taking place within my family. The reality is that grief impacted my whole identity as well as the individuality and security of my family. Although my children and I were trying to get back to some "normalcy," it was hard. Her death felt like an un-survivable moment, and when I turned to God in those moments when my heart was crushed, and I was in deep grief, I chose to trust Him. I realized the grieving process was not something that Christians were exempt from. Our hearts ache, our families hurt, and some are torn apart. I knew I still had to trust that God would bring us through no matter what we were experiencing.

Second Year

Moving into the second year was considerably more difficult but for different reasons because not only did I have to heal from Ginneria's death, but with the complexities of the legal system. I had to prepare myself emotionally to go through the upcoming court trial alone. In this journey, I soon found out that the criminal justice process is slow, frustrating, and sometimes insensitive.

March of 1985, the trial for David Gladney was starting, and it knocked the wind out of me and brought me to my knees. This caused me a lot of stress because I had to relive the night Ginneria was murdered. The thought of reliving that December night and hearing firsthand testimony from the witnesses who were there with her when she was murdered was going to be really traumatic for me to listen to. I was informed that the State's Attorney's office would fly me back to Chicago once the jury had been selected and that the trial would take about four to five days. After I was given all the information, I asked if I could be there during the jury selection but was told that I could not. A week later, I received a call from the State's Attorney's office informing me that the jury had been selected and that the jury consisted of seven men and five women. The individual expressed that the State's Attorney was pleased with the makeup of the jury and that the trial was going to start the following week.

The day the trial started, and throughout the duration of the trial, I sat in the second row behind the State's Attorney. I was also able to have a clear view of David Gladney; he and his attorney were on the opposite side, showing no remorse. His family was seated two rows behind him. I was informed earlier that I would not be able to show any kind of emotions in front of the jurors, and if I found myself getting emotional, I had to leave the courtroom, or I would be escorted out since the judge didn't want the jurors seeing me becoming emotional because it might cause jurors to be empathetic toward me. Although I understood the rationale behind this, I also felt that this was insensitive. The pressure to hold your emotions in during an emotional time seemed unreasonable, at best. So, throughout the trial, when I felt myself becoming emotional, I would hold on to a picture of Ginneria that I had as if I could draw strength from her and not break down. The last thing I wanted was to be asked to leave the courtroom. I wanted to hear everything that took place that night.

During the trial, the witnesses testified that on the evening of December 7, 1983, Marvin Gladney, along with Ginneria, Stacey, Juan, Jason, and David Gladney, drove together to a liquor store. At that time, Stacey gave Juan money for liquor and cigarettes, but he was unable to make the purchase. When Juan returned to the car, he said that he couldn't purchase the cigarettes and liquor and that he gave the money to David to purchase it. When David got back to the car, he had not purchased anything and didn't give Stacey all her money. She was missing eighty-five cents. An argument ensued over the money as Marvin drove the group about four blocks away, parked, and ordered David, Juan, and Jason out of the car, and he proceeded to search them. He then recovered the eighty-five cents from his brother, David. Marvin then told Juan and Jason to get back in the car, leaving David and Marvin outside of the car. The argument escalated, and Marvin pushed David to the ground and then returned to the car, only about two steps away. However, before Marvin could drive off, David opened the driver's side door where Marvin was seated. David then fired six shots into the car, shattering all three windows on the driver's side. Ginneria was shot in the head, and Stacey was also shot. Marvin then drove to the hospital, which was about five minutes away. Once they arrived, Ginneria was pronounced dead on arrival. I later learned the detectives arrived at the hospital and took Juan, Jason, and Marvin into custody so they could take their statements. After taking all their statements, David was arrested and read his Miranda rights. David subsequently confessed to the shooting, contending that he only intended to frighten his brother. As simple as this story can be told, the consequences were nothing but.

As I sat there in silence, listening to all the witnesses over the four and a half days of the trial and looking at the person who murdered my child, it just tore my heart open, opening up all those emotional wounds again. While sitting there, his family continually stared at me with angry looks as if I were the reason for him being there. This was really upsetting. But the toughest day of the trial was when the State's Attorney called the medical examiner to the stand. It was heartbreaking when the medical examiner's office gave their report regarding the autopsy and the results stating that Ginneria was shot twice in the head, shattering her brain. Hearing that shook me to my core. At the end of each day, I went back to my hotel room feeling exhausted and overwhelmed. I felt so helpless and alone especially being in the courtroom with no family there to support me.

At the conclusion of the evidence and testimony, the attorneys gave their closing statements. After the closing statements, the judge gave the jurors instructions and dismissed them to the jury room to deliberate. The waiting seemed endless; it went on late into the evening hours. After the verdict was reached, everyone was notified to come back to the courtroom, and once everyone was there, the judge had the bailiff bring the jurors back into the courtroom. After all the jurors were seated, the foreman handed an envelope to the bailiff, and the bailiff then handed the envelope to the judge. My eyes were glued to the envelope. It possibly contained the words I wanted to hear, GUILTY. The judge then opened the envelope, looked at it, and then handed the envelope to his clerk, who read the verdict aloud. David Gladney was found guilty of aggravated battery and murder. There was a gasp of disbelief among David Gladney's family. I sat there and cried. I was relieved that the person who was responsible for my child's death had been found guilty.

A month later, David was sentenced to concurrent terms of twenty-five years for murder and twenty years for aggravated battery. He served twelve and a half years. Although I was upset with the sentencing, no amount of time served would have brought Ginneria back. Our lives will never be the same, but life had to go on.

The Third, Fourth, and Years Beyond

Moving through the third year was a year of transition. Not only were we trying to move forward, but we also had to work on rebuilding our lives. We still had surges of sadness, loneliness, and pain because we still missed Ginneria so much. The fourth year was a year of change. Even though grief was a part of our lives, the immensity of my daughter's death and the enormity of my pain gave my life renewed purpose and urgency to help and support others. During those years, I learned that grief was a process, and you have to go through that process until it brings about acceptance. Even though the journey was hard, I continued to read the word of God, which gave me encouraging words to comfort my spirit and turn my sorrow into joy. Forgiveness was another important part of my healing. When you forgive another, you let go of a burden. I remember sitting in my room, and I heard clearly in my spirit God telling me to forgive David Gladney—to let go of the anger, bitterness, and resentment I had toward him. I asked the Lord, "Are you really telling me to do this? You want me to forgive this person after he murdered my child." I told God that I didn't know if I could do that. He basically said to me that that was the only way I would be able to get past all the hurt and pain I was holding onto and find peace. It's not uncommon to have trouble forgiving others and oneself, and I know that Jesus teaches that forgiving is a spiritual act because he pointed out again and again that when you do not let go of any thoughts or feelings that keep you from forgiving, you will not find peace and joy. I didn't know if I could do that because I was immersed in my pain, anger, hate, bitterness, and resentment toward this person. I wanted to feel better; I wanted to have joy and peace again, but this was an act. I didn't know if I could or if I wanted to. After a while, I asked the Lord to forgive me for holding on to all the feelings that were holding me back and not allowing me to forgive. Hard was an easy word that came to mind, but it did not come close to capturing how I felt. But when I did, I welcomed the Lord's forgiveness and found the strength in my heart and clarity of mind to forgive David Gladney. By letting go and forgiving, God gave me inner peace, and that's when I was able to grieve freely and begin to truly heal and rebuild our lives. I take nothing away from my grief journey, and I would not say everything was and is one hundred percent because it is not. We still hurt, and we're still walking and managing this grief journey after all these years. However, God knows us, and he can feel the pain of our grief. When you have a relationship with Him and one another, you can get through anything.

Life has never been quite the same since the day Ginneria was taken from us thirty-eight years ago. This journey has been difficult for all of us and was the biggest challenge God has given us as a family. Through it all, we persevered because the Lord gave us the strength, and kept us submerged in his love, and prevented us, especially me, from going crazy. I was blessed to have a wonderful daughter, and I got to love her for seventeen years and five months, and the nine months while I carried her in my womb. I gave her life, but she gave me so much more. She gave me a lifetime of love and immeasurable memories. I would often wonder how life would have been different had she still been with us today and all that she would have accomplished. If my daughter taught me anything, she taught me about grief. She taught me that we should live every day loving, caring, and creating precious memories that will comfort us after they're gone. She taught me that pain and joy can coexist. She taught me that grief teaches us to be true to our feelings and ourselves. She taught me that I can navigate through just about anything—pain, hurt, anger, bitterness, and anything else I am dealing with. I miss my child so much, and my heart is broken, but I believe God was preparing my heart through all the pain and suffering I experienced in my life. He was teaching me what a true heart of compassion and unconditional love looked like for those who are experiencing the pain of grief.

For those of you who are reading my journey through grief, who too have lost a loved one, I know that it hurts and it's hard, but I want to say to you, allow yourself to go through the grieving process; don't run from it and don't suppress it. Don't treat your grief as if it were a stranger. You can send away or deny. Grieve what is lost. Grieve honestly. Grieve lovingly. Grieve patiently. Grieve compassionately until you are able to release your pain. There is no other way back to wholeness but by facing and acknowledging your loss. This is my word of comfort to you, and it comes from Philippians 4:6-7 (Amp), which says:

Do not be anxious or worried about anything, but in everything [every circumstance and situation] by prayer and petition with Thanksgiving, continue to make your [specific] requests known to God. And the peace of God [that peace which reassures the heart, that peace], which transcends all understanding, [that peace which] stands guard over your hearts and your minds in Christ Jesus.

My journey today is not about grieving my daughter's death but turning a tragic situation into honoring her memory by providing grief support services to families who are going through their grief journey. I am not the same person I was thirty-something years ago. I am happy for the person I have become in the aftermath of Ginneria's death. I am leading a life that I would have never dreamed for myself. Surprisingly, over the course of many years, we made great progress even though I had no rulebook to follow on how to cope and how to help my children cope with what they were experiencing. But I prayed a lot.

Reflection
The Death of a Child

Losing a child is the loneliest, most desolate journey a parent can take. One of the toughest challenges a parent faces when a child dies is learning how to support and comfort their surviving children. As a parent, we are expected to have all of the answers, but in times like these, there are no words. What do you do or say when you, yourself, are experiencing so much pain? You may find that you have become so preoccupied with your own grief that you're overlooking the needs of your surviving children. There is nothing else on this earth that is more difficult than the death of a loved one, especially if it is a violent death. It is something that affects the lives of the entire family. In fact, actually experiencing it is the only way for you to really know and understand this level of pain and suffering, especially if it's a child's sibling. Immediately, you are faced with two extremes, the loss of your child and the ongoing daily demands of your surviving children. There are times when you can barely help yourself get through the day, let alone tending to the needs of your grieving children.

It is important for parents to recognize that their children, too, are grieving the loss of their brother or sister. Also, remember that each family member grieves differently in their own way. It is not uncommon for surviving siblings to become consumed with thoughts that they could have somehow prevented their sibling's death. Over the course of time, they may imagine various scenarios on how they could have somehow saved their brother or sister. Their thoughts are flooded with the "what if's" and "if onlys." They may resort to drugs or alcohol to deal with the negative feelings, or in more serious cases, the surviving siblings may lose their will to live and begin having suicidal thoughts. Through this experience, I am eternally grateful that my four remaining children have gone on to live fulfilling lives, but to this day, all four of them, particularly Deshone, have their moments when they are overwhelmed with emotions after the loss of their sister, Ginneria. Today, they are in their 50s and yet the bond with their sister and the heartbreaking memories of her death are still very much alive.

Guilt is a powerful emotional roller coaster ride. After Ginneria's death, I began to feel guilty that I didn't get to say goodbye. I didn't get to spend as much time with her on the day of her death, and I didn't get her the "goods," which was the candy she asked for. Fortunately, I now know that feelings of guilt in grief are normal. We may feel guilt for continuing to live when our loved one has died. We feel guilty for things we may have done or said and later wished we had not. We also feel guilt for things we feel we should have done or said and somehow didn't. You may also agonize and tell yourself, "If only I'd done something differently, this never would've happened." Sometimes though, there simply isn't anything you could have done differently.

I reflected on everything that happened since receiving that phone call and grew more upset by the minute. The staff in the emergency room was deceitful, extremely unsympathetic, inconsiderate, and lacked any ounce of compassion. No one deserved to be treated that way! As a parent, that was the worst thing imaginable. Feelings of pain, distress, helplessness, and devastation are beyond words. Unbeknownst to me, the experience that I went through at the hospital due to my daughter's death became the birth of the Family Trauma Advocacy Program. I want you to know my heart joins with yours with compassion. Although none of us can fully understand the circumstances and unique experiences of another person's life, it's comforting to know others are willing to walk with you through pain, grief, and despair. I want you to know I consider it a privilege and a blessing to come alongside you to encourage you and be a companion as you walk your personal trail of tears. My purpose isn't to try to give you answers. It's to help you find your answer. It may be that you are the one sorrowing, or it could be you are sharing in the struggle of a child, family member, or friend. All of our lives touch others, so it's inevitable that we take on the load of the people we love. As my children have all become adults with their own families, I am beginning to understand the obvious but somehow surprising truth that you are a mother as long as you live.

Reflection
Coping with the Murder of a Loved

Losing a loved one as a result of a murder or violent death is one of the most traumatic experiences a family will face. The process of grief and bereavement is very different when a death is the result of homicide. This is also true of other violent deaths. Families are left not only with the sorrow of the loss but also with the profound powerlessness. Individuals and families can become trapped in the trauma of their loss as their lives become defined by the violent death of their loved ones. As the devastating reality of the murder is replayed over and over in the minds of the family, it also often appears in the headlines of the news over and over again. Experiencing this type of grief is like no other. It is intense and overwhelming, and it leaves tremendous emotional pain and disruption. Likewise, it is often challenging to understand and even more difficult to come to terms with.

Although there is no one way to grieve, the following list provides some important steps for healing. These are some suggestions in ways to cope:

- ❖ **Give yourself permission to grieve so you can heal.** Decide every day that you will make the choice that your healing and joy will return. Even though your future may be quite different from the one you had, it can still be a good one. Happiness and hope can be yours again. Choose life.
- ❖ **Embrace your feelings.** Grief can bring many different feelings to the surface at any time, and some with enormous intensity. Acknowledge these feelings and accept them as part of the natural grieving process. Don't hold in anger, sadness, or longing. These are important feelings that, once expressed, help you heal.
- ❖ **Grieve at your own pace.** Grief doesn't have a timetable and can be exhausting. It takes a lot of energy. Allow yourself plenty of time to do everyday activities, and don't over-schedule yourself. Rest when you feel yourself getting

exhausted. Do what you need to do and feel what you need to feel to heal for the process to unfold. No matter how difficult things may seem, healing does come.

- ❖ **Be patient with yourself.** You can never get over grieving in a month or even a year. The pain you have experienced will diminish over time. Expect that even years later, you will occasionally have feelings of sadness. Give yourself permission to mourn in your time.
- ❖ **Support.** While there may be times you are coping with loss when you'll wish to be alone, it's also important to have support in those times when you might need it.
- ❖ **Keep the faith.** Remember that intense grief doesn't last forever. Keep the faith that you will heal and be whole again.
- ❖ **Learn as much as you can about the grieving process.** The more you learn about the grieving process, the more it will dismiss the myths surrounding grief. The more you learn, the more you will recognize that your grief is normal.

CHAPTER 9

Remembering My Sisters

> "Be devoted to one another in love. Honor
> one another above yourselves."
> **Romans 12:10 (NIV)**

Eloise

There was nothing quite like the bond I had with my siblings. The sibling bond, particularly among my sisters, was one of the most significant relationships I had. It was like no other. No matter how far apart we were, we were always connected. No one understood me better than they did. They grew up with me, cried with me, and laughed with me. They were there during the good and bad times. This was especially true for my sister, Eloise.

Eloise has always been there for me when I needed her most. I could always go to her with anything that I might be struggling with. My sister and I have always been extremely close through everything. She was nine years older than me, and even though there was an age gap, it didn't make a difference. My sister had a big heart, and she loved her family. Having a sister like her was one of the greatest gifts I could have had growing up. No one knew me the way she did. We had a special "sibling bond," and we shared a connection. Our bond was something I cherished, and I was so blessed to have had her as my sister. Her support was second to none.

When our brother, Sonnyboy, drowned, our family experienced a tremendous traumatic loss. I was scared and lonely, but during this time, we banded together for strength and support. My siblings and I worked through the pain, and we grew even closer than ever. One evening, while lying in bed crying, Eloise came over, picked me up, held me in her arms, and told me it was going to be all right. This may have been the first time I cried in her arms, and it definitely wasn't the last. Also, I remember after Sonnyboy's funeral, I was walking down the street with her, holding her hand, and thinking about how blessed I was to have her with me and her support during this time. Her commitment and my sense of knowing that she was there was reassuring for me. As I glanced into her eyes, they affirmed her love for me.

Eloise helped me in so many ways. Growing up, she taught me to be truthful, kind, and to never lose faith. Through her, I've learned to have self-confidence in myself and stand up when kids were trying to bully me. She just reaffirmed what my grandmother taught both of us. I could trust her over anyone to tell me the truth. If I did something inappropriate, she didn't have a problem telling me whether it hurt my feelings or not. She was straight up and honest.

Unfortunately, Eloise's twenties marked a period in her life where she suffered loss and trauma that changed her in ways that is difficult to fully grasp. Eloise married at the age of twenty and divorced five years later, and it was during her time of separation when she experienced a horrific and violent act. Eloise was a victim of sexual assault. The evening this occurred, Eloise made plans to go out with friends. I remember her putting on a red "Shimmy" style dress with fringes, black patent leather shoes, and dangling pearl earrings. She was so excited as she dressed for the evening and she looked beautiful. Unbeknownst to me, when my sister returned she would never be the same. Early in the morning hour, a friend of the family found Eloise wandering around in a daze and brought her home. I remember my sister coming into the house and seeing her face bruised with her eye and lip swollen, and her face was wet from tears. As I looked at her, she kept saying, "I'm here," "I'm okay," and "everything's okay." Beyond those words, she never discussed what happened and she did not receive any counseling to help her process her trauma. This violent act lingered with my sister for years in a negative and destructive way. She began drinking excessively, and her relationships and her ability to trust and connect with others became challenging. You could always tell when she was reliving what happened to her because she would become quiet and self-isolate. Eloise's spirit just slowly faded away.

Soon thereafter, she began drinking excessively. Dealing with my sister's alcohol addiction was consuming. It took a toll on the family in different ways, especially her children. Despite her drinking, Eloise was always there for her family. She was a dedicated mother, and she really loved her two girls and took very good care of them. I admired her style. She made sure to show her girls how much she loved them with a simple expression of love and encouraging words. She listened, she played, and she laughed with them. Eloise didn't take motherhood for granted, and I'm so grateful to have learned from her about being the best mom I can be. Nonetheless, addiction comes with a cost, and even with the best intentions, it affects those close to you.

Eloise showed signs of alcohol abuse around the age of twenty-five or twenty-six. I was concerned about her drinking and if she was becoming an alcoholic. I wanted to do whatever I could to help to encourage her to stop. I often felt helpless. I didn't know what to do to save her. When the family tried to talk to her about her drinking, she became really upset and didn't want to hear it. Eloise would just change the subject. She was in denial and didn't consider herself an alcoholic. This cycle of communication continued for years. I understand now, but I didn't know then that alcoholism is a progressive disease and no one chooses to be an alcoholic. My sister probably wanted to stop drinking, even more than we wanted her to, but she didn't know how. We tried to get her into a detox facility, but there were none at the time for her to check herself into.

After I moved to Chicago years later, Eloise and I talked several times a week. I remained in a constant state of anxiety and worried about her constantly. I loved my sister very much, and I struggled with how I could help her. I was at a loss about what I could do. When we talked, she was always upbeat and wanted to know what was going on with the kids and me. When we talked, she always listened with love and compassion. She loved to talk about her dog, Poochie. She took that dog with her everywhere she went. I was her support system, and she was mine. We encouraged and motivated each other. She was my inspiration, and unquestionably she was constantly there for me, and I was there for her. That's why it hurt me so to see her in that state. Sometimes, I could tell she had been drinking, and it made me so sad. My heart broke each time as I felt so powerless. My sister, my rock, was destroying herself with alcohol, and I didn't want to lose her. What hurt most was that I knew she was drinking herself to death. We had many lifelong memories that will never perish from my mind, and the bond we had was unbreakable. The difficulties we encountered growing up together only made us stronger and kept us closer. I have realized about my life that my sister and I had been through pretty much everything together.

After our grandmother died, Eloise's drinking became even more severe. I am convinced she died of a broken heart. Eloise and I were the closest to our grandmother. Her death devastated the family, but Eloise took it the hardest. She adored my grandmother, and she really struggled with accepting her death. I knew her life had become distorted because she focused more on drinking to cope with her grief. She went in a downward spiral and didn't want to live anymore. Her drinking had gotten so bad that it started to affect her health. The week my sister died, she started hemorrhaging from her nose and mouth. It wasn't unusual for her to have nosebleeds. However, this time, it was worse. She later started coughing up blood. She was immediately taken to the hospital, and after being examined, the doctors informed my family that she had to be admitted. Upon further examination, we learned Eloise was hemorrhaging internally. They would have to take her to surgery to stop the bleeding. However, because her blood was not clotting, and given she was too weak, the doctors were unable to perform the surgery to stop the bleeding. All we could do at that point was wait and pray. My sister lapsed into a coma and died three days later. She died as a result of hemorrhaging from the esophagus on April 10, 1984, four years after my grandmother's death and just four months after the death of my daughter, Ginneria. My one regret is that I was not there at the hospital when she died, and I was not there in the way she was always there for me. Furthermore, I didn't get a chance to hold her the way she always held me and to say goodbye.

The thing I remember most about my sister was that she was like a mother figure to me, and she took care of us while my mom worked. She taught me the true meaning of sisterhood at a young age. Throughout the years, I was proud to have an older sister to look up to, to protect and guide me. Through her, I learned the importance of unity, teamwork, and compromise. I also learned from my sister the importance of standing up for myself, being humble, and always apologizing or admitting when you're wrong. Eloise encouraged me to be patient and keep a positive attitude no matter what life throws at me. These simple lessons changed my whole outlook on life. I am so very grateful that my sister took the time to help mold me when I was young. When I got married, she was there whenever I needed her. Eloise was right there by my side after my greatest losses, with the death of Lionel, our grandmother, and Ginneria. For that, I will forever be grateful for my sister.

Edna

Each one of my sisters truly inspired me. Edna showed me what it means to be a survivor. The greatest test for Edna was her extraordinary courage when she was diagnosed with Huntington's disease at the age of thirty-five. Huntington's disease is an inherited progressive (degenerative) brain disorder. Symptoms of Huntington's disease include a loss of cognitive abilities, emotional control, and most visibly jerky and involuntarily movements. It also causes slurred speech and difficulty swallowing. Unfortunately, parts of the brain deteriorate and break down over time. I had never heard of Huntington's disease until Edna was diagnosed with it. Over time, it became harder for her to walk, think, reason, swallow, and talk. It was difficult to watch her suffer through it. Throughout the years, she became physically weaker, and we witnessed her rapid decline. However, she had enormous strength and handled every challenge she encountered with dignity. It wasn't easy, but every challenge Edna faced, she faced with courage and determination. Though there were times she had moments of extreme struggles, she never once gave up and at no time complained. Her strength and courage were remarkable with all she was going through. However, it was incredibly difficult for me to watch my sister's life deteriorate before my eyes. Watching her go through this affliction made me realize that strength does not always equate to independence. In fact, it can sometimes mean the opposite. Being strong doesn't mean standing alone. It can mean having an army stand with you. My sister recognized when she needed help, and she asked for it. She had the determination to keep living. Her strength was being patient when it may have been so easy to fall apart.

As I watched my sister go through this horrible disease, it broke my heart. I was my sister's caregiver for a little over five years. As I watched her decline, the need for a higher level of care became inevitable. I eventually had to place her in a nursing home. For three years, I visited my sister three or four days per week, alternating on the days the center bathed her to make sure she had a bath every day, and her bedding was changed. On Friday's I picked up her dirty clothes and dropped them off on Saturday mornings when I picked her up so we could spend the day together. I would take her to the mall, which she enjoyed, and after lunch, I took her home with me so she could sit on the patio while drinking lemonade. Edna also enjoyed listening to music and watching television. Later that evening, we would have dinner, and afterward, I gave her a bath and took her back to the nursing home.

On Sunday mornings, I would pick Edna up for church. She loved to hear Pastor Smokie Norful sing, and she listened to his sermons when she was unable to attend church. After church, we went out for lunch and then to my house, where she spent the rest of the day. After dinner, I would give her a bath and then take her back to the nursing home. I did this until her condition worsened to where she was wheelchair-bound, and I was unable to take her out. I never once heard Edna complain, nor did she ever ask God, "Why me?" Rather, she took it as an opportunity to grow in character and resilience.

Edna epitomized grace and exhibited true and genuine humility when faced with adversity. There was not a single day that I didn't think of how her life had been altered and how she handled it with dignity. I realized that if Edna could wake up each day and face the world and all its challenges and never complain, I had no reason to do less than that. Every challenge she faced made her an incredibly tenacious person. Edna showed me how important it is to be independent, persistent, and unapologetically individual. She also taught me what it means to be a strong woman of faith, courage, and determination. It's in part because she met each obstacle knowing that she had the love and support of her family, and she trusted and had faith in God. Edna would always say, "I love my Master, and He loves me." Whenever she saw me, she would always greet me with a big smile and say, "I love you, truly I do." Edna had such a positive attitude, and she was always more concerned about others than herself. The nurses told me the day before she died that she told them how great they were and to tell me that she loved me.

In caring for my sister, I learned to see her disease as an awakening. Without it, I would not have known the true meaning of courage and its role in triumphing over obstacles. Not a single day goes by where I don't think about my sister. Edna gave me hope that there are people in this world filled with compassion, courage, and determination. She carried a heavy burden for quite some time, knowing that one of her children and possibly her grandchildren will be affected by this disease. Unfortunately, Edna's eldest daughter was diagnosed with Huntington's disease in 2014, and her granddaughter in 2019. My sister died on August 12, 2012, and her daughter died on April 22, 2019.

Janet

Every once in a while, we come across someone who truly lives a life of caring for and helping others. These individuals perform so many acts of kindness that come from a pure and giving heart. One individual, I knew firsthand who exemplified this was my remarkable sister, Janet, who we called "Dooley." Dooley was one of the most extraordinary people I knew. She was in a league of her own. Dooley was a compassionate and empathetic person by nature. She had such an unselfish heart and genuinely enjoyed helping those in need. I can truly say she had a servant's heart and a willing spirit. Dooley would go above and beyond to help others. She had such an unselfish heart, and she genuinely enjoyed trying to make a positive impact on others' lives.

Dooley volunteered at shelters, where she cooked and served meals. She also provided clothes to the homeless and took care of those with disabilities. Dooley took in the homeless and loved and cared for them as well. You could also depend on her whenever you needed something. I have seen her do so much for others wherever she went. If you called her any time of the day or night, you could always expect to hear her say her favorite words, "I'm on my way." She saw the good in everyone no matter where they came from or what they might have done. She wouldn't judge a person based on what they looked like or what she heard about them. I am so proud of my sister, the person she became, and the love she poured out into those in need.

In 2002, Dooley was hospitalized and diagnosed with a ruptured brain aneurysm. Before going to the hospital, she had been complaining of a headache for several days. During that time, the headache worsened even though she was taking pain medication. The pain had become so intense that Dooley had to be taken to the emergency room. The doctors examined her and performed x-rays, after which we were informed that she had a ruptured brain aneurysm and her condition was serious. Immediate surgery was necessary, but it could not be performed until they were able to reduce the swelling in her brain. The doctors also shared that Dooley may not survive given the swelling and bleeding in the brain. We were so scared for her. The doctors began giving her medication to reduce the swelling, and eventually, the swelling had reduced enough for them to perform the surgery.

The surgery took about ten hours. The doctors were able to stop the bleeding, and later we were told that the bleeding was coming from behind her eyes. Several days after the surgery, we were informed that she was blind in both eyes and that she might not regain her sight, and if so, she would have limited vision. But God! After a week, her eyesight returned, and when Dooley's vision was tested, she had 20/20 vision. She said she was able to see better than she had before the surgery. After eight weeks of recovery, Dooley was back, providing service to those in need. There was no stopping her. Dooley was back to her old self, during what she loved—taking care of others. Over the years, Janet continued to suffer from headaches; she took medication to manage the pain.

After Hurricane Katrina hit New Orleans in 2005, my mother and two of my sisters, Doris and Dooley, moved to the Chicagoland area a few days later. Another sister, Joanette, came about a week and a half later. At that time, I had an opportunity to reconnect with my sisters for three years, especially with Dooley. We had always been close even though I lived in Chicago, but during this time, I was especially grateful that our relationship deepened and grew into a very special friendship. When Dooley moved from New Orleans, she encountered an environment far different from the one she had become accustomed to. New Orleans was where our entire family lived. She had never lived any place other than

New Orleans. She was leaving behind all her friends, and I knew this would be a different experience, not only for Dooley but also for my other two sisters and my mother. Their entire lives were uprooted, and they experienced a traumatic event. However, Dooley adjusted quite well. She found an apartment and picked up where she left off, just in a different city. She contacted homeless shelters in the area and began volunteering. She did that for two years before returning back to New Orleans. Shortly after returning to New Orleans, she went back to what she most enjoyed, helping others.

My family is close-knit. Every Sunday, we had dinner at my mother's house, even as adults. During one of the Sunday dinners, Dooley complained that her head was hurting more than usual, and one week prior, the doctor prescribed her a new medication because the old medications were no longer reducing the pain from her headaches. The family noticed that Dooley's mood was somber, and she wasn't her bubbly self. She was acting rather strangely that day. She didn't want to drink her beer, which she enjoyed, nor did she smoke her cigarettes. She just sat quietly in the den watching television. During dinner, Dooley ate very little. She said she didn't have an appetite and proceeded to take her medication and lie down. It was not uncommon for Dooley to have headaches for days at a time, and she would take her medication and relax and feel fine afterward. About an hour or so, she got up complaining that her head was still hurting. Mom asked her if she wanted to go to the hospital, but she said, "No," she wanted to wait and see if the new medication would eventually give her some relief. Dooley also expressed she wanted to wait around because she wanted to see our sister, Doris, who was driving in from Tennessee (she moved there after leaving Illinois). Doris later shared that Dooley called her several times during her drive back to New Orleans, and she thought it was odd that she kept calling. She said Dooley wondered what time she thought she might be arriving at Mom's house because she wanted to see her before leaving for home. Upon Doris' arrival, everyone was so excited to see her because she hadn't been home in four years. Soon thereafter, Dooley decided to head home because she was tired, and her head continued to hurt. But, before leaving, she took another pill and hoped that by the time she made it home, she would feel better. At this point, Mom was really worried about Dooley and insisted that Joanette spend the night with her.

Dooley assured Mom that she would be fine, and Joanette proceeded to drive Dooley home.

Joanette dropped Dooley off at home at about 9:30pm. Once Dooley got out of the car and walked up to her front door, she stopped, looked around, and called out to Joanette. She said, "I love you." Joanette said it wasn't what she said. It was the way she said it. Joanette added that the feel of it was somehow different this time. Joanette then waited until Dooley got inside her house before she drove off. Joanette shared that she actually sat there a bit perplexed and unsettled for a brief moment before driving off but also had a sense of comfort knowing Dooley was safe inside.

Doris received a call from Dooley between 12:00 and 12:30 a.m. asking her if she could take another pill because she still had a headache. What I didn't mention was my sister, Doris, is a nurse. Doris reminded her that she had taken her medication before heading home and not to take anymore. Doris suggested she give the medication a chance to work and for her to get some rest. She also suggested that she would come and bring her to the emergency room, but Dooley declined and said that if she was not feeling any better in the morning, she would go to the hospital. Doris told her if she changed her mind to call her. Dooley said she would, and they said good night.

Early the next morning, Joanette called to check on Dooley to see if she was feeling any better and to let her know that she was on her way to her house after checking her blood sugar reading. However, Dooley didn't answer the phone. Once Joanette arrived at Dooley's house, she noticed her car in the driveway so, she got out of her car, walked to the front of the house, and began knocking on the door while calling out her name. After a few minutes and no answer, Joanette proceeded to walk around to the side of the house to peek inside the window. She started knocking on the window while calling her name again. Still no answer. She began to think that perhaps Dooley may have left with our niece, Monique, to run errands, which was not unusual because that's what she did on Monday mornings. Dooley always started early, so Joanette decided to wait for a while. She waited for an hour then decided to go to her granddaughter's house, about ten minutes away, to wait a bit longer. Once she arrived, she called Dooley again, and still no answer. Joanette then called Monique, and she didn't answer. So Joanette and her granddaughter, Ericka, went back to Dooley's house, hoping she had made it back home. This time, Ericka got out of the car and knocked on the door while calling out Dooley's name. Yet again, no answer. At this time, Joanette began to worry that something may have happened to Dooley. She then called Mom and told her that she had been trying to get in touch with Dooley and she was at Dooley's house. She shared that she had been calling her, she had been knocking on the door while calling out for her, and nothing. Joanette then asked Mom if she or Doris had heard from her. Mom answered and said she hadn't as well. This, too, made Mom worried, and she then told Joanette she would call our nephew Marvin to stop by because he had a key to Dooley's house. At that time, Doris said she was on her way to Dooley's house and asked Mom to stay home in case Dooley was with Monique, and they decided to visit Mom.

Once Marvin arrived, he unlocked the door, and he and Ericka began calling out Dooley's name. He then started walking through the house. As he entered her bedroom, he found her in a kneeling position as if she had been praying. He then turned her over, laid her on the floor on her back, and immediately began checking for her pulse. Her pulse was faint, and straight away, he began trying to resuscitate her. A short time later, the paramedics arrived and started providing her care. Joanette called me to let me know what was happening. However, she said that she could not go inside the house because she was afraid. One thing you have to understand about Joanette is, she doesn't do well under uncomfortable situations. At that time, I told Joanette to call me once she found out anything. After hanging up the phone, all I could do was pray that Dooley was okay. No sooner than I hung the phone up, it rang again, and Joanette was on the other end crying. She told me Dooley was dead. For a moment, I couldn't breathe. Joanette's words knocked the wind out of me. I heard those words again, and never can I be acquainted with them. I truly believed that when Marvin found her in that kneeling position, she had been praying and asking God to send someone to find her. She could sense that God answered her prayers. I'm eternally blessed that I had such an amazing time with her for those two years when she lived near me after Hurricane Katrina. Janet, my beloved Dooley, died on October 7, 2013.

Reflection
Coping with the Death of a Sibling

Grieving the death of a sibling at any stage of life can be difficult. As each sibling experiences this significant loss, you will be dealing with your own deep feelings of pain and grief. The death of a brother or sister is a great loss, and many of us will experience it more than once. When you lose a brother or sister during your adult life, you may experience the same feelings if you lost a sibling in childhood. That was the case for me. After the death of my sisters, I had many of the same feelings as I did in my childhood when my brother died. Losing my sisters brought back memories of my brother and his death, and it released a floodgate of pain and heartache again. The only difference was their death brought a deeper, more intimate pain, but I believe it was because of the relationship we had (the trials we experienced together) as adults, which was a deep and intimate relationship. I am reminded in this moment of Eloise and how she played an integral part of my formative years and being there to comfort me when our brother died. We shared critical childhood experiences that created a special bond.

If you are surviving siblings, you will find that you will mourn regardless of the type of relationship you had with your sibling, and you have the right to grieve in your own way. During this time, your feelings will run high in your family in the weeks and months after the death, so try not to judge one another in the way you are grieving. Family members and friends may not understand the role your sibling may have played in your life, so it is important to communicate your feelings to them and receive their support. It is helpful to know that you are not alone and you are not forgotten. Know that your love does not end with the death of your brother or sister. You can and will carry them with you. Also, remember what you shared together and what they brought into your life will never change. Moving on with your life does not have to mean forgetting your loved one. In fact, allowing yourself to hold your loved one in a special place in your heart can help you be okay to move on with your life.

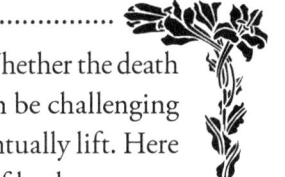

The death of a sibling can be extremely difficult. Whether the death was from a prolonged illness or sudden tragic loss can be challenging for quite some time. With time your sadness will eventually lift. Here are some ways to manage your grief and help yourself heal:

- ❖ **Accept the reality of the loss**—This can come suddenly, and for some, it will take time.
- ❖ **Acknowledge and accept your feelings**—The first step in coping with the death of your sibling is to acknowledge your pain and give yourself permission to grieve your loss.
- ❖ **Share your feelings with your family**—The entire family is grieving; sharing and talking can help you navigate and release difficult emotions together as a family.
- ❖ **Survivor's guilt**—You may feel guilty for living when your sibling didn't get to grow up or finish their life's dream. You may even feel guilty about moving on with your life after the death of your sibling, or you may feel like you failed to protect your sibling, especially if it was a violent death. Regardless of the reason, let go. Forgiving yourself and letting go of the guilt is a crucial part of healing.
- ❖ **Give yourself time**—Siblings are among the closest relationships we will ever have. They are our best friends, our protectors, our secret sharers, and our teachers. So, give yourself as much time as you need to mourn and recover from their death.
- ❖ **Take care of yourself**—Experiencing a death is emotionally and physically draining. This is a good time to pamper yourself. Eat nutritious foods, take naps, indulge in your favorite activities, go out with friends, and exercise. If you notice signs of depression, seek professional help. It is important that we not only take care of our physical health but also our mental health.
- ❖ **There is no closure**—Know that there will come a time when you arrive at a place of acceptance, even peace of mind, where you are able to move forward with your life and cherish the memories you have.

CHAPTER 10

I'm Ready to Go

> "I have fought the good fight, I have finished the race, I have kept the faith"
> 2 Timothy 4:7(NIV)

Nothing can prepare you for what it's like to lose your mother. Over the years, I have provided grief support to many individuals who experienced the death of their mother. I felt sad for them and offered words of comfort to help them get through their grief. But I had absolutely no idea how excruciating their pain was, to no longer have their mother with them. I could not imagine or fully grasp the gravity of their loss until it happened to me when my mom died. My mom often talked about her mom and how the death of her mother affected her. She would say, "If you haven't lost your mother, you can't possibly comprehend and understand the pain someone goes through until it happens to them." Losing my mother was a pain like no other pain. Sometimes, the pain was crippling, and it hit at unexpected times. One minute I was fine, and the next minute, I'm experiencing an unimaginable agony and crying uncontrollably because the pain was unbearable. If you have lost your mother, then you're probably sitting and nodding your head, saying, "Yes."

My mother's name was Bertha, and she died suddenly and unexpectedly in October 2015. She was the last member of her generation, which meant the end of an era for my family. I have no more blood aunts or uncles on either side that are living. The death of my mom saw a generational shift in the structure of my family. My siblings and cousins became the leading generation.

I loved my mom more than I could even explain. Her death completely tore me apart. My mom was my best friend, and I always imagined her being there for me. She was such a core part of my life, as well as my siblings. Now, there is such a void she has left in our lives since her death. There is not a day that goes by when I do not think about my mom. I miss talking on the phone with her and her going over her day with me. What hurts most is, I didn't get a chance to talk with her the day before she died.

On the morning of my mother's death, like many others, I was on my way to work. After parking my car in the parking lot, I got out and waited on the Pace Express Bus to go to downtown Chicago. As I was getting on the bus, I received a call. As I answered the call, I heard my brother on the other end crying. At that moment, I asked him, "What's going on?" He said, "Mama is dead. Mama is dead." I froze. Hearing those words brought me back thirty-five years when I heard those same words. I was thinking, "My Lord, there goes those dreadful words again," when my mom called to tell me that my grandmother was dead, crying as she said them, or when she told me my husband, Lionel, died. My mom had been living with my brother, Champ, for about one month before she died because we felt it best that there was someone to keep an eye on her. Mama would get up between 5:00am and 6:00am, and he would make her coffee. When Champ realized Mom had not gotten up to get her morning coffee, he went into her room to check on her. As he entered Mom's room, he said she appeared to be asleep, but then he noticed she was lying on her side in a fetal position. He then walked over and leaned toward her. Mama wasn't breathing. He then turned Mom over on her back and raised her arm up. It went limp. At that point, he knew she was dead. He then called the paramedics and the family.

I could not believe what I had just heard! My mom was dead. I called her the night before, but I was unable to talk with her because she had already gone to bed for the evening. I just sat there on the bus and started crying. Before I knew it, the bus was moving, and unfortunately, I was unable to get off the bus because it was already headed to the I-55 expressway to downtown Chicago. In that moment, I couldn't move. My body and my feet felt like lead. I was paralyzed in my thoughts. I was in a state of shock and disbelief. My heart was utterly and completely shattered, and I kept repeating to myself, "I can't believe this. This can't be true. Champ must have made a mistake, and he'll call me back to tell me the paramedics were able to revive her and that she was on her way to the hospital." But a part of me knew it was true. My mom was dead, and I'd never see her again. I then buried my face in my hands and cried, blocking everyone and everything out. The pain and heartache of losing her were numbing. I missed my opportunity of being close to my mom on her last day. I didn't have the chance to kiss her goodbye, stroke her hair, or hold her hand for the last time. My ride downtown on that bus will forever be with me; it's etched in my memory. After getting my composure, I called my husband and children to let them know that Mom had died.

Upon arriving at my office, I informed the staff that my mom had just died and I was going to go back home. The bus returning home didn't leave from downtown Chicago for another hour, so I started making phone calls, checking on my family. As I was leaving my office to take the bus back home, I received a call from my daughter, Kim, letting me know that she was on her way to pick me up. Instead, I told her not to because I wanted to take the bus so I could have some time alone.

Reflecting on the Impact of This Incredible Woman

On the bus ride back home, I laid my head against the window with my eyes closed, reflecting on the impact of this incredible woman and the life she gave me. Mama was deeply sensitive and extremely intelligent, with an almost perfect memory. Mama was the person who taught us to never give up and to always keep our heads up. She was the one who was there to lean on when we couldn't fix our own problems or if we would just want some advice. She always knew what to say or when to say nothing and to let us try to do things on our own. Her influence affected the way we lived our lives. As I journeyed home, I thought about the moment we are born. We know our mothers. We know the sound of their voice, and we feel the comfort and warmth of their arms. I felt truly blessed to have had such a special person in my life and to have been connected with her all these years later in the same way as when I was born, knowing her voice and the comfort of her arms.

When I think of my mom, I can hear her contagious laughter and see her beautiful smile that would melt your heart. It was heartbreaking to know that I would not be able to hear that laugh and see her infectious smile anymore but in my memories—memories that will never capture the true essence of her. I already began to miss hearing her voice. I called my mom every day; it was something my sibling and I did. Mom really enjoyed talking to her children. Mom raised nine children, and she was a continual presence in our lives. Mom was not just Mom. She was an extraordinary mom. She was the glue and the sustaining force that held our family together. For Mom, happiness was being with her family. She was the one who kept in touch with all the family members and spread everyone's news around. She was the one who arranged get-togethers that kept us connected, and her house was the hub for everyone. With everything she had to go through, she managed to push through every obstacle and keep her faith through every one of her trials. Mama kept her priorities intact and her family together, which is why she impressed upon my siblings and me to always be there for one another and to love each other unconditionally. Her children and family were the most important things in her life. This is a wonderful legacy and an example for us to follow—keeping our focus on what is truly important, not only when life is easy but when it is also difficult.

As I reflect on the extraordinary person my mom was, I am reminded of the compassion and care she had for people, which led to a career working in the hospital taking care of the sick. (Mama eventually retiring as a surgical technician.) She had the biggest heart, and her character won her many friends. We were taught to be kind to all people, no matter where they came from or their circumstances. Mama taught us that even though people could be cruel, it did not mean we needed to retaliate with more cruelty. I would often see her cry when she was hurt. The pain showed in her eyes when she felt that she had been wronged. But she easily forgave and let things go without holding a grudge. She lived her life by example—forgive and let go. What's in your heart reflects on your face, she would say. Her character of forgiving and letting go is one of her precious gifts to me. In addition to this, Mama taught us about accountability, truthfulness, and honesty, as well as the importance of faith, moral principles, and personal responsibility.

Beginning of

My mom had a stroke in 2012. The doctors said the stroke primarily impacted her right side, which caused her not to be able to walk. She became totally dependent on others. Mama lived alone, so my sister, Janet, moved in with her during her time of recovery. As Mom began her recovery, she struggled with walking, relying on her left side, and using her left arm and leg since her right side was weakened by the stroke. After several months of therapy and hard work, she was able to do everything she could do before the stroke. Once again, she enjoyed what she loved doing, and that was cooking, especially Sunday dinner for the family. I strongly believe the reason she recovered so quickly was because of her faith and belief in God and family. I remember my mom always having a strong faith in God and she took spirituality very seriously.

For the most part, a year after Mom's stroke, everything was going great until my sister Janet died suddenly and unexpected. After Janet died, Mom really struggled with her death. Mom was devastated, and it appeared as though she lost her will to live. Mom slowly withdrew from life and stopped doing the things she had once enjoyed, like cooking her favorite foods and watching her favorite television shows. However, she continued to read her Bible and listen to music. During this time, Mom also began going back and forth to the doctor two and three times a week even though they said there was nothing physically wrong with her. Though they gave her medication to calm her anxiety, she began to get worst. She was struggling with depression and experiencing confusion. I called my mom several times a day to check on her, and she would always tell me that she was tired and was "Ready to go." I would then ask her if she was giving up on life. She would say, "I just want to go home to be with my Savior."

My siblings, along with other family members, were constantly going over to the house to check on her. Not only did Mom's life drastically change after Janet's death, but so did my siblings. Despite the changes in Mom's condition, the family tried to keep a sense of normalcy around her. My siblings still gathered at mom's house for Sunday dinner, and she insisted on cooking. My sister, Joanette, always went over on Saturday and stayed with Mom until Monday. Three and half weeks before Mom died, the family was at her house on Sunday. For the most part, Mom wasn't herself, and she seemed to be quiet. My sister left on Monday but felt a little uncomfortable leaving. Mom assured her that she was fine. On the following Wednesday, Joanette decided to go over to the house to check on Mom and noticed that she seemed a little confused and disoriented. At that time, Joanette asked Mom if she had taken her medication. Mom had several medical conditions, including diabetes, congestive heart failure, and chronic obstructive pulmonary disease. Joanette was concerned she was not taking her medications, so she called my brother and me and told us that Mom was acting strange. Not only that, but she felt as though Mom should not be home alone anymore. I called and asked my sister to put Mom on the phone. Once Mom got on the phone, I asked her how she was feeling. She told me she feeling fine, but she was feeling a little confused earlier and didn't remember if she had taken her medication. I then asked her if she wanted to go over to my brother, Champ's house, and she said, "No." Mom said that even though she was a little confused, she wanted to stay at her own house and insisted that's how it was going to be.

Persuading Her to Leave

Shortly thereafter, my brother arrived and tried to persuade her but couldn't. He could not persuade her that she could not be alone because she needed someone to make sure she was taking her medication on time. Getting her to leave home and all that was familiar to her was not an easy task. I failed to mention that Mom was also stubborn. Since my sister and brother could not persuade her to leave, I told my sister to put Mom on the phone again. I then told her that if she would go over to Champ's house for a few days, she could then come to Chicago and visit me later. She was excited to hear that an agreed to go to my brother's home. After a few days, we agreed that Mom was not well enough to fly and decided she should wait a couple of weeks before leaving.

During the time she was at my brother's house, it seemed as if she was doing fine. But, on the other hand, when I called her, she would say, "I'm ready to go home." I then would explain to her that she was not well enough to go home, and as soon as she was well enough to fly, she was coming to Chicago. She would reply, "Okay, but I'm talking about my other home."

Events Leading Up to Her Death

The events that took place leading up to Mom's death and what would follow afterward were so surreal that it seemed almost as if she knew she was about to die. That Monday, three days prior to Mom's death, she kept saying she was going to die and needed to see her children. She insisted on talking with each one of us to say "Goodbye." This was rather unsettling because there was no indication this was going to happen, not from a medical position. Nonetheless, my brother, Champ, called my sisters to tell them what Mom said, and all of them, with the exception of my youngest sister, Wanda, made their way to see her. My sister, Joanette, went there on Tuesday and spent the day with her. Joanette said she and Mom sat on the porch enjoying each other's company, and when Mom got tired, they both laid in the bed together talking. While lying in bed, Joanette recalled Mom running her hand through her hair and telling her how soft it was. When Joanette would spend the weekend at Mom's house, they would always lie in bed together and watch television while Mom ran her fingers through her hair. After a while, Joanette got up and went into the living room to talk with Champ. Upon going back to the bedroom, she heard Mom praying, so she stood by the door. As Mom was praying, she heard her say, "Lord Jesus, I'm ready to come home. Please take me now." Joanette shared that all she could do in that moment was cry. She later told us what happened and sadly said, "Mama is ready to leave us." None of us knew it would be so soon.

My sister, Doris, went over on Wednesday. Mom told Doris that she was so happy to see her because she would be leaving her soon and wanted to say goodbye. Then and there, Doris told Mom to stop talking like that because she was going to be all right, and she was going to be around for a long time. Mom then turned to Champ and told him to take care of his sisters and that she didn't have much time left. Afterward, Mom then asked to see my sister, Wanda. Champ tried calling her, but she didn't answer. Eventually, my brother was able to get in touch with Wanda, and she told him that she was on her way. Unfortunately, Wanda never showed up, and my mom died without seeing her.

Never Got a Chance to Talk with Her

Wednesday evening, I tried to call to talk to Mom. Champ informed me that Doris was there spending time with her. I told him to let her know that I called and I'd talk with her later. When I called again, she was taking a nap. Later that evening, I called back, and Champ told me Mom was tired and had gone to bed. I was like, "I've been trying to talk with her all day but haven't been able to." I then told him I would call her in the morning. I was heartbroken. I never got a chance to talk with her the night before she died. Her death shook the core of my foundation.

Coping with Mama's death and learning to live without her has been really hard. Life after the death of my mom was difficult, and if I didn't know that it was normal to experience grief years after a loss, I think I'd be feeling pretty crazy right about now. As the years past by, my feelings of loss changed, and I've noticed that lately, they're fixated on the passage of time. I've actually found that the more time I place between my mother and me, the more I ache for the past. My mother was "home," and now that she's gone, I'm faced with the reality that I'll never be able to see her again in this lifetime. If you're wondering when you'll get over the sadness, speaking from my experience, if you ask me, my answer is never.

Each year as the anniversary of her death approaches, I find it hard to describe my feelings. Sometimes, I feel sad, and other times grateful to have had her in my life for the time she was. Sometimes, I feel deprived of her not being here with the family and me. I also go through so many other emotions and feelings that catch me off guard. Life after a loss can be so perplexing and complex.

At the beginning, I cried a lot, and over four years later, the pain is still as sharp as it was when I first lost her. Not a day goes by where she doesn't pop into my thoughts. There were times when I felt so guilty not keeping my promise. I would think to myself, if only I were there during that time, she might not have died. I was looking for answers, but in the meantime, I was blaming myself. Thoughts such as, "What if I had gone to New Orleans to get her instead?" or "If only I had done…?" These questions stayed on my mind as I felt the need and desire to find an explanation to lessen my pain. It took me a while to understand that it wasn't my fault, and there was no way I could have prevented Mom from dying.

I got through each day by keeping myself very busy, and to this day, I still don't know if I can truly say I have reached a state of acceptance that she is gone. However, I have realized that maybe this is okay. I'm so thankful that a year and a half prior to Mom's death, we, as a family, would have family prayer (via conference call) time every Sunday evening, and some of her children, grandchildren, and great-grandchildren would call in to join in prayer. Mom would be the first on the line. She truly enjoyed it. Her favorite saying was, "When you take one step, God will take two." Every time I think of my mom, I start to feel that maybe I am becoming more like a true piece of her. I hope I am making her proud today as she is right there, smiling at me from heaven.

Reflection
Coping with the Death of a Parent

A mother's love is irreplaceable, which makes their death incredibly painful. There is no love like a mother's love, and no stronger bond than a bond with a mother. My mother was my best friend and my sounding board. We had an unbreakable bond, and we had a special relationship. We sometimes don't often think of them as the noticeable anchor, but in truth, they hold a place in our generational timeline. They have been there since the moment we were born, and even though we know they will die someday, how do we imagine someone that has always been there, suddenly gone. I couldn't imagine my world without my mother, but I had to learn how to cope without her. Learning to cope was a long and difficult process. My mother's death affected me emotionally, psychologically, spiritually, and physically. I felt numb at times and empty too. When I lost her, I went into denial. It was easy to bury what had happened because I was living far away in Chicago, and she was living in New Orleans. I thought that it was going to be easier since I was living so far away. However, that didn't last long. I had to do a reality check and face that my mother really died, and nothing was going to change the fact that she was never coming back.

After a parent dies, we often reflect on them. Perhaps we realize for the first time all they did for us as children. Mothers are the ones who may have played a major role in our growth and development during our formative years. For some of us, when we become parents, we appreciate the challenges our own parents must have gone through. We gain a new perspective of their lives.

As you reflect on the memory of your parent, whether you are alone or walking through it with a surviving parent, you are beginning the journey through the stages of grief. Here are some suggestions in coping with your loss.

- ❖ **Recognize the scope of your loss.** Coping with the loss of a parent means learning to live without a person you have known for your whole life who may have played a formative role in your growth and development. Parents have shared in important moments in your life and have been invested in your well-being.

- **Allow yourself time to grieve.** After the loss of a parent, you may feel angry, upset, numb, depressed, and anxious, all of which can be intense and perhaps unfamiliar. Nonetheless, all of these feelings are appropriate given the scale of the loss. Grief is a uniquely individual experience, and different people, even within the same family, will process loss and express emotions in different ways at different times.
- **Give yourself time.** Acknowledge and embrace your emotions without feeling that you need to "get over" your feelings or move on. When it feels comfortable to do so, find the time to reflect on the past and hold onto memories.
- **It's important to express your feelings.** Take time to cry, and don't be afraid to share your tears with other mourners. Talk openly with family members and friends. Express your anger if you are feeling it. Lean on your friends. Family members and friends may not know what to say or how to talk and support you, but you can help them by simply telling them what you need.
- **Keep talking about how you are feeling as much as possible.** It may not always be easy to put into words, but try to explain to others around you how you are feeling. Close friends and family will want to help you as much as possible but won't always know how, so telling them how you feel and what you need from them will be helpful.
- **Take care of your health.** It can be very easy to neglect your physical needs while grieving. However, this is a time when taking good care of yourself is crucial. As difficult as it may seem, making every effort to get adequate sleep, eating nutritionally balanced meals, and exercising are excellent ways to relieve stress and anxiety. Make sure to mention to your physician that you have experienced a loss. Knowing this will help to make other decisions that may be helpful to your physical health.

- ❖ **Seek counseling or a grief support group.** There is a lot of support out there, and many people find comfort in speaking to people outside of their friends and family.

Being a part of a community that has shared experiences with you can be healing and empowering.

CHAPTER 11

His Name Was Cyler

> **"He heals the brokenhearted and binds their wounds"**
> **Psalm 147:3 (NIV)**

Being a grandmother is one of the greatest joys of my life. When I found out I was going to be a grandmother, I could not have been more excited. Over the years, God has blessed me with fifteen grandchildren and four great-grandchildren. Once they were born and after seeing them, I fell in love with each one of them immediately. These experiences were like no other, and my excitement never lessened. I wanted to protect them and love them and be there for every milestone in their lives. Throughout their lives, their hugs, kisses, and smiles just melted my heart. My little great-grans, every time they see me, they run with their arms wide open, calling me, "Granny, Granny," to give me a hug and a kiss. This has truly been a blessing and a balm when I'm having a hard time. Their smiles make everything feel possible.

Seeing them together is a pleasant reminder of how my family has grown, and I feel extremely blessed to have the opportunity to be around to make a difference in their lives. I am grateful for the love and joy that they bring to my life. Just when I thought it couldn't get any better, I found out I was going to have my fifth great-grandson. I was super excited; my heart expanded even wider for another special little person to have a place in my heart.

Just prior to me finishing this book, I experienced the death of four family members. Within three months I lost, my nieces, Deedra and Ginnel, and my nephew Eddie and, prior to them, my long-awaited great-grandson, Cyler. I had prayed for Cyler before he made his entrance into this world. My heart ached upon hearing of the death of my much-loved great-grand baby. My very being was overcome with anguish.

After Cyler died minutes after his birth, the hospital allowed my great-grandson to stay in the room with his parents for twenty-four hours. Our family had an opportunity to hold Cyler, cuddle him, and love on him, even though he was not alive. When my grandson Clive, Cyler's father, walked in the hospital room, I noticed the pain and sadness on his face. As he held his firstborn baby boy with such tenderness and love, it broke my heart as I watched the tears stream down his face and disappear onto his shirt. I sat there in awe and yet powerless because there were no words I could say that could ease or take his pain away. I remember when Clive was younger, and he would hurt himself. I was able do something to make it all better, but now he was hurting, and there was nothing I could do to make him feel better. I would have done anything to take his pain away, yet my heart was heavy in grief as I sat there and grieved Cyler's death.

After a while, Clive gave the baby to his mother, Ariana, and she laid him on her chest and just stared at him while she cuddled her baby. I had to hold back my tears to appear strong, but inside, I was broken. My brain just could not process it. I kept saying to myself, "This is not supposed to be this way. I was supposed to be spoiling baby Cyler. This hurts too much, and it's just not fair."

At times, the atmosphere in the room was somber and muted, with bursts of smiles as everyone tried to create balance. Constantly taking the "emotional pulse" of Clive and Ariana, we were very sensitive to allow them the time to be parents and grieve in the way they wanted, without judgment. What we all found amazement and comfort in was that during the twenty-four hours we had him in the room, Cyler never became cold to the touch, nor did his body stiffen up. He stayed warm and soft. We experienced a transformation come upon his face as if he were alive. He never looked like he died, only asleep.

The anguish of losing a child at any age is hard. There is no age or point in time that makes it any easier. No parent is ever prepared to face the death of their child, and no grandparent is prepared to lose their grandchild. The loss of my great-grandchild touched me in a way that caused me to experience grief like no other. I not only had to witness my grandson's loss but also the pain of my daughter and her losing her grandson. What Cyler's death taught me was today is all we have, and the little moments you share count; love continues even after death.

CHAPTER 12

The Birth of a Ministry

"Comfort, comfort my people, says your God"
Isaiah 40:1-11 (NIV)

The Death of a Stranger

I am no stranger to death, but none of my experiences could have prepared me for the emotions I felt on this specific evening thirty years ago. I have worked with families of homicide and violent crime victims for over thirty years. I started with the Cook County State's Attorney's Office and then with my organization, the Family Trauma Advocacy Program, under the umbrella of Parents Against Gangs. I've provided free comprehensive grief support services to thousands of families in the Chicagoland area and across the country, providing crisis intervention and grief services. Nevertheless, on this particular day, I was called to a Trauma One hospital. I received a call from the social worker and was informed that a family of a fifteen-year-old female was there, and she had committed suicide.

Upon my arrival to the hospital, the nurse briefed me on the family and stated that the patient had been pronounced dead and the family had just been informed. The nurse also informed me that the name of the patient was Elizabeth (name changed to protect identity), and her father, brother, and sister were in the quiet room at the hospital waiting to view her body. At that time, the nurse and I walked over to the quiet room. Once inside the room, I noticed that the family was huddled together as they were crying and holding onto each other. As soon as the father saw us, he began saying, "Why would she do this?" He repeatedly asked, "What was going on with her?" When her father finished talking, the nurse introduced me and informed him that I was a family advocate and that I was there to provide grief support to the family. Soon thereafter, the nurse left, and I began to share what steps the family would need to take care of and what to expect. Like most families whose loved one commits suicide, they are left trying to make sense of what happened and what or why he/she took their own life. For many, the question is "Why?" "Why did they do something like this?" "Why is this happening?" This family shared that they never saw it coming because she gave no indication that there was anything wrong. While speaking with the family, I learned that she was a typical, carefree teenager who exhibited healthy relationships with friends and family alike. On the outside, she was a girl who was loved by so many people, and she never complained about anything. After talking with the family, I then asked them if they were ready to see their daughter and sister. The father said they were. Before I escorted them to where she was, I went to where Elizabeth was to make sure she was prepared for viewing. Upon entering the room and looking at her, my heart ached for this beautiful young girl. I noticed the bruise around her neck because she hung herself. I then went back to get the family and accompanied them to the room where she was. As we reached the room, her father and siblings stood at the entrance of the door for a minute and just looked at her. Her father then slowly walked in and laid his body across hers as his children stood crying on both sides of him. It was an emotional moment for me, but I composed myself in that space. I then stood outside the room to give the family some privacy and quiet time. Although, in many cases, supervision is typically enforced to ensure that the family does not remove the body from the stretcher (yes, I've seen it happen), in that moment, I felt it best to give them that time alone.

When the family finally left the holding room, I was left standing alone with Elizabeth, and it brought back so many memories. They were memories of my own experience of losing someone so special to me, someone so young with so much life left to live. After a few minutes, the nurse told me that the transport was there to take Elizabeth to the medical examiner's office. I then waited to make sure the family had left the hospital because I didn't want them to see her being wheeled out and placed into a police van. To my surprise, I never knew until then that remains were transported to the medical examiner's office this way. The officers pulled onto the emergency room ramp, and one of the officers rolled the stretcher out of the emergency room area. Once the stretcher was on the ramp, the other officer exited the van, and both officers grabbed hold of the bag and tossed her onto the back of the van. I just stood there with my mouth opened and in shock. I began to think of the family and how they would feel to witness such disregard for Elizabeth. There was no respect shown for her body.

Finally, the day's events were over, or so I thought. When I left the hospital and started driving home, I saw a police transport van pull in front of me, and instantly, I was flooded with uncontrollable emotions. They were feelings of pain, hurt, anger and sorrow. The grief I was experiencing was very familiar, but I hadn't actually experienced such powerful, unexpected emotions in quite some time. In fact, it had all become so overwhelming. I began crying so hard I had to pull my car over to collect myself. I began sobbing even more at the thought that the officers may have handled my daughter, Ginneria, in the same way with the same disrespect. This case was hard for me because not only was this my very first case, but it involved the death of the first young girl I had seen after Ginneria's death. To see the hurt and pain this family was experiencing was hard for me to witness. The memories took me back to a place in my own life where grief was all too familiar. Elizabeth was my trigger. I wasn't quite sure where it had all come from, but I'm sure it had a lot to do with Elizabeth. After listening to her father describe her and all of her youthful qualities, it reminded me so much of my own daughter.

Although commonalities exist among people who have experienced a certain type of loss, individual grief is as unique as the person experiencing it. Here are some tips to help you cope:

- ❖ **Grief is a Journey** - It is a challenge to give yourself permission to grieve when you live in a culture that wants you to "get over it." However, when you allow the grief journey to take place and give yourself the time you need to express your emotions, you will come to find peace and healing.
- ❖ **Give yourself permission to grieve** - You give yourself permission to grieve by recognizing the need for grieving. Grieving is the natural way of working through your loss. Remember, it is neither a sign of weakness nor absence of faith.
- ❖ **Everyone's journey through grief is unique** - No one is exactly like you, and the relationship you enjoyed with your spouse was one-of-a-kind. As a result, you will grieve in your own unique way. Don't compare your grief experience with that of others. The path of everyone's grief journey is different and there is no timetable on grief.
- ❖ **Grieving is a process** - As time goes on, you will adjust to your new life and the pain will diminish. This does not mean you will forget your loved one. It only means you have accepted the death and can begin to live each day in the present, savoring the memories as part of your past as you begin a new life journey.
- ❖ **Don't suppress the grieving process** - Whatever you do, don't suppress the grieving process. You have been wounded, and have a multitude of emotions welling up.
  Experiencing the death of a spouse affects your head, heart, and spirit, and working through them helps in the healing process. Grief work takes a great deal of work and energy. Some emotions you may feel are fear, disorientation, anger, confusion, despair, and guilt, to name a few. These emotional feelings are a natural response to the death of someone we loved. You may

also feel like you are going "crazy" or something is wrong with you. These thoughts and feelings are a normal part of your grief journey as well.

- ❖ **Express your feelings** – I used to think I shouldn't cry or express how I was really feeling about the loss of my husband. But then I realized that we built a life together that didn't last as long as I expected. So, I accepted that I had a right to grieve and not be ashamed. Talk about the type of person your husband or wife was, and the activities you both enjoyed together. Although it may bring tears, joy, and laughter, feel and express those wonderful memories you shared. Allow yourself to talk about the circumstances surrounding the death, your feelings of loneliness and what's hard for you, and the specific things you miss about your spouse. This too helps in your healing journey. Healing beings when you express your grief experience honestly.
- ❖ **Take care of yourself** -You may not feel like resuming the activities you did before your loss and that is perfectly okay. Take time to listen to your body, it will guide you through this process.
- ❖ **It is okay to laugh** - Humor is an excellent stress reliever and it's not being disrespectful. Your loved one would want you to enjoy life's laughter.
- ❖ **You are not alone** – When death occurs, we often feel we are alone in this healing journey, but we are never alone because Jesus says that he will never leave you or forsake you. On the other hand, there are friends, family and so many people who truly want to see us move past our pain and embrace our life again. While you may take time to be alone and reflect on the life you shared with your spouse, don't forget that there are others who love you and are there for you when you need them. For those who do not have a healthy, positive support network, I recommend you join a support group to connect with others who too are journeying through their grief.

Encouraging Scripture Verses While Coping with Grief

As much as death is a topic that most people try to avoid—it is unavoidable. Each and every one of us will have to face this traumatic and devastating experience at some time. There is no right or a wrong way to grieve. Everyone grieves in his/her own way. The Bible is a powerful source for support and comfort in times of grief. Scripture tells us that God will comfort those who mourn so that we may comfort others. When you are faced with loss, and it feels as if the grief will never end, turn to scripture to find strength. As a believer, I turned to God's word to find strength and comfort while I grieved. Here are some that helped me:

Scriptures: from the New International Version (NIV)

Psalm 23:1-6 (NIV) "The Lord is my shepherd, I lack nothing. **2** He makes me lie down in green pastures, he leads me beside quiet waters, he refreshes my soul. He guides me along the right paths for his name's sake. Even though I walk through the darkest valley, I will fear no evil, for you are with me; your rod and your staff, they comfort me. You prepare a table before me in the presence of my enemies. You anoint my head with oil; my cup overflows. Surely your goodness and love will follow me all the days of my life, and I will dwell in the house of the Lord forever."

Psalm 31:9-10 (NIV) "Be merciful to me, Lord, for I am in distress; my eyes grow weak with sorrow, my soul and body with grief. **10** My life is consumed by anguish and my years by groaning; my strength fails because of my affliction, and my bones grow weak."

Psalm 34:18 (NIV) "The Lord is close to the brokenhearted and saves those who are crushed in spirit."

Psalm 147:3 (NIV) "He heals the brokenhearted and binds up their wounds."

Isaiah 26:3 (NIV) "You will keep in perfect peace those whose minds are steadfast because they trust in you."

Revelation 21:4 (NIV) "He will wipe every tear from their eyes. There will be no more death or mourning or crying or pain, for the old order of things has passed away."

2 Corinthians 1:3-4 (NIV) "Praise be to the God and Father of our Lord Jesus Christ, the Father of compassion and the God of all comfort, who comforts us in all our troubles so that we can comfort those in any trouble with the comfort we ourselves receive from God."

1 Peter 5:7(NIV) "Cast all your anxiety on him because he cares for you."

Matthews 5:4 (NIV) "Blessed are those who mourn, for they will be comforted."

John 14:27 (NIV) "Peace I leave with you; my peace I give you. I do not give to you as the world gives. Do not let your hearts be troubled, and do not be afraid."

Matthew 11:28-30 (NIV) "Come to me, all you who are weary and burdened, and I will give you rest. Take my yoke upon you and learn from me, for I am gentle and humble in heart, and you will find rest for your souls. For my yoke is easy, and my burden is light."

John 14:27 (NIV) "Peace I leave with you; my peace I give you. I do not give to you as the world gives. Do not let your hearts be troubled, and do not be afraid."

Jeremiah 17:14 (NIV) "Heal me, Lord, and I will be healed; save me, and I will be saved, for you are the one I praise."

Matthew 7:7-8 (NIV) "Ask, and it will be given to you; seek and you will find; knock, and the door will be opened to you. For everyone who asks receives; the one who seeks finds; and to the one who knocks, the door will be opened."

2 Corinthians 1:3-4 (NIV) "Praise be to the God and Father of our Lord Jesus Christ, the Father of compassion and the God of all comfort, who comforts us in all our troubles so that we can comfort those in any trouble with the comfort we ourselves receive from God."

Isaiah 41:10 (NIV) "So do not fear, for I am with you; do not be dismayed, for I am your God. I will strengthen you and help you; I will uphold you with my righteous right hand."

Isaiah 43:2 (NIV) "When you pass through the waters, I will be with you; and when you pass through the rivers, they will not sweep over you. When you walk through the fire, you will not be burned; the flames will not set you ablaze."

EPILOGUE

Writing this book has been a healing journey for me. Through writing I understood that the tragedies and losses we experience change the trajectory of our lives, and as we journey through life we are faced with unknowns and questions that we grapple with in search of answers. We often hear that grief is like a roller coaster, but my lived experience has taught me that life itself is the roller coaster and grief is the inevitable twist we endure from time to time. Just when you are in a place where your life is leveled and coasting, a shift happens.

On August 26, 2021, as I was completing this book, my great-granddaughter Rebecca was diagnosed with stage 3 cancer; a neuroblastoma of the adrenal gland. Nine months later we were told that her cancer has progressed to stage 4. As I reflect on Rebecca and her journey my heart is heavy, and I am in a place of processing the road she has traveled, as well as what lies ahead for my family. Her story is to come…

CPSIA information can be obtained
at www.ICGtesting.com
Printed in the USA
LVHW101522160722
723674LV00002B/12